God-Optional Judaism

GOD-OPTIONAL JUDAISM

ALTERNATIVES FOR CULTURAL JEWS
WHO LOVE THEIR HISTORY, HERITAGE,
AND COMMUNITY

JUDITH SEID

CITADEL PRESS
Kensington Publishing Corp.
www.kensingtonbooks.com

CITADEL PRESS books are published by

Kensington Publishing Corp.
850 Third Avenue
New York, NY 10022

All Kensington titles, imprints, and distributed lines are available at special quantity discounts for bulk purchases for sales promotions, premiums, fund-raising, educational, or institutional use. Special book excerpts or customized printings can also be created to fit specific needs. For details, write or phone the office of the Kensington special sales manager: Kensington Publishing Corp., 850 Third Avenue, New York, NY 10022, attn: Special Sales Department, phone 1-800-221-2647.

10 9 8 7 6 5 4 3 2 1

Printed in the United States of America

Library of Congress Card Catalogue Number: 2001087603
ISBN 0-8065-2190-2

CONTENTS

Part Four. Now What?

ACKNOWLEDGMENTS

I'd like to thank my colleagues the leaders in the Secular Humanistic Jewish movement, whose ideas I've integrated and whose support has been invaluable. Among those whom I've consulted while writing this book are Deet Newman, Aviva Panush, Debbie Klemptner, Hershl Hartman, Miriam Jerris, Toby Dorfman, Stacie Fine, Adam Chalom, Susan Lerner, Mike Prival, Barry Swan, Eva Goldfinger, Shane and Leslie Dyson, and Roberta Feinstein. I've also been enriched by the work of my colleagues Len Cherlin, Julie Gales, Sherwin Wine, Dan Friedman, Renee Kogel, and Rhea Seagull. Special thanks go to Bennett Muraskin for making sure my history was accurate and to Ruthy Seid and Lynne Portnoy, who took out a lot of words.

Thanks to Laura Markham, who brought my name to the attention of my editor, Carrie Cantor, whom I thank for calmness in the face of my terror at this whole process.

I also thank the people whose stories I've told in this book. You'll recognize yourselves, even though I've changed all your names.

I was lucky to be brought up in the Secular movement by my parents, Ethel and Seymour Seid, who were also born into the movement as children of Sam (Shloime) and Celia (Tsivia) Zuckerman and Yossl (Joseph) and Regina Seid.

Special thanks to David Gates, who is my most steadfast supporter and giggle-partner, and to our children Moses, Rivka, and Micah, who put up with being the rabbi-equivalent's kids.

And, of course, I thank Max Rosenfeld, for having been himself.

INTRODUCTION

Marian believes in the power of prayer. She just doesn't believe there's anyone she's praying to. "I believe that praying creates an energy for good in the world," she explains. "I don't feel that I'm praying to someone who then acts on those prayers. Instead, it's like my prayers spread out away from me in every direction, and that energy creates goodness and help."

Marian, now in her fifties, joined a Reform temple when her children were small. She sent her girls to religious school but never felt at home at the Reform temple, and she stopped attending when they left for college. Her belief in an external god had waned over the years, and she reached a final break with traditional belief when Orthodox relatives made unkind comments about the Jewish status of her daughters, who are adopted. "I realized then that I couldn't believe in a god who would make people act mean and stupid. But," she says, "I still feel intensely Jewish. I crave that Jewish connection."

Like many who grew up in religious Jewish traditions, Marian can't imagine not being part of the Jewish community, but she feels that she can't let her beliefs be known. "I don't talk much about what I believe," she says. "It's personal. And I don't want people to judge me."

The rabbi of Marian's congregation acknowledges that many of his congregants are not traditional believers. "Probably more than half of them are atheists or agnostics" is his off-the-cuff estimate. His Conservative colleague in their small Midwestern college town has a similar estimate. His guess is that up to one-third of his congregants don't believe in a self-conscious god who acts in history and in people's lives.

These estimates are confirmed in a recent poll of Los Angeles Jews (commissioned in 1998 by the Jewish Federation of Greater Los Angeles and reported on in the secularist magazine *Jewish Currents* and other periodicals). Only 41 percent say they have no doubts about the existence of some sort of personal god.

The Reform movement claims 1.5 million of America's 5.5 million Jews as members and the Conservative movement 1 million. If the polls and the rabbis' estimates are correct and representative, there are over 1 million North American Jews who belong to religious congregations but don't believe in the religion taught there.

The Reform and Conservative rabbis above were speaking about Jews who are currently affiliated with synagogues. But what about those who don't belong to religious congregations? The 1990 National Jewish Population Survey, available in many libraries and on-line, shows that only half of America's Jews, representing 41 percent of Jewish households, are affiliated with any congregation. The Los Angeles poll showed only about one-third of Jews currently belong to synagogues. Of course, this is a narrow definition, measuring only religious affiliation. Many committed Jews are members of Jewish Community Centers or social action groups such as B'nai B'rith, the Anti-Defamation League, American Jewish Congress, the Organization for Rehabilitation and Training (ORT) (a women's organization that provides education and training for Jews and non-Jews throughout the world), Hadassah, or the National Council of Jewish Women.

While most American Jews do affiliate with a congregation at one time or another, at any given time at least half of America's Jews are unaffiliated. Jews tend to affiliate with synagogues or temples when they are or have children of school age. They respond to family pressures or their own feelings that their kids need some education about their heritage. Because many Jewish parents had little Jewish education, have little to do with the organized Jewish community, and do little that is ritually Jewish in the home, they feel they cannot adequately educate their children themselves. In order to get some—any—Jewish education for their children, they allow their children to be taught things that they themselves do not believe. They affiliate with the temple or synagogue their friends or their children's friends attend, and after their children become Bar or Bat Mitzvah, most drop their memberships. Religious congregations are not meeting their needs as Jews.

Karen and Ray fit this pattern of sometime affiliation. Both were raised in liberal Jewish households, but neither belonged to a warm, caring congregation, and neither felt the sense of community they were searching for. As adults, they joined an Orthodox congregation that offered them warmth and caring and they remained members for years, enjoying the community and the fervor of the celebrations but never quite believing in the religion they were taught. Finally, the dissonance between their beliefs and their actions made it impossible for them to remain Orthodox, and not finding the commitment, depth, and passion that they wanted in other movements, they dropped out of Jewish life entirely. Karen and Ray thought that they could not have Jewish heritage without dogmatic religion. They believed that they could not do and say Jewish things that didn't include statements of belief in and praise of a powerful and sometimes vengeful god who meddled in human lives and history.

Several years later, after having been transferred to the Midwest, Karen and Ray stumbled on a Secular Humanistic congregation and realized that they could, indeed, pass their heritage on to their children as members of a community that did not demand specific beliefs or rigid practices. Karen says, "This is what we were really looking for. We're so grateful to have found a place where we can be Jewish in a way that is comfortable for us." Karen and Ray's family fits into the 20 percent of American Jews who told the National Jewish Population Survey that they are ethnically, but not religiously, Jewish. How many more of these Jews have no idea that they can find a home in Jewish life? How many of them, like Karen and Ray, have given up hope of finding a Jewish community or a Jewish way of practice that will allow them to express their true beliefs as well as their commitment to their Jewish roots?

Ray and Karen weren't comfortable in a religious congregation because they didn't believe what they were taught. But discomfort with religious congregations can be the result of things other than religious ideas. Sometimes traditional attitudes toward life choices have made synagogues uncomfortable places. Ed and Jeannie have been happily married for fifteen years. They have two children who are connected strongly with the Jewish heritage their father brings them. Jeannie was not born Jewish and has not made a formal religious conversion. "I'm Jewish in my heart," she says, "but I don't really believe in any religion." That Jewishness is not accepted in most religious congregations, and most movements won't consider her children Jewish. Ed and Jeannie had a Jewish home but no Jewish community, and they felt that lack. They joined the Jewish Community Center to let their children be around other Jews so they would not feel so lonely and different.

Melanie and Kate's relationship is also a long one. Melanie was brought up Jewish and Kate Christian. Until their children reached school age, they mostly ignored their cultural and religious heritages, but they always knew they would raise their children to be Jewish. When their oldest daughter was eight, Melanie and Kate went looking for a Jewish congregation in which a lesbian couple could feel comfortable and accepted. Even though one rabbi in their town welcomed them, they never felt quite at ease in the congregation. Melanie, who grew up in a religious congregation, started noticing that the prayer language assumed heterosexuality. Kate noticed that she wasn't accepted because she wasn't Jewish. The congregations wanted to list only Melanie as a member, leaving Kate's name out of the congregational directory. Melanie and Kate kept looking until they, also, stumbled on a Secular Humanistic Jewish congregation where they were not only accepted, but welcomed.

Bonnie is the single parent of an adopted mixed-race child. She never thought much about religion but felt that her son should have a Jewish education. Because the boy was not converted officially, he was not welcome in most Jewish Sunday Schools. And because her child is non-European, his Jewishness was always in question. Bonnie found a Jewish home in a Secular Humanistic Jewish community where her child is accepted as a Jew.

The families in these stories did conform in at least one important way to Jewish norms—they were families with children. But a growing number of American Jews are single or don't have children. What about them? It's not easy to find an authentic way to be Jewish if you are single or don't have any children. You don't join a congregation because you don't have any kids to put through religious school; it's expensive, and there's nothing there for you. You don't have a seder or make Shabbes at home—those are family things and it seems silly to light candles all alone, especially if you have nothing to say over them because you don't really believe in the Ruler of the Universe who sanctified his Chosen People with a commandment to light Sabbath candles. But if you don't join a religious congregation, and there's nothing you can do or say at home alone to confirm your Jewishness, how can you express your identity?

What are the options for cultural Jews who are just as fiercely attached to their Jewish heritage as religious Jews are? How can they express their Jewish roots and commitment to the Jewish community? How can they find ways to celebrate Jewish holidays, educate themselves, and be part of the Jewish community and still maintain their integrity? How can these Jews find an authentic, inclusive Jewish life?

This how-to book helps answer those questions. It will help you find a way to be Jewish without being religious; to understand Jewish history without seeing Jews as "chosen" or as the particular concern of a patriarchal deity; to celebrate holidays and life-cycle occasions; to find or create the community you need so you can be the kind of Jew you want to be. And it will help you explain to others just what kind of Jew you are.

I

WHAT KIND OF JEW AM I?

1

Sit Down, Shut Up, and Pray

Before I learned Hebrew, I used to enjoy the occasional Saturday morning service I attended for Bar Mitzvahs and the monthly Shabbes get-together of my *chavurah* during which we would "make Shabbes" and sing the blessings. I loved the singing together, the use of an ancient language, the melodies, the sense of being part of my community. Then I ruined it all by learning what I was singing about, and I have never been able to regain my pleasure in those services.

The same thing happened to Dan, an anthropologist who learned Hebrew after earning his PhD. "I knew something about a lot of cultures and a lot about a few," he says, "but very little about my own. So I set out to study Judaism." What Dan found disappointed him mightily. "I thought I must have been saying something really profound," he admits sheepishly. "I couldn't believe it when I realized that all I had been doing was singing praises to God over and over again. I can't imagine a god who would really need all that adulation. After all, if he's a god, he already knows how great he is! What a waste of time and good music."

Dan believes in something he can't quite define, but it's not a personlike god who takes pleasure in people "buttering him up." The god he feels connected to is a sort of collective emanation of goodness from people. He had always felt he was adding to this collective force for good when he participated in religious services, and he still misses the feeling he got from being part of that community. But now he says he would just feel silly saying over and over again how great and glorious is a god that exists as a self-conscious persona, sitting, as Sherwin Wine has said, "like an Oriental potentate" accepting the adulation of his subjects.

Dan's understanding of religious services impelled him to look for, and find, a Jewish home in the Secular movement, a Jewish congregation where he can say what he really believes to be true.

A Quick Look at the Shabbes Service

What is it that you're saying if you pray at the morning Shabbes service? A typical Conservative service begins with preliminary readings of psalms and other prayers. This is where the first episode of cognitive dissonance occurs. The Conservative prayer book includes Psalm 136 with its chorus "For His loving-kindness endureth forever" and its praises of this loving and kind God: "Him that smote Egypt through their firstborn." When you take a look at what this psalm is saying, it really is quite shocking. We are praising God for killing the innocent little firstborn sons of the Egyptians, and we continue extolling that God's loving-kindness.

After the preliminary prayers is the Barchu, or call to prayer, a short blessing read by the leader of the service and repeated by the congregation: "Bless the Lord who is praiseworthy." "Bless the Lord who is praiseworthy for all eternity." Following that, there are more prayers and the recitation of the Shema. This is an old statement, found in the Bible, probably originally meaning to affirm the commandment to have no other gods before the god of the Hebrews. It probably originally meant "Listen, Israel, YHVH is our God, only YHVH." Now, however, it is generally translated as "Hear, O Israel, the Lord our God, the Lord is One."

More prayers follow and then the central prayer—the Amidah—is said. The Amidah is a set of nineteen blessings in the Orthodox and Conservative services. The Reform and Reconstructionist movements have omitted or changed a few of the blessings to accord with their beliefs. The first blessing reminds God of the merits of the patriarchs and asks that God, remembering the love of the patriarchs for him, bring a redeemer to their descendants. The second praises God for bringing the dead to life. The third—the Kedushah—praises God for being holy. The rest of the prayer includes statements of chosenness, including that God loves us particularly and delights in us, has exalted us above others, and draws us near to him. It continues with pleas for God's understanding, protestations of repentance, and requests for forgiveness. Then come prayers for redemption and healing and rain, the gathering in of the exiles, and restoration of judges. The twelfth blessing was inserted later than the others and is really an imprecation against non-Orthodox Jews. It says, "May the slanderers have no hope," and asks God to cut down his enemies and crush the arrogant. It continues by asking God to arouse his compassion for the righteous and godly and the "remnant" of the sages of Israel and "true" converts. It asks God to reward those who trust him. The next prayers ask for a restoration of the Temple in Jerusalem and the sacrifices at the Temple; these are generally omitted in Reform services. Finally, the prayers ask God to rebuild Jerusalem and reestablish the hereditary kingship of the House of David. The concluding prayers ask for happiness and for God to accept the prayers. They thank God for his blessings and ask for peace.

After the Amidah and a few more prayers of praise comes the Torah reading. The Torah is the scroll that contains the first five books of the Bible. A portion is read each week of the year so that the whole thing is read every year. In addition, a Haftarah—a section of the other parts of the Bible—is attached to each Torah portion and read with it. There are blessings before and after the Torah reading, and these again stress that the Jews have been chosen of all the people to receive the "Torah of Truth" from God. Some congregations insert a *d'var Torah*—a sermon about the Torah portion—at this point in the service.

The Torah reading is followed by more prayers and, in some movements, the Musaf, or additional service, which is mostly a repetition of what has already been said. The last portion of the service is marked by the Aleynu, praising God for being the Creator and for not making us like the other nations, and looking forward to the day that God will be God of the whole world. It is followed by the Kaddish for mourners. A song of praise to God, the Kaddish asserts that he is the Creator and asks that his kingdom be established on earth soon, and for peace for the Jewish people. The conclusion of the service includes the familiar songs Mi Kamokha, praising God for being God, Lord, King, and Savior, and Adon Olam, which says that God is the only Creator and will be the King forever; that he is one and unique; that he is a savior and a refuge.

The service, especially the Amidah, is really a snapshot of the diverse Jewish people and includes progressive and reactionary elements in the same breath: yearning for peace, health, and good harvests; smug self-righteousness; and wishes for the return to animal sacrifice and for the utter crushing of anyone who doesn't follow the party line. Mainly, though, it's a litany of lavish adulation of God, who concerns himself with the world.

Who Cares About the Words?

Singing together creates a sense of community that is central to the Jewish experience. The prayer book—*siddur*—which has been in its current form for several hundred years, includes psalms, prayers, and readings from the Bible and from some of the finest of Hebrew poets from ancient to modern times. The services are sung to melodies that evoke both our ancient and our more recent past. Then why not just participate in services for the history, the connection, the community and ignore or redefine what is offensive or counter to our true beliefs?

Well, lots of people do just that. The Reconstructionist philosophy is based on that idea. Reconstructionists posit a god who is unrecognizable in the prayers they say, but they sing these prayers anyway, meaning something quite different from the literal meaning of the words. Many Jews belonging to Orthodox, Reform, and Conservative congregations do the same. For them, the act of participating in the service means they are connecting themselves to their heritage, their ancestors, and other Jews everywhere. The words are not what's important to them. The meaning is in the activity, not the words.

This is certainly a valid choice; it works for them. But it doesn't work for everyone. Some of us are just constitutionally unable to say what we don't believe. We understand that words have literal meanings and transcendent meanings, but we are not willing to ignore the literal meanings to achieve the transcendent. In this we are in very good Jewish company. Many Jews have died because they would not say what they did not believe. Our martyrs throughout the ages refused to convert to Christianity or Islam and died terrible deaths; they were burned or flayed alive, decapitated or disemboweled. The penalty for refusing to say what they didn't believe was cruel. For us, here and now, saying what *we* do not believe poses only a slight social handicap, but such dissembling dishonors our martyrs and their sacrifice.

Because It's There

There are other valid reasons that nonbelievers belong to religious congregations. Rhonda, a cultural Jew whose parents were nonreligious but always belonged to a synagogue, was genuinely surprised to find that there are congregations of cultural Jews. Her parents, she is sure, never heard of any such thing, even though they lived in New York, where such congregations, fraternal groups, and schools for children abounded. And they would never have conceived of starting a group themselves.

Becky, too, has always belonged to a religious synagogue, but not because she doesn't know about other alternatives. Becky knows she could have started a new *chavurah* or congregation, but it seemed like way too much work. Becky attends a Reconstructionist synagogue with a Sunday school for children. Like many others in all the movements, she does not particularly relate to the words said in the services and she doesn't particularly like the school, but it's there. It's available. Members don't have to take the time that they'd rather spend on their families, their careers, or other interests, to work on something new. Families are so busy now. Most two-parent families have two working adults; kids have to be carted from sports to lessons; there's homework; there are community responsibilities; and, sometimes, if we're lucky, there's a cup of hot tea and a mystery novel. Starting something new takes more time and energy than many of us have.

Starting a new group is hard, but even belonging to a Secular Humanistic or Cultural congregation or *chavurah* can be time-consuming. Most are cooperatives, run by the members, with no paid staff, or only part-time help. Eileen left a busy, active, friendly Secular organization for her local Reform temple. She explains, "I just got tired of having to make everything I wanted happen. Sometimes, I just wanted to come to something that was already there, that I didn't have to invent and work on." Eileen, as a member of a religious congregation, can attend Friday night services whenever she feels like. Nobody has to scour the city for speakers and adult-education teachers—the rabbi is there to speak and teach. The Sunday School doesn't demand the participation of the parents. It's a relief for Eileen to have a Jewish place to go, a place that she does not feel responsible for. And she can continue to celebrate holidays at home in a Secular Humanistic fashion.

Art's reasons for belonging to a religious congregation also have to do with its established existence. He wouldn't mind working to build a new congregation, but, like most Jews, Art's Jewish education stopped at his Bar Mitzvah, and he, like so many others, freely admits that he doesn't remember a thing from Sunday school. Art is not happy with the religious content of his congregation and its Sunday School, but he doesn't feel he knows enough to do something different on his own. And, like most others, he's busy with his career and his family and doesn't feel he has time to embark on a serious study of Judaism and Jewish culture and history.

Marcia grew up in a Zionist Secularist home. When she had children, she wanted them to learn Hebrew. The Secularist supplemental schools didn't teach Hebrew then, and she and her husband felt that the only alternative was a synagogue school. Now, many Secular and Humanistic Sunday schools do teach Hebrew, but it is nearly impossible to learn a language by attending one class a week. A religious congregational school doesn't really teach Hebrew, either, but many kids do learn to decode Hebrew in order to read aloud, whether they understand what they are reading or not. And they do sometimes learn enough Hebrew to understand the prayer service, and that's a start.

If you really want your kids to learn Hebrew, you can send them to a Hebrew-speaking private school, but most of these are religious. You can move to Israel. Or you can make learning Hebrew a family activity. There are computer and book-based texts for home learning. Jewish Community Centers and other organizations offer conversational Hebrew classes, or you can hire a Hebrew-speaking college student as a tutor or even a Hebrew-speaking day-care provider. All of these are ways to make Hebrew a part of your home, instead of something that you send your kids to learn.

Rhonda, Becky, Eileen, Art, and Marcia can be found in every Reform, Conservative, and Reconstructionist congregation in North America. Belonging to a religious congregation is "good enough" for them only because no established alternative has presented itself. All of them will probably continue to belong to these congregations, but they can still enrich their Jewish lives with activities and rituals that are meaningful to them. An authentic Jewish home life can be created by remolding what they already do into a Jewish form that suits them. Does the family eat dinner together on Friday nights? Why not add a candlelighting and song? It takes only a minute and you can say and sing something that is truly meaningful to you instead of religious prayers. You don't have to give up your congregation and what it offers. You can add powerful cultural experiences to your own home life.

What Makes Congregations Work

Of course, many people who belong to religious congregations really love them and the religious services. These congregations are working, even for those who don't believe in any gods.

Mark and Rachel belong to a Conservative congregation in a Midwestern college town. Rachel is an agnostic who says, "I never thought that theology was very important to Jewish identity, culture, or practice. But culture is. And to me, the liturgy, Torah reading cycle, holidays, etc., are all part of that culture, and an important part." Rachel belonged, for a while, to a Reconstructionist *chavurah,* but found its practice too erratic. She calls herself a "traditionalist" and enjoys the ritual and consistency of the services she attends at the Conservative synagogue. Her husband, Mark, is an outright atheist, who is not offended by God-language because it just doesn't mean anything to him. What he loves about his congregation is the way his kids can participate. His young son and daughter know all the songs and sing with joy and gusto. They feel part of a community, and that's what Mark thinks is important about being Jewish. If his kids get that sense of community from a religious congregation, he can live with that and even enjoy it.

That sort of community and belonging is important for Jewish life, and congregations that offer it are attractive to people of any religious outlook. Janice and Jonah belong to a large Reform congregation in suburban New Jersey. They feel at home in their temple, a place where the rabbi knows their names and the names of their two sons. In an era when so many people move away from their original communities, change jobs often, and are generally pretty isolated from their neighbors, a congregation can meet the need most people have to be known and to be part of a community.

Barry's Reconstructionist congregation in a major Midwestern city offers him a different sort of satisfaction. He enjoys the intellectual challenge of grappling with traditional texts, of bringing new writings into juxtaposition with old, of thinking through the meanings of biblical writings and commentaries. And he likes the commitment to social action. When Barry acts on a political belief, he, like many of us, acts as a Jew, and he wants a Jewish context in which to express those beliefs. His congregation sponsors speakers and takes public stands. Barry, a former member of the now-disbanded progressive organization, New Jewish Agenda, is proud to be a member of a congregation that is active in the world and that does some good other than just satisfying the intellect and emotions of the membership.

The religious congregations that are working for cultural Jews are those in which everybody sings, those where a sense of community is pervasive, those that afford the members an opportunity to act Jewishly in the world.

Whether you're lucky enough to belong to one of these congregations or not, you can honor your own religious and spiritual beliefs while still maintaining your congregational membership, or you can take a deep breath, gather all your strength and energy, and join or start a cultural *chavurah,* or congregation, of your own.

2

Jewish History

Judaism is a historical process, not a philosophical formula.—Theodore Gaster

Remember your fifth-grade American history class? Remember learning this story?

And God hardened the heart of King George III and he laid great taxes upon the American colonists. Then did God speak unto Tom Paine, and he spoke saying, 'I am the Lord. You shall go unto the people and say unto them, yea, verily, shall you tell them. And they shall have one vote for one man and then shall no man tax them without representation.' And Tom Paine went and wrote what God had told him. And when the people heard this there was a great wailing for, lo, they had not adhered to the word of the Lord. And they rose up and God strengthened them.

Well, okay, you probably learned it a little differently. You probably learned about the political and economic situation of the time, about the political movements, and about the people who were the critical thinkers of the time. It probably never occurred to you that American history and the history of all the countries that ever interacted with America were controlled by some supernatural power who was concerned primarily with America. It would be foolish and ethnocentric and improbable in the extreme.

We are willing to accept that American history and European

history and Chinese history are all products of events and movements and people. Why on earth are we supposed to believe that only Jewish history is a product of a supernatural force working on the entire world to influence the Jewish people? But that is exactly how Jewish history is taught to our elementary school kids in Jewish day and supplementary schools. God controls all the different countries and people around ancient Israel in order to teach the Jewish people a lesson. Everything that happens to the Jews is because God is making a point. The great Jews were empowered by God. No human action can thwart God's will.

In teaching this, we are teaching our children that human action is futile, that people working together can have no effect on history, and that ordinary people, who are not possessed by the spirit of God, can't make any difference in the world. We are teaching them that effects have no causes other than God, making political and social and economic systems irrelevant. Of course, most of us don't want our children to believe this, and, in fact, most of our children won't believe this when they grow up, anyway. So what are they getting from their Jewish school education? Only the message that what they learn in Jewish school is not true and not relevant to their lives.

And they are getting another pernicious message from the organized Jewish community: the Orthodox Official Story, which says that all Jews were always Orthodox in exactly the way Orthodox Jews are today, that the Orthodox are the only real Jews, and that they are the only key to Jewish survival. If you go to a fund-raising dinner for Chabad, a Hasidic movement, for example, you'll find that most of the people there and most of the big donors are not Chabad Hasidim. In fact, most of them aren't even Orthodox. The room is full of Reform and Conservative Jews who have bought the Official Story. They are contributing to a movement they don't adhere to because they believe they are supporting "the real Jews," the ones who will ensure the continuity of the Jewish People. This is not true and has never been true. Orthodoxy is a *modern* invention, and the Jewish people has been a diverse group since its beginnings and continues to be one to this day.

The Orthodox mind-set is based on a profoundly ahistorical understanding of Jewish life and tradition that can be traced back to the beginnings of the rabbinic period around 100 BCE. Not long ago I heard a Chabad rabbi explain to a group that Esther in the Purim story "went to the rabbis and asked them to write her story." Now, Esther is a fictional character in a historical romance set at least four hundred years before it was written. And Esther, if she existed then, could no more have talked to a rabbi than she could have talked to an astronaut. Rabbis hadn't been invented yet. But this Chabad rabbi really believes that all Jews were always just like him. He is convinced that Abraham kept kosher, even though God hadn't yet given the commandments, and that Ruth converted to Judaism by going through a *mikveh* ritual and going before a board of three rabbis—and this about a thousand years before there was such a thing as a rabbi! The Orthodox are certainly entitled to this belief, but believing it doesn't make it true. The effect of accepting the Official Story is that non-Orthodox Jews of every kind end up feeling that they are not good or authentic Jews. And some of them just say, "If this is being Jewish, the hell with it," and leave Jewish life altogether. Both they and the Jewish community are poorer for their loss.

The Real Key to Jewish Survival

So, if God didn't make things happen in Jewish history, and if all Jews were not always Orthodox, what is the real message of Jewish history? What really happened and what does it mean?

Ellis Rivkin, in the introduction to *The Shaping of Jewish History* (1971), says, "Jewish history gives evidence, not of the triumph of a single form, belief, or set of practices, but of the proliferation of many forms, ideas, beliefs, and practices—as many as survival necessitated." The key idea here is not just that Jews have always been a diverse people, but that this diversity is a good thing, a trait that enriched the Jewish community and allowed it to survive for thirty-five hundred years. Judaism is the creation of the Jewish people in all places and at all times through their dynamic interaction with the cultures they came in contact with. Our capacity to act and adapt and diversify is what allowed our survival as a people.

Ancient and Classical Times

The Torah is not our national history. It is a mythology that has become part of our national history, a historical fiction that can give us some outlines and some general ideas about the people who lived when it was being written. It includes stories that the people remembered and interpretations that the establishment attached to those stories. It is full of anachronisms and other details that help us to differentiate between the time the stories were written and the time the stories are supposed to have taken place.

Jewish history is a constant struggle between the advocates of unity and the advocates of diversity. And it isn't always the leaders who are in favor of unity, as one might suppose. Some kings, priests, and prophets in ancient times were advocates of diversity. We don't hear all their voices, since their points of view did not prevail, but we see evidence of them all over the Bible and in later historical accounts.

A quick reading of the historical books of the Bible and the Prophets gives a taste of this diversity. Prophets preached against other prophets, calling them "false." Each of these prophets had followers who disagreed on what social and political actions were right. In the language of the times, this meant that they disagreed on what God wanted. The kings of Israel in the north and Judah in the south allowed and even supported worship of many gods (even in the Temple in Jerusalem), including the sky god and fertility gods and the goddess Astarte. These are the gods of the "high places" and "groves" that are often preached against in the Bible. This constant preaching against the worship of other gods only shows how prevalent such worship was.

There was also intense disagreement over whether sacrifices could take place anywhere, at any holy shrine, or only in Jerusalem. (In the seventh through fifteenth centuries BCE there was even a working Jewish temple where sacrifices were made in Elephantine, on an island in the Nile.) In each of these cases, the Bible supports the winners; the stories of the losers are often simply not there. But evidence of the diversity is everywhere in the polemics against the opposition and sometimes in other ancient documents discovered in modern times.

Who is a Jew, according to the Bible? The Bible accepts as a mem-

ber of the people anyone who lives as part of the ethnic community. In practical terms, this means people whose fathers were
members of the Hebrew tribes or women who marry Hebrew men.
The ancient Middle East was patrilocal; women went to live in the
families or tribes of their husbands. Therefore, men who married
"out" brought new Hebrews into the community and women who
married "out" left the community. There was no ritual of belonging or of being expelled.

Jews in Babylonia spent the generations of exile there accom-
modating themselves to Babylonian life to the extent that when
they were allowed to return to Israel around 450 BCE, very few
went. They were well integrated into Babylonian life as farmers,
soldiers, canal managers, business agents, spinners of wool, and
even as slaves. They sometimes gave their children Babylonian
names, even the names of Babylonian gods. Under both the
Babylonians and Persians, they enjoyed a significant degree of self-
government.

By the time of Alexander the Great, in the 300s BCE, more Jews
lived in Alexandria, Egypt, than in Jerusalem, and Jewish life was
exceedingly diverse, even, perhaps, as diverse as it is today. During
the period of the Greek and Roman empires, there were among the
Jews fierce nationalists, like the Maccabees, who carried out the religious rites for purely political reasons; Sadducees, who were up-
holders of the sacrificial cult and who did not believe in the afterlife
or the Oral Law of the rabbis; and Pharisees, adherents of the new
rabbinic form, which preached another, oral, revelation alongside
the written Torah (a sort of Jewish "new testament"). Just before
and after the destruction of the Second Temple in 70 CE, during the
failed rebellion against Rome, various ascetic, mystic-Gnostic
groups (sects with a mystic knowledge of spiritual things), and
messianic groups flourished. But the majority of Jews everywhere
in the Greek and Roman empires of 300 BCE to the first century of
the common era were, while still firmly self-identified and practic-
ing Jews, also modern and assimilated Hellenists, like Philo of
Alexandria, whose histories are still read today.

In various places, women had the right to divorce their husbands (which is not allowed under today's Orthodox Jewish law),
to run businesses, and even to testify in court (which is also not allowed in today's Jewish law). Jews were valued members of merce-

nary armies, as well as farmers, craftsfolk, and merchants. They gave their children Greek names like Alexander and Jason (which now sound like Jewish names!), just as we name our kids Scott and Jennifer. They sent their children to Greek schools, not Jewish schools, just as we send our kids to public schools, not Jewish day schools. They played organized sports and read philosophy and studied astronomy and mathematics and literature, just as our kids play soccer and we read popular science journals and literature and works in scientific and technical fields. They wrote Jewish fiction in Greek and Aramaic just as Philip Roth and Cynthia Ozick and Saul Bellow and Grace Paley write Jewish fiction in English. Most of them spoke Aramaic or Greek and didn't know a word of Hebrew. There is even substantial evidence of widespread intermarriage between Jews and Hellenized Egyptians. The majority of Jews in the Greek empire were much like us.

After the Romans destroyed the Temple in Jerusalem (amid bitter and bloody fighting among factions of the Jewish community) late in the first century CE, the writings that came to constitute the Jewish Bible were finally canonized by assemblies that accepted some and discarded other historical and religious texts. Biblical scholars generally agree that the authorship of stories in the Bible span a thousand years and were written down or composed by priests, courtiers, and prophets with different religious and political viewpoints. (If you're interested in how the Bible developed, I'd recommend Richard Elliott Friedman's *Who Wrote the Bible?*) The writings that found their way into the Bible include both parochial viewpoints and reflections of diversity and humanism, as do the writings that were excluded but have been preserved as Apocrypha and Pseudepigrapha. The latest writings date from the Greek empire, just before the Romans gained ascendancy.

It was during Roman times that the rabbinic form of Judaism rose and flourished. After the destruction of the Second Temple the Temple-oriented Sadducees lost their legitimacy, and after the Romans finally put down the last Jewish rebellion in 135 CE the nationalist zealots had been destroyed. Rabbinic Judaism, with no competitors left, became the dominant form of religious Judaism, and it was under the influence of the rabbinic establishment that the Oral Law was expanded and written down.

These writings, some apocalyptic and some interpreting biblical laws, became the Mishnah and other books that are Mishnaic in nature but didn't get included in the Mishnah itself, which is the core of the Talmud. Of course, even these works show the diversity of Jewish belief and practice at the time. There are lists and lists of those who "have no share in the world to come." Although Orthodox scholars believe that this is a literal reference to an afterlife, the phrase, according to Rabbi Samson Levey of Hebrew Union College, the Reform movement's rabbinic seminary, was used to mean that people who believed certain things were not good Jews, or perhaps not even Jews at all. (This is the first appearance of the idea that being Jewish is defined by particular religious beliefs.) The existence of these strictures demonstrates the existence of Jews who opposed the rabbinic interpretation of what Jews had to believe, whether organized in nonrabbinic communities like the Essenes, who were probably Gnostic dualists, or just ordinary Jews living their daily lives.

For example, take a look at Mishnah number one of the chapter called Sanhedrin in the order of the Mishnah called Nezikin. Here are the people that the Mishnah says "have no share in the world to come": the one who says that resurrection of the dead isn't in the Torah; the one who says that the Torah is not from Heaven; and the *apikorsim*. An *apikores* is one who does not believe that God is watching humans' daily lives. It's interesting and significant that this philosophy was so widespread there was a word for this belief. Today we might call an *apikores* a "heretic" or "freethinker."

The Gemara, the later writings in the Talmud, adds that *apikorsim* include atheists and those who deny the coming of a Messiah from the House of David. (This would include the entire Reform movement!) At least one scholar from Mishnaic times, Elisha ben Abuya, was castigated and expelled from the academy for his atheism.

The Gemara also includes discussions about the masses of Babylonian Jews and the problem the rabbis had because the people commonly did not follow the increasingly complex rabbinic laws on keeping kosher, on family purity, or on observing the Sabbath. Clearly, all such nonrabbinic beliefs and practices were common in the time of the Mishnah, which was completed about 200 CE, and the Gemara, which was completed about 500 CE. In fact, there are scholars who believe that the work of the rabbinic establishment, the minute detail of the law, and the endless discussions, were tolerated by both the Babylonian authorities and the Jewish masses as a way to keep the intellectual elite happy and busy and out of politics or economic affairs.

The Middle Ages

Whether under Byzantine, Roman, Babylonian, or Visigothic rule, Jews in the Middle Ages were astoundingly diverse and participated freely in the workings of both the social and economic worlds of the majority cultures as they left agricultural pursuits and began to play a huge role in the world of commerce and trade. Jews of Northern Africa and Persia were international merchants with routes from Spain to China and India, living among and interacting extensively with other peoples. Rabbinic Judaism was forced to adapt, and Jewish laws forbidding certain economic transactions and social interactions between Jews and non-Jews were relaxed and finally disappeared entirely.

The majority of Jews in the early Middle Ages (500–1000 CE) lived in Spain, North Africa, and the Middle East, and most spoke and wrote in Arabic. Business and love letters along with great works of Jewish philosophy and poetry were written in Arabic, and the poetry echoed Arabic forms and themes. Documents from the Cairo Genizah (archives) indicate that Jews engaged in the same sexual practices as their neighbors, including concubinage and homoerotic relationships. And even one Exilarch—the ruler of the Jews in Babylonia—was said to have married the daughter of a Sassanian Persian shah. It is generally supposed that Mohammed was influenced not by rabbinic texts but by ordinary Jews of the area who had little or no formal rabbinic education and transmitted the Judaism they knew to him.

One of the ways we see the extent of assimilation is in the laws that were made by the non-Jewish rulers who were trying to stop it. In all the places Jews lived, whether under the rule of Christians, Muslims, or others, from time to time we see laws forbidding intermarriage with Jews; eating, celebrating holidays, or bathing with Jews; using Jewish doctors; owning businesses together with Jews;

and conversion to Judaism. These laws were made to stop common existing customs, and they were made over and over again, which suggests that they were impossible to enforce.

We tend to believe that Judaism is strongest when Jews are oppressed and that freedom is a threat to Jewish survival. Understanding that the Jews have survived as a people despite long periods of economic prosperity and social acceptance should make our current comfortable situation less frightening to those who want to wall off Jews from the rest of society.

The variety and complexity of Jewish economic and social expressions were mirrored by the religious and philosophical variety and complexity in the Jewish world of the Middle Ages. Multiple religious forms abounded both in the early and later Middle Ages all over Europe, the Middle East, and North Africa. While those official interpreters of the tradition whose deliberations were recorded in the Talmud were codifying and explaining Jewish beliefs in their own way, other codifers and interpreters were writing rival texts, many of which were found in the Cairo Genizah.

Four main movements in Jewish life vied with rabbinic Judaism for the allegiance of the masses throughout this long period, and all of these movements have echoes in today's diverse Jewish world.

Messianism

Messianic movements abounded in Jewish communities in Europe and the Middle East. Although Cyrus the Great was called messiah by the Jews returning to Israel in the fifth century BCE, the word *messiah* did not have the meaning we now associate with it. In fact, when Rabbi Akiva called the military leader Bar Kochba messiah in the second century CE, he did not seem to have in mind much more than a military leader sent by God to set up a Jewish state. Jesus was recognized as a messiah in his own time, but his godhood was not recognized even by the early Christians, who were just beginning to break with Judaism a century after his death. It was during rabbinic times that messianism took on religious, rather than political, significance in Judaism.

The early Middle Ages was a time of rising messianism among both Jews and Muslims. The best known of these early messiahs is Mohammed, the father of Islam, who, according to some Islamic texts, was regarded by some prominent Jewish converts as the messiah. We know about others mostly from the diatribes written against them in the rabbinic texts, including works by Maimonides and Sa'adya Gaon and by Muslim and Christian adversaries of their own messiahs as well. Some of these messianic movements sparked armed uprisings against the establishment religions and sometimes even against the civil governments. Some of these messiahs could cure disease. Some changed religious law or taught reincarnation or claimed descent from the House of David. They were diverse, and each of the messiahs we know about had many followers, enough to provoke the rabbinic establishment into attacking them both verbally and sometimes physically.

The later Middle Ages had its share of messiahs as well. After the expulsion of Jews from Spain, David Reubeni and Shlomo Molko each gathered thousands of followers in Turkey, Greece, Italy, and Iberia. Molko's messianism penetrated into France and Germany, where he was burned at the stake by the Office of the Inquisition.

During the very late Middle Ages, two messiahs captured the imaginations and loyalty of huge numbers of Jews in Europe. Sabbatai Zevi, a mystic, declared himself the messiah in 1666. Bands of prophets like those in biblical days formed and traveled about through Eastern and Western Europe, Africa, and the Middle East, spreading the word. Entire communities of Jews in Poland, disheartened after the Chmielnicki massacres of 1648, abandoned their homes and everything they owned to go to Israel. When Sabbatai Zevi converted to Islam under threat of death, some of his followers were devastated. But others believed that the true Sabbatai Zevi had not converted, but had ascended to heaven. Sects of mystical adherents rose in Turkey, Greece, Italy, and Poland, in spite of declarations of *herem,* or excommunication, by the official Jewish leaders. Remnants of the Sabbatean sect still exist in Turkey.

Jacob Frank, in the next century, came into contact with Sabbatean messianism when he visited Salonika, Greece. Frank declared himself the messiah and led a moderately successful cult centered on sexual activity as a means to mystic unity. Frank and his supporters converted to Catholicism so that they would be protected from the anger of non-messianic Jews.

Jewish messianism flourished throughout Jewish history, and it was such a powerful idea that rabbinic Judaism gradually had to adapt its own notions of messianism so that it could appeal to the masses of Jews and keep them from following self-declared messiahs. Some Orthodox Jews believe in the concept of a messenger from God, who will lead the Jews and change the world so that all will worship the true God, an idea articulated in the late biblical and early rabbinic ages. The Reform movement has declared that there is no individual who will be sent by God, but rather that the messianic age, which we are all responsible to bring about, will be a time of universal justice as envisioned by the prophets. The Lubavitch sect of the Hasidic Jewish movement is riven by controversy over whether the late leader of the movement, the rebbe, Menachem Shneerson, was the messiah. It remains to be seen whether the rest of the rabbinic establishment will still consider as Jews those who believe that the messiah has come.

Mysticism

Mystical movements related to earlier Gnostic movements were popular during the Middle Ages, beginning in the immediate post-Talmudic era, around 500 CE, in the Middle East and becoming a primary Jewish form in Europe in the 1500s through 1700s. Mystic Judaism says that mystic knowledge—wisdom achieved by direct knowledge of God—is beyond Talmudic knowledge, and that mystic adherents know more than those who study only Talmud and Jewish law. This was a radical idea because up until this challenge Talmudic sages had been considered the elite among the Jews.

Messianism, magic, astrology, demonology, mystic union with God, mediation between people and God, reincarnation (including into animals), numerology, and all sorts of supernatural phenomena were subjects of study. Numerous movements all over the Jewish world formed schools and wrote books that influenced and changed rabbinic Judaism. The Zohar, which is the primary work of Kabbalah (mystic knowledge), was written in Spain in the 1300s and collects mystic, dualistic/demonological, and astrological ideas from earlier and contemporary Jewish and Albigensian (dualist) proponents. The dualistic nature of kabbalism is apparent in the

Zohar's insistence that Jews are by nature linked to the sacred spheres while non-Jews are, by their very essence, linked to the impure. This dualism is also seen in the mystic idea that the heavenly and earthly spheres are linked in a system of mutual influence in which earthly actions influence heavenly spheres.

Modern Jews are typically amazed at the variety of religious beliefs propounded by devout and prominent Jews of the time. Among the varied beliefs that we now think of as less mainstream but that were propounded by religious leaders of the time are a belief that God has a measurable physical body; a sort of pantheism in which God is seen in everything; and a mystic union with God in which the person who achieves this union comes back to the world with supernatural powers. This last idea is echoed in the later stories of Hasidic rabbis who are miracle workers. There was also a strong strain of asceticism, which echoed the asceticism of the Essenes and other early Gnostic Jews. Rabbi Isaac Luria, perhaps the best known of the Safed mystics, urged Jews to save the souls of the world by constant self-mortification, not eating, not sleeping, and not enjoying life.

Mystical movements are profoundly upsetting to the establishment because mystic knowledge is an alternative to the authority of the rabbinic texts and traditions. By the 1700s, in order to meet the popular challenge of the mystics, rabbinic authorities were forced to show that mystic knowledge is compatible with revealed (that is, rabbinic) authoritative teaching. In doing so, they legitimized one of their strongest opponents and, in fact, adopted so much of the mystic ethos that a sort of superstitious Judaism took over much of the Jewish world, so that mystic movements, although they seemed to be outside the mainstream, became part of modern rabbinic tradition, which changed dramatically during the Middle Ages. Rabbis began to accept and even practice the mystic arts to the extent that even such rabbinic stalwarts as Bahya ibn Pakuda included mystic teachings in their writings.

Mystic movements still exist and, in fact, look back to the writings of the Middle Ages as well as to modern charismatic mystic leaders. Writings from some branches of the Jewish Renewal movement include accounts of "received" knowledge and communing with and conversing with dead rabbis of the past two thousand years. Hasidic sects also maintain mystic traditions, including those of the rebbe, as the head of each sect is known, as an intercessor between people and God. The rabbinic ideas of careful, detailed observances (like being careful to bake the matzah within exactly eighteen minutes of adding the water, or moving the Shabbes candles only if they are on a tray with a mundane object like a saltshaker), the importance of *kavanah* (concentration/attention to the symbolism of the actions performed), and *tikkun olam* (the perfection of the physical world in order to complete the Creation) are taken directly from the mystics.

Karaism and Other Nonrabbinic Judaisms

The Karaite idea arose in the 700s, alongside Islam. Karaism was a radical rebellion against rabbinic Judaism that grew, contracted, died out, and rose again all through the Middle Ages. It denies that rabbinic interpretations of Torah and rabbinic law are "Torah from Sinai" and insists that each Jew has the authority to read and understand the Bible. Karaites are to Judaism what the Protestant Reformers were to Catholicism and seem almost like modern fundamentalists in their total reliance on the source document. Like modern fundamentalist leaders, Karaite leaders, such as founder Anan ben David, denied the validity of biblical interpretation but then demanded that their followers accept the leader's interpretations.

While the first Karaites believed that only the Torah—the first five books of the Bible—were valid, later some Karaites accepted the entire Jewish Bible. Karaites were prominent in the study of Hebrew language structure and established an academy in Jerusalem in the 900s. The internally diverse Karaite movement spread all over Persia, northern Africa, the Middle East, Spain, Turkey, Cyprus, and up into the Balkans and the Crimea, and from there into Poland and Lithuania. The movement was prominent enough to have been denounced by such rabbinic leaders as Sa'adya Gaon and Maimonides, who tried, over a period of several hundred years, to have Karaites expelled from the Jewish community. Nevertheless, the Karaite movement clearly had an influence on rabbinic Judaism, as even Abraham ibn Ezra quotes Karaite writings.

But Karaism was also a political and social movement against elitism and hierarchy in Jewish life and such prevalent practices as the buying of rabbinic positions by those unqualified to hold them. The Karaites were particularly attractive to poor Jews who were overwhelmed by the meticulous detail and ritual demanded by the rabbinate. (This is ironic, however, since the Karaite rules are, in many respects, stricter than the rabbinic rules.)

There are only a few thousand Karaites living today, but parallel elements appear in both modern rabbinic Judaism and modern secular Judaism. The Reform movement says it bases its religion on the Bible rather than on the Talmud and later rabbinic works, although the movement has tended in recent years to take on more rabbinic traditions. The Reform religious movement, like the biblical religion, does not believe in an afterlife and does not believe that rabbinic laws are God-given. The anticlericalism of the Karaites is also echoed in the early Secularist movement of the 1700s, which was strongly anticlerical and remains at least suspicious of official rabbinic leadership.

Also during the rise of Islam, another sect, the Isawiyya, was formed in Persia, spread as far as Spain, and lasted at least into the twelfth century. Evidence of the Isawiyya exists in both Muslim and Jewish texts of the time. The Issawiya believed that Mohammed and Jesus were true prophets, but not prophets to the Jews. They venerated rabbis and allowed intermarriage with rabbinic Jews but held different views on a number of ritual matters.

Philosophy and Freethought

Just as in classical times, not all forms of Judaism were concerned primarily with religious observance. During the Middle Ages, philosophy flowered among the Jews. While many Jews interested in philosophical thought were also religious adherents, other Jews were not interested in observance or were Freethinkers.

Hiwi al-Balkhi, who lived in the 800s, probably in Persia, is known only through the writings of his opponents, both rabbinic Jews and Karaites, who suppressed his work, evidently believing it to be a threat. Hiwi argued that the Bible is internally inconsistent and that the god of the Bible and the rabbis was neither just nor compassionate but whimsical and limited in knowledge and power.

Freethought was not confined only to the world of Jews under

Islam. Kalonymos ben Kalonymos, one of a family of famous
European Jewish poets, poked fun at the practice of perpetual
study of arcane ritual. Susskind of Trimberg, a German Jewish
minstrel of the 1200s, wrote poems that praised Freethought.
Rashi, a European rabbinic leader of the 1000s, wrote blisteringly
about Jews who publicly desecrated the Sabbath by transgressing
the restrictive laws. Judging from his strictures, there must always
have been Jews who did not believe that the Sabbath should be
kept holy in the way the rabbis believed it should.

The Spanish Jews, primarily under Islam, were integrated into
cultured society as poets, scientists, doctors, and philosophers.
They wrote and communicated primarily in Arabic and Spanish
rather than the Hebrew that few Jews were familiar with. Famous
poets and philosophers such as Solomon ibn Gabirol certainly believed in a god, but this was a god of Platonic essence and in no
way a rabbinic god of providence or imminence. Even the great
Maimonides did not believe in the rabbinic god, although he
thought it was good for the masses to believe in such a god. In fact,
the mystic rabbis of Christian Western Europe bitterly opposed
him and succeeded in suppressing his work for several hundred
years.

By the time of the Crusades, beginning in 1096 and lasting three
hundred years, the rabbinic authorities in many places had coercive
powers. While there is some evidence that Jewish communities in
Spain had actually carried out the death penalty against heretics,
most of the power of the community was based on the *cherem,* or
excommunication. Upon a declaration of *cherem,* a person was removed from all economic and social ties to the community, and
none of his or her actions or teachings could be discussed. Because
of the efficacy of this power, we have little extant material from
nontheistic or antitheistic Jews and have to rely on the writings of
those who inveighed against them. Nonetheless, we can see the influences of these Jews in modern non-Orthodox rabbinic Judaism.
Maimonidean and earlier ideas of a distant god, barely more than
a prime mover, are common among Reform and even some
Conservative Jews, including those who cling to traditionally religious prayer and ritual. Biblical criticism and the understanding
that the Bible was written over a period of a thousand years by
multiple authors has become entirely mainstream. The notion that

not all religious law is absolutely binding is the basis of all non-Orthodox Judaism. Today's Secular and Humanistic Jews are only one outgrowth of the philosophical and freethinking strain of Judaism from biblical times through the Middle Ages and on to the present.

Modern Times

Jewish diversity has continued into the present. During the last three hundred years, rabbinic Judaism has ensured its survival and continued hegemony by continuing to change and adapt in relation to both the outside world and non-rabbinic Judaism within the Jewish world, just as it has since its inception.

Modern Judaisms result, just as classical Judaisms did, from the interaction of Jews and the surrounding societies. The late 1600s saw a general diminution of Jewish self-rule in Europe. In Eastern Europe this resulted from oppression; the contraction of Jewish self-rule in Western Europe resulted from the emancipation of the Jews.

In Eastern Europe the Jews had generally been economically successful and had been allowed a high degree of autonomy and self-government. Following the upheavals of 1648 and the subsequent national border shifts that put most Eastern European Jews under Russian rule, Jewish life became much more difficult. Traditional Jewish occupations were forbidden to Jews and their movement was restricted. Many Jews lived in small self-governing communities, but the romantic shtetl in which everyone was poor but pious and happy is little more than a myth. Norman Cantor, normally a strong proponent of the superiority of Ashkenazic Jewry, writes in *The Sacred Chain* (1994) that the small self-governing Jewish communities were ruled by a strong and often corrupt alliance of the rabbinic establishment and wealthy Jews; any individual freedom was stifled. The poor were exploited and lived in misery. Crime abounded, and the communities were periodically overrun by hoodlums who, encouraged by the state, ransacked homes, raped, and murdered.

The rest of the Jews, those who lived in rural areas together with Christians and those who lived in the larger cities in the Pale of Settlement, had less communal autonomy than shtetl Jews, although, because the force of community was less, they had more personal autonomy. Their lives were, nonetheless, made miserable by anti-Jewish laws and actions.

In the West, the growing emancipation of the Jews and sporadic acceptance of Jews as quasi citizens demanded that as a condition of emancipation the Jews give up their communal autonomy and identity. The emancipated Jewish idea *"a yid in der heym; a mentsh oifn gahs"* (a Jew at home, a plain human being in public) was a demand to reduce Jewish life to religion and to forgo all national identity other than the identity of the state in which the Jew was living.

The conditions in Eastern and Western Europe and the Jewish responses to them created the five types of Judaism we see in the modern Western Jewish (Ashkenazic) world: Hasidism, Liberal Judaism, Modern Orthodoxy, Zionism, and Secularism.

By this time, Eastern Jews, those who lived in the Middle East and Northern Africa, were a small minority of the Jewish world, which is why their modern history is not included here. Nonetheless, it is an interesting history and includes much of the same diversity found in Ashkenazic Jewry.

Hasidism

Hasidism is a mystic movement, originally a radical challenge to the authority of rabbinic Judaism. The early movement held two seemingly incompatible ideals: the ordinary individual's joyous union with God and the mystic, intercessionary power of wonder-working rebbes. When Hasidism arose in Eastern Europe in the 1700s, it was attacked fiercely by the rabbinic establishment, and Hasidim were routinely excommunicated. The most important rabbi of the time, the Vilna Gaon, decreed that Jews could not marry Hasidim, which meant that he did not consider the Hasidim to be Jews at all.

Nonetheless, the movement was extremely popular, since it had the mystic's advantage of direct revelation and spiritual experience without the need for tedious rabbinic study. The purpose of obeying Jewish law, in prior rabbinic thought, was to gain rewards in the afterlife. Hasidism held that the purpose of obeying Jewish law was to gain ecstatic communion with God. In fact, Hasidic leaders taught that even mundane acts could lead to communion with God, if pursued with attention and intent—a very Zen notion that has been carried forward into the modern Hasidic-style Jewish Renewal movement.

But there was yet another seemingly paradoxical strain, a strong ascetic component. Rabbi Nachman of Bratslav, one of the best known of the early Hasidic leaders, emphasized joy and dancing while also encouraging his followers to fast and engage in other forms of self-denial and discomfort. The Bratslaver Hasidim, in fact, resorted to magical or miraculous thinking to the extent that they were prohibited from consulting doctors. Both exuberant and ascetic strains existed among the opulent courts of Hasidic rabbis and among impoverished followers.

The Hasidim were roundly attacked by the rabbinic establishment, which even arranged for the government to imprison Hasidic leaders. Over time, however, in response to the challenges of the Enlightenment, Hasidism and rabbinic Judaism came to a mutual toleration, and each adopted some of the other's ideals and flavor. The most successful Hasidic sect today, the Lubavitch, or Chabad, movement, stresses study and learning as much as does non-Hasidic rabbinic Judaism, and the Hasidim have become just as clerical as the rabbinic establishment. At the same time, mystic ideas have entered rabbinic Judaism, and ordinary rabbinic Jews now feel entitled to spiritual experiences facilitated by the religious establishment. This sort of ecstatic spiritual experience is new in rabbinic Judaism and appeared as an accommodation to Hasidic successes.

Hasidim, the most visible of the Orthodox Jews, have been outstandingly successful in portraying themselves as "the real Jews." Every great Lubavitch function is attended by ordinary modern Jews who donate large sums to Hasidic institutions because they have been led to believe that those institutions are carrying forward the Judaism of the ages. In fact, Hasidism is a modern Jewish movement no more connected to the religion of Abraham or Moses or King David or even Rabbi Hillel than is any other Judaism of modern times. Not only is it a modern movement (although it has roots in the mysticism of the Middle Ages), but it has been, for most of its existence, a fringe movement despised by the rabbinic establishment. In only three hundred years of existence, this movement has succeeded in positioning itself so that modern Jews believe that Hasidim are the authentic Jews who represent a pure strain of Judaism from ancient times to the present day. They could not have done this without the failure of the other movements to teach a Jewish history based on facts rather than on mythology.

Liberal Judaism

The Jewish Reform movement arose in Western Europe at exactly the same time as the Hasidic movement arose in Eastern Europe. The eighteenth-century Reform movement, which spawned both the modern Reform and the modern Conservative movements, was primarily an attempt to make Jews more acceptable to the Christian majority, but there was also an element of the movement that truly sought to reform Judaism because it saw Judaism the way the Christian majority did: backward, superstitious, lacking in decorum, and somehow debased. In that time, it was also commonly believed that Jews committed more crimes than others. The extent to which this conception was held is illustrated by Moses Mendelssohn, who defended the Jews by stating that the Jewish criminality rate was about the same as the rate among non-Jews.

In 1810 the first Reform Jewish school was opened in Germany. Services were conducted by a single leader and were dignified, organized, and accompanied by organ music. Soon the Reform movement added a sermon in German (or the native language of the area) and replaced Bar Mitsvah with Confirmation. Abraham Geiger, one of the early reformers, even called for an end to circumcision. For a brief period, in an attempt to further imitate Protestant mores, services were held on Sundays, both in Europe and America, but that innovation didn't last long.

These were all changes in form, not content. Not long after, however, the Reform movement began to take the religious positions it holds today, including the denial of the coming of a messiah and the resurrection of the dead, and the elimination of the prayer asking for the restoration of the Temple in Jerusalem, with its animal sacrifices.

Moses Mendelssohn, who is known as the Father of Reform

Judaism, was the most prominent proponent of the Jewish Enlightenment, called in Hebrew the *Haskalah,* which began in the 1700s,
seeking to modernize Jews by bringing the Enlightenment to the
Jewish community and opening Jewish life to secular knowledge.
Mendelssohn wrote philosphical works that defended the immortality of the soul and the existence of God. He translated the Torah
into German so that ordinary Jews could study it to learn German.
His own commentary was included. This translation was immediately banned by rabbinic authorities.

Now most of us think of Liberal (Reform and Conservative)
Judaism as mainstream, but in the 1850s the Board of Deputies of
British Jews, which was supposed to be a representative body of all
Jews, wouldn't allow Reform Jews to be seated. And it wasn't until
1999 that Israel's Supreme Court declared that non-Orthodox
Jews must be seated on municipal relgious councils. Furthermore,
there is an ongoing debate in Israel about whether non-Orthodox
converts to Judaism are to be accepted under the Law of Return,
which allows all Jews into Israel and grants them immediate citi-
zenship.

Even today, one of the attacks the Reform community endures is
that Reform leads to the end of Judaism. Opponents of Reform
point out that the children of Moses Mendelssohn converted to
Christianity. This is perfectly true. It is also true, however, that the
son of the Orthodox chief rabbi of France likewise converted to
Christianity, as did the son of the founder of the Lubavitch Hasidic
movement.

Modern Orthodoxy

What we now think of as Orthodoxy is a modern creation, a reaction to Hasidism and Reform. It was invented to defend the concept of the Oral Law against both those who denied it and those
who claimed it could be superseded. The Oral Law doctrine, long a
rabbinic mainstay, holds that all of Jewish law, including that
which is made today or will be made tomorrow, was given to
Moses by God on Mount Sinai and handed down through a chain
of elders, prophets, and learned men to the rabbis of today.
Therefore, all decisions that are made by accepted (Orthodox) rabbis are really the word of God.

In opposition to the Hasidic movement, which teaches that individuals can have direct knowledge of God, just as the prophets did, the new Orthodox in Eastern Europe, who called themselves Misnagdim ("those who fight against" the Hasidim) proclaimed that revelation ended over two thousand years ago and that the only source for religious knowledge is the extant texts and the interpretations that can be teased (or forced) out of them. This was the basis for their excommunication of leaders of the early Hasidic movement.

In opposition to the Reform movement, which denies the validity of the Oral Law as God-given, the new Orthodox in Central Europe in the 1700s and 1800s proclaimed not only that the Oral Law was divine but also that only those who believed this were capable of understanding and interpreting Jewish law as rabbis. This is the basis for their current denial of Jewish identity to those who convert under non-Orthodox auspices. It is also the basis for their 1945 excommunication of Mordechai Kaplan, the founder of the Reconstructionist movement.

The position of this new Orthodox movement, led by Samson Raphael Hirsch, was that it has the only direct line back to Moses and is therefore the only true interpreter of Judaism. The more that other branches of Judaism accept that they, themselves, are only offshoots of the true Jewish stem, Orthodoxy, the more the Orthodox position is validated. Only attention to the real history of the Jewish people can show that all branches and movements of Judaism are formed from Jewish roots and are nourished by the same surrounding soil. This includes Modern Orthodoxy, which formed itself through interaction with other Jewish branches and a modern society. Although formed in reaction to other Judaisms, it integrated some of their ideas: decorous worship, secular education, the attention to personal spirituality, modern dress (as opposed to the dress of the Hasidim), and sermons in the vernacular.

Secularism

We tend to think of Freethought and Secularism as modern outgrowths of the Jewish Enlightenment of the 1700s and 1800s, but this dates the Secularist movement at least a century too late. There is evidence that there was a major antirabbinic movement among the bourgeoisie in Europe, including Germany, Holland, and Italy, by the 1600s. Italy, especially, was home to a liberal Jewish movement in the mid-1500s that included such scholars as Azariah de Rossi, who pointed out the contradictions between Talmudic beliefs and scientific knowledge, and Leon da Modena, who, although a rabbi himself, attacked many rabbinic precepts and asserted that historical evidence is more to be believed than is revelation.

Further, the dating of Secularism to the 1800s ignores the influence of the Jews from Spain and Portugal. Many of these Jews fled to the Ottoman Empire, where they and their descendants participated in progressive Secular organizations. Some Conversos—those who converted to Catholicism under the Inquisition—(and some of their children and grandchildren) came back to Judaism after being exposed to both Catholicism and Protestant anticlericalism. Judaism was a voluntary choice for them, and they were inclined to feel that the form of Judaism they practiced and the amount of clerical authority they chose to accept was also a matter of choice. Sephardic Jews of the 1600s, such as Uriel da Costa and Baruch Spinoza, were among the first Secularists and Freethinkers.

Uriel da Costa (1585–1640) was born and raised a Catholic, but when he was a young man, his family, then living in Holland, reverted to Judaism. Da Costa publicly challenged the idea that rabbis had the authority to declare God's will, and was excommunicated and cut off from the entire Jewish community. Sometime later, he renounced his views to allow his mother, who alone had not shunned him, back into the Jewish community. Although he endured immense humiliation, he was desperate to reestablish his connection with the Jewish people. Nonetheless, he could not continue to profess what he did not believe and finally killed himself.

Baruch Spinoza (1632–1677), who was a child when da Costa died, had an easier time. Spinoza had a Jewish education but became involved in the dissent movement, which led to his excommunication. Spinoza's excommunication was not as onerous as da Costa's, since Spinoza had Freethinker friends among both Jews and Christians. He wrote that biblical laws were not binding and that Moses did not write the Bible. He demonstrated that the Bible itself contradicted the teachings of the rabbis. Spinoza did not believe in any supernatural self-conscious god, but rather called the workings of nature and the universe "God." Nowadays the idea that the Bible has numerous sources is accepted by all but the most fundamentalist of Jews, but in the 1600s saying so was grounds for excommunication.

Not only philosophers but also many ordinary Jews were Secularists. Joseph Suess Oppenheimer, for example, who worked for the Duke of Wuerttemberg, is described as "not observant." Oppenheimer, nonetheless, refused to convert to Christianity, even when threatened with death.

These early secularist thinkers were active at the same time as the Sabbatean messianic movement, which is a phenomenon of the Middle Ages. The forerunners of the Secularist movement, often thought of as a radical modern movement, date from a hundred years before the founders of Hasidism, which positions itself as traditional!

The Jewish free thinkers of Western Europe tended to integrate into Christian society. They often went so far as to make "dry baptisms," becoming nominal Christians in order to be able to study in the universities or gain other positions, even though they were not believers. Some Eastern European Jewish free thinkers also integrated into the society of free thinkers from every cultural background. But Eastern Europe also saw the development of communal ways to be a secular Jew, and the Secular Jewish movement we know today stems from these Eastern European secularists.

It was in the mid-1800s that Jews began to self-identify as Secularists and to form a philosophy and a movement. The writers of this time were influenced by the Romantic era in which they lived, an era in which "peoplehood" had been discovered and idealized. Secularism was based on the idea that there was a distinct Jewish national spirit that had been created over the centuries of Jewish experience and that this national spirit, or "peoplehood," rather than religious dogma, was what defined being Jewish.

The movement's philosophies were expounded by scholars who founded a number of branches within the secular movement: Political Zionism, Cultural Zionism, Labor Zionism, Diaspora Nationalism, Socialism, and Yiddish Nationalism among them. We now think of Zionism as a trans-movement phenomenon, but at its inception it was almost entirely a Secularist movement and its most important leaders were Secularists.

The leader of the non-Zionist wing of Secularism was Simon Dubnow (1860–1941), a historian and the originator of the idea of Diaspora Nationalism, which holds that Jews should have national rights as Jews within the nations in which they live (sort of like Native Americans in the US). He believed that Jewish communities should develop autonomy in social services, education, culture, and legal matters, much as they had for the preceding two thousand years. Mordechai Kaplan's vision of the Reconstructed Jewish community, serving all the needs of its members, owes its form to Dubnow.

Another proponent of Secularism was Chaim Zhitlowsky, often called "the father of the Secularist movement." Zhitlowsky (1865–1943) wrote, traveled, and lectured widely about Secularism, socialism, and Yiddishism. He was one of the first thinkers to show how Jewish holidays could be celebrated in nonreligious ways.

The flowering of Yiddish culture in theater, music, fiction, and critical, philosophical and historical writing, journalism and education made Jewish nationalism a reality. In Europe and America, Yiddish newspapers, journals, and theaters abounded. Political, economic, and philosophical conversations were carried on in Yiddish. Love songs and labor songs and political satire were sung in Yiddish. Poems and stories about nature, love, politics, and the human condition were published. Yiddish, the thousand-year-old language of 80 percent of the world's Jews, seemed to be at the heart of Jewish national expression.

The faction of the Secularist movement most opposed to the insistence on the value of a specifically Jewish identity was the Bund, the Jewish Socialists. The Bund began as a self-help society of workers, providing funerals, insurance, and celebrations, as well as strike assistance and a Jewish workers' presence in the larger labor movement. This faction was composed of two separate but intertwined sets of members, the trade unionists and the socialists. Despite its presence in the national and international socialist and labor movements and its avowed universalism, the Bund's later ideology provided that the Jews should have the same national and cultural autonomy as all other ethnicities. At the same time, Jewish labor activists became leaders in national labor movements in Europe and America.

Between 1910 and 1950, several networks of Jewish supplementary schools *(kindershule, mittlshule,* and *hekhereh kursn),*
communal organizations and self-help societies flourished in the
United States. Organized under ideological umbrellas, Zionist,
Yiddishist, and *linkeh* (leftist), these institutions affected the lives
of what has been estimated as over half of American Jews.

Three things killed Secular Jewish expression at midcentury:
The Nazis, Stalin, and America. The Nazis wiped out not only
Jews but also Yiddish culture. Stalin waged war on Yiddish culture
and killed Jewish cultural leaders. In America, Jews were offered
the opportunity to be prosperous Americans—but the price was
giving up their specific national and cultural identity. In only a
quarter of a century, from the early 1930s to the mid-1950s,
Yiddish Diaspora Nationalism, the product of a millennium, was
destroyed. Jews who wanted to retain their ethnic and cultural
identity were faced with the longstanding Western European
dilemma: how to be nonreligious Jews and also citizens of the
countries in which they lived.

Those Jews who retained cultural rather than religious identity
were marginalized by the Jewish establishment and were red-baited
during the McCarthy era. The few remaining Secularist federations
fell apart and did not rejoin in an active movement until the
Congress of Secular Jewish Organizations was founded in 1965,
bringing together the isolated shules and Secularist groups that had
survived. In that year, Harold Gales, of the Jewish Parents Insitute
in Detroit, called together leaders of the various organizations and
formed the precursor to the CSJO. Leaders and members of the
CSJO meet for an annual conference with workshops, perfor-
mances, discussions, and meetings (not to mention singing and
dancing). For the last twenty-five years, a teen and young adult
conference has been held concurrently. In addition to the yearly
conference, CSJO members exchange holiday programs, curriculum materials, and speakers, and graduates of CSJO Sunday
schools often teach in CSJO Sunday schools where they're attending college. CSJO is actively involved in publishing, in social action, and in helping new Secularist communities to establish and
publicize themselves.

Zionism

Zionism began as part of the Secularist movement in Eastern Europe. It was a radical revolt against the rabbinic understanding of exile and redemption. The rabbinic authorities prayed for the return to Zion and the reestablishment of the Temple, but they did not believe that they should act to make this prayer a reality. Only the coming of the messiah would re-create Israel as the home of the Jews, and it was arrogant of humans to believe they could accomplish this. The bulk of the religious establishments (Liberal, Modern Orthodox, and Hasidic) were firmly anti-Zionist.

Zionism is now seen as the dream-made-reality of Theodore Herzl. Herzl, however, was the leader of only one faction of Zionism, Political Zionism, which held that the Jews needed an independent state. Herzl did not originally insist on historic Israel, but the Political Zionist movement soon settled on Israel as the place most likely to gain support. Herzl saw a new Israel as a modern Western state and was successful in lobbying Western European countries to support its establishment.

Before Political Zionism, autonomous groups of mainly young Eastern European Jews had started settling in Palestine after the oppressive May Laws of the early 1880s. These are the pioneers who cleared swamps, built kibbutzim, and created a homeland for themselves in historic Israel. This Zionist movement began without a particular ideology, but later those who actually moved to the land and began to work and live there were Socialist Zionists, members of the Poale Zion. While the earlier settlers had established communal settlements because they were practical, the Poale Zion established communal settlements because they believed that this was the ideal way to live. These ideological socialists were led by Ber Borochov, who wanted to normalize the Jews economically and create a society in which Jews were farmers and workers as well as intellectuals and shopkeepers.

Others, such as A. D. Gordon, believed that working the land would transform the Jew into a better person. In this, he was very like the leaders of the early Liberal movement, who believed that the Jewish character had become debased through economic marginalization.

Ahad Ha-am (1856–1927) was the proponent of Cultural

Zionism, the idea that the Jewish spirit could not be expressed out-side of Eretz Israel, the Land of Israel. Ahad Ha-am was not a Political Zionist—that is, he did not believe that Jews had to have a state. He believed that the best and most creative Jews should move to Palestine and create a new Jewish culture to invigorate the Jews of the rest of the world. His disdain for the Eastern European religious Jewish culture based on impractical piety and ritual prac-tice is prevalent in Israel today. This widespread attitude has had unfortunate results, such as the denigration of the Yiddish lan-guage and culture.

Some religious Jews were also Zionists. There were a few reli-gious Zionist groups among those who settled in Palestine in the 1880s, and there was support for Zionism among the Sephardim of the Balkans. Some religious Jews supported Herzl's Political Zionism because they believed Jews needed a haven. The bulk of the Zionist movement, however, was secular.

It seems hard to believe, now that Zionism has practically be-come the organizing principle of modern Judaism, that it was very recently rejected by every major Jewish religious movement. All the religious movements except for a few Hasidic sects are now strongly pro-Israel. This turnaround of the Orthodox and Liberal establishments was accomplished in less than half a century, the time between the rise of Hitler in 1933 and the Six-Day War in 1967. The profoundly Secularist notion that the Jews themselves could create a new Jewish homeland in Israel, without the inter-vention of any gods, has become a mainstream notion in rabbinic Judaism.

Secular or Secularist?

Along with the growth of diverse Jewish expressions has been the general secularization of modern society, and Jewish society in par-ticular. Here we have to differentiate between a secular Jew—one who is only involved in the general world and not involved in Jewish life—and the Secularist Jew—one who is deliberately in-volved in both the universal and the particular Jewish world.

The Holocaust, and Jewish religious reactions to it, have con-tributed to the secularization of the Jewish world. Although some

Holocaust survivors became stronger in their faith, others lost faith entirely, believing that if a god existed, he would have stopped the Holocaust. Others became angry at a god who would turn his back on his people. Still others were infuriated by the stand of certain Hasidic and other Orthodox leaders who said that the Holocaust was a punishment for the Jews because they had strayed from the Law. One prominent rabbi said that diseased limbs have to be amputated. When challenged as to how one million children could be considered to have strayed from a law they were not yet obligated to keep, one Hasidic leader replied that sometimes a schoolboy gives a wrong answer with his mouth, and his teacher strikes him on the hand for punishment, meaning that some individual Jews were punished for the transgressions of other individual Jews. Horrified by this viewpoint or simply deciding that being Jewish was not "worth it," Jews abandoned religious Judaism. Some found their way to Secularist communities; others just became secular, not necessarily denying their Jewish heritage (though some did), but not celebrating it in any way, either.

Even among nominally religious Jews, those who belong to a temple or synagogue when their children are of Hebrew school age, many are secular in every way. They do not keep kosher, go to services, or even believe in a provident god. They also don't speak Hebrew or Yiddish, seek out Jewish literature and music, or learn Jewish history. Their tie to Judaism is sometimes merely gastronomic. That is, they like lox and Chinese food.

These are Jews that the Secular Humanistic Jewish communities you'll read about in the next chapter can serve. The forty or so affiliates of CSJO and SHJ, the independent shules and Workmen's Circle groups (and the organizations in Europe, Israel, South America, Australia, and the former Soviet Union) can help provide a home so that these secular Jews can become Secular Jews.

A look at rabbinic Judaisms of today shows that, far from an unbroken chain from Moses to this very day, what presents itself as mainstream Judaism is a complex amalgam of ideas and beliefs assimilated into the Jewish psyche through contact with outside cultures and diversity within Jewish life. Who are the "real" Jews? We all are.

3

Alternatives to the Big Three

If you've found a home in religious Judaism, you are a minority in American Jewish life. Although most American Jews are affiliated with religious congregations at some, or several, points in their lives, at any given time most Jews do not belong to religious congregations. Where are all those Jews going for community? Where do they find spiritual nourishment? Where do they find answers to the really big questions about the meaning of life and the finality of death?

There are three responses to those questions. Some Jews find their spiritual homes in non-Jewish religions. Some don't seem to require spiritual homes. And some find homes in Jewish alternatives to the Big Three of traditional religious affiliation—Orthodox, Conservative, and Reform.

Other Religions

Eastern Religions

Since the mid-1970s Jews have been involved in the Eastern religions, primarily Buddhism. In fact, the leaders of the movements that brought both Hinduism and Buddhism into American life are almost all Jewish: Richard Alpert (Baba Ram Dass), Allen Ginsberg, Jack Kornfeld, and Sharon Saltzberg, among many others. And large numbers of Jews (who still identify themselves as Jewish as well as Buddhist or Hindu) and former Jews are active in American forms of Eastern religions. What attracts Jews to religious practices so foreign in belief and culture from their own?

Buddhism has important aspects that differ from the Judaism most American Jews grew up with. It provides a meaningful atheism that answers the question of human suffering and the ultimate goal of existence. It exalts the Quiet Mind. It provides direct spiritual experiences. And it is universal.

Some of the most dedicated "Jew-Bu"s are Jews looking for the meaning of existence and not finding it in traditional Jewish religious forms. The idea of a single god who is both good and powerful doesn't make sense to them and neither do the official explanations of why bad things happen to good people. Neither the Hasidic idea that the Jews killed in the Holocaust somehow deserved their suffering nor the popular new notion of an emotionally strong but physically weak god provide for them a god worth worshiping. Jewish god-concepts insult their intelligence and moral sense, but they are people who care about the meaning of life, and they are looking for answers. Buddhism provides those answers. It provides both an explanation for the question of human suffering and an assurance that death is not the end—explanations and assurances that are rare in Jewish life.

Jewish life is noisy. Prayer is communal and sung or chanted. Study is conducted in pairs, and everything is discussed at length. Families interact with questions, jokes, arguments, and constant discussion. Jewish life, with its admiration of activity and the active mind, seems to be entirely incompatible with the Buddhist desideratum of the Quiet Mind. Buddhism teaches the way of attention, not distraction. It focuses on the present, the moment, in a way that Judaism, which is impelled by history, does not. Buddhism exalts qualities besides the intellect, which is explicitly valued in Jewish life. Some people, despite being born Jewish, are just not suited to the active and interactive Jewish style. Those who value the Quiet Mind find a comfortable home in Buddhism. There may be Jewish ways that would suit them, but these ways are rarely taught and are not accessible to the majority of Jews.

In his 1994 book *The Jew in the Lotus* (HarperCollins, San Francisco), Rodger Kamenetz quotes Joseph Goldstein, a leader in the American Buddhist movement, as explaining that he felt Judaism's path "involved following the vision, the law, of someone else's experience." Goldstein, like many others, did not want to follow someone else's experience; he wanted to have his own experience of truth. Certainly there are Jewish mystic practices that provide just this direct experience, but the purveyors of the Official Story have demoted this minority practice into near nonexistence. Jews who want authentic spiritual experiences are forced by their lack of education in Jewish alternatives into the fold of other religions.

The universalism of Buddhism is attractive to many Jews who have been turned off by the emphasis on the separateness of Jews. Even those who were not taught that the Jews are God's Chosen People have been brought up to feel that gentiles are different, if not inferior. Jews tend to be proud of Jewish Nobel Prize winners and wince when they see a Jewish name in a story about crime or corruption. We care more about Jews than we do about others. Even those who have been brought up with the most universalist values, the most sense of solidarity with oppressed peoples everywhere, seem to retain a sense of difference from others. And many see *different* as meaning *better.*

Buddhism is essentially a solitary religion, focused on the individual. While this can be attractive to those of us with universalist values, Buddhism also teaches that suffering is illusory, so Buddhists don't tend to take on social action or charitable works as community responsibilities to the extent that Jews do. While it is true that the bodhisattva does help others through his compassion, the task of becoming bodhisattva does not involve helping others; rather it is mostly concerned with attaining one's own spiritual perfection.

Western Religions: "Some of My Best Jews Are Friends"

Cherie was born Jewish. She considers herself Jewish. She sends her daughters to Jewish Sunday school. But Cherie attends Friends Meeting and participates in the Quaker religious services. What is she gaining there that she doesn't find in the Jewish community?

"I was looking for a true spiritual experience," she says. "I wanted to be somewhere that God could talk to me, instead of me talking to God. I wanted quiet and contemplation. I didn't want a lot of noisy, empty words." For Cherie, the traditional Jewish ritual prayers didn't open a two-way spiritual gate, and she hasn't found any Jewish setting in which she can have the direct kind of religious experience that she treasures. Friends Meeting, in which there are no ritual prayers, fits her needs. In a Quaker religious service, everyone just sits quietly unless he or she has something to say. Anyone can stand and speak at any time. Much of the time, everyone is silent, receptive.

Cherie retains her Jewish identity and feels herself still to be religiously Jewish. However, her religious affiliation is not Jewish, so she relies on her family life for Jewish connection, and as the older generation of her family nears the end of life, this connection becomes thinner every year.

Felicia is Jewish and Al is an Armenian Christian. Both are close to and cherish their heritages and families. Although they've been married for ten years, neither is entirely comfortable with the other's religion or ethnic identity. Each feels excluded by the other's tradition. Both, however, agree that their children should have a religious community. They have chosen to affiliate with the local Unitarian Universalist church, an active, friendly Humanistic congregation that doesn't offend either of them, but doesn't satisfy them, either.

Laura also belongs to a Unitarian church, a more overtly religious church than Felicia and Al's. She joined because she was looking for community, and the church provides one. She enjoys the discussions and fellowship and has made friends. Laura's mom is her only surviving family member, and she's not interested in Jewish life at all. Laura misses being around Jews and Jewish culture, but she hasn't found a community of Jews that has welcomed her as the church community has.

Cherie, Felicia, Al, and Laura are looking for a Jewish connection but aren't finding one that meets their needs. None feels able to create a new Jewish community, so each has settled for a "good enough" alternative. Cherie's spiritual needs are met; Felicia and Al's need for religious education for their children is met; Laura's social needs are met; but none has a way to express the Jewishness to which they feel connected. And their connection to being Jewish becomes more tenuous over the years. If, in the future, they find their way back to the Jewish community, they run the risk of finding themselves strangers within it.

Being "Nothing"

It wrenches my heart every time I hear a kid say, "I'm nothing." Of course, the kids I'm talking about don't really believe they're nothing. They are soccer players, musicians, friends, members of families. They have lots of identifications. They have personal identities. But they have no group identity. Their parents have never told them that they belong to any intermediate group between family and humanity. These kids know very well that others have group identities and sometimes can tell you the group identities of their parents and other relatives. "My mom is Jewish," they'll say, "and my dad is Christian. And I'm nothing."

Though it sounds sad to me, these chidren don't usually seem to be suffering and neither do their parents. The parents do not feel the need for a group identity and are not looking for a spiritual community of any kind. They find their satisfaction in work, in music, in family life, in social and political action in the environmental or women's movements, in gardening, or in any of hundreds of other activities that they can drop into when they feel the need. Likewise, their children are perfectly satisfied with stitching together a coat-of-many-colors life, picking and choosing from the wealth of choices available.

Problems arise, though, because of this wealth of choices. When we belong everywhere, we belong nowhere in particular. While this feels fine to lots of folks, a sense of rootlessness can affect some, and when they go looking for a grounding source, they may find destructive authoritarian cults or religions that fill that need. Or they may find spiritual paths that cut them off from their families and other ties, so that in finding a place for their future they lose their past.

If a person doesn't have a need for a particular community, there's no way in our modern world to force him or her to belong. All Jews nowadays are Jews by choice. It's an entirely voluntary identity. Those of us who care passionately about that identity have the obligation to make it available to the seekers, to be sure that there's a home for every Jew, a community that will fill that particular person's needs. A diverse and accepting Jewish community is the only way to make that happen.

Jewish Alternatives

Modern Jewish life, like that of the past, is complex and rich with religious and cultural alternatives. The growth of the Reconstructionist and *chavurah*-based Jewish Renewal movements attests to the pull of traditional religious worship (Reconstructionist) and personal spiritual content (Renewal). These religious alternatives coexist and interact with old-style Secularism, ethnic Jewish expressions, and a modern Secular Humanistic Judaism that is more accepting of spiritual interests.

The Reconstructionist movement, established by Mordechai Kaplan as an encompassing ethnic community, has moved far from its roots. It is now concerned with religious services rather than culture and community support and has a strong interest in social justice. The services (based on the Conservative practice) are egalitarian, and prayer language is also demasculinized. Some Reconstructionists omit references to the Chosen People while others retain them. There is room for the addition of poetry and expansive interpretations, and, in smaller congregations, services often include congregational discussions of the Torah portion.

The language and form of Reconstructionist prayer is recognizably Conservative, but the theology is not. While the Conservative movement believes in the authority of halacha, Jewish law, and an actual being who is God, Reconstructionists retain prayers addressing a self-conscious external deity while their theology does not include such a supernatural being. Kaplan set forth no specific creed, however. He specifically said that Reconstructionism is not any particular idea about God, but rather a method of dealing with the idea of God, a method that "consists in treating Judaism not as a static, or even as a dynamic, system of beliefs and practices, but as the sum of all those manifestations of the Jewish People, which are the result of its will to live and to make the most of life." Kaplan allowed each Jew his or her own god-concept.

For many who are sympathetic to the community orientation and social conscience of Reconstructionism, the god-concept remains a problem. Kaplan's definition of "the sum of all those manifestations of the Jewish People" seems to be a good definition of Jewishness but has little to do with any conventional understanding of the word *god*. And even if the word *god* means just that, it is jarringly uncomfortable to some to refer to this god as just or merciful or powerful, and almost nonsensical to address it directly as one does in prayer.

The Jewish Renewal movement appeals to many of the same people who are attracted to Buddhism. It stresses a spiritual approach to Judaism and is in many ways a modern Hasidism. Renewalists seek a direct spiritual experience and are receptive to mystic Jewish traditions. Although among Jewish Renewalists one finds those who are practical and political, it is the mystic and devotional components that set this movement apart from the others in Jewish life. The Renewal movement has established teaching seminars and camps, and its leader, Rabbi Zalman Schachter-Shalomi, has begun to ordain many rabbis who are working to expand the movement.

The old Secularist movement is exactly the opposite of the Renewal movement. It consists of those whose Jewishness is primarily cultural and is steeped in Yiddish and socialism/trade-unionism. It also includes the fraternal self-help societies, such as Workmens Circle/Arbeter Ring, which created insurance and burial cooperatives and free-loan societies. This anticlerical and fiercely atheistic Secularism was the dominant Judaism in America from the 1880s to the 1950s. It is rooted in positive cultural and social ideals and total rejection of religion and everything having to do with religion.

The old Secularist movement was my Jewish home. I grew up attending an after-school and Saturday program that taught Yiddish, Jewish history, literature, and music. My *kindershule* engaged in social and political action based on the lessons of Jewish history and progressivism. I knew what I believed in, and I certainly knew what I didn't believe in.

"Just" Culture

The old Secularist movement declined as more and more Jews entered the middle classes and as Yiddish increasingly became irrelevant. If we left our homes for cities with no Secularist institutions and married those who didn't speak Yiddish, we had no communal structure for our Jewish life, no rituals to bring Jewishness to our consciousness, no forum to express ourselves as Jews. And in our modern America, where so many adults work outside the home, it is just too hard to take time away from the family to organize something new. Without a communal framework, many of those who grew up in the Secularist movement came to think of themselves as "just" cultural Jews.

The idea that culture or ethnicity is somehow less important than religion is a new one in Jewish life and one I've started to run into more and more when I meet with couples for whom I'm going to perform wedding ceremonies. It's not uncommon for one member of the couple to be an ethnic Jew and the other a more-or-less religious Christian or Jew. Typically, both members of the couple feel that the one with the stronger traditional *religious* faith should guide the religious identity of the household. They believe that cultural and ethnic identity is not as important or meaningful as religious identity. The culturally Jewish member of the couple almost invariably feels a great sadness at giving up his or her identity, but this sadness is not honored by our society, which exalts religion over ethnic or cultural identity. We are expected to behave as if our cultural and ethnic identity were only American and as if that American identity really had its own cultural content, separate from the ideals of Western democracy and accessible and acceptable to all Americans.

This attitude, that we are all Catholics, Protestants, or Jews by religion only and Americans by culture, ignores and delegitimizes the role and meaning of ethnic and cultural identity. Religion is a part of culture, but only one part. It is culture that gives us our folk wisdom. It is culture that gives us our social and political ideals. It is culture that gives us our language, our music, our way of relating to others, and our expressive forms. It is culture that makes us human. The denigration of ethnic Judaism as "mere" cultural identity shows a flawed and narrow understanding of what an ethnic culture provides us as human beings. Cultural and ethnic identity are as valid and deeply felt and important as is religious identity.

One of the reasons Jews who don't believe in an external self-conscious god end up in religious movements of one kind or another or choose to be "nothing" is that they haven't found a place that would allow them an authentic expression of their own Jewish identity, an identity based on culture, ethnicity, ideals, and an exhaltation of the human spirit.

Some Jews have, however, found such a place in the modern Secular Humanistic Jewish movement, in organizations affiliated with the Congress of Secular Jewish Organizations or the Society for Humanistic Judaism. This movement, which is connected to the older Secularist movement, represents an extraordinarily diverse population. It includes Jews who are attracted to the way Secular Humanistic Jews maintain a democratic Judaism expressed by Liebman Hersch, who said, "It is not the result of study of facts, but a manner of behaving in regard to facts" and Yudel Mark, who said, "Secularism is antidogmatism." Along with Chaim Zhitlowsky's statement that "Religion is a private matter," these tenets express the essence of the Secularist movement, an openness to all that the Jewish People has created.

Because of this openness, all sorts of people are attracted to the movement, including intermarried couples, those who grew up Secularist, Jews from other movements who are uncomfortable with religious god-concepts, religious Jews who just feel comfortable in cultural settings or who like the Sunday schools in the movement, and seekers, those looking for a community and spiritual home that will respect their own personal beliefs.

A Secular Spirituality

The great generational difference between the traditional Secularists and the present cultural Jews is the difference in the way the generations think about spirituality.

Because we recognize that we are more than our bodies, that we are different from the other animals in some qualitative way, that we need rest and music and love, we have come to ask if we also need what is called a spiritual or even religious experience, a feeling of congruence, order, and harmony, the feeling of being part of something larger than our individual selves. This need may be hardwired into us, part of our human systems, part of our need to make order out of a world of chaos. Secular and Humanistic Jews are beginning to embrace the notion of spirituality because we want to be able to access that experience, an experience many Secularists enjoy in other environments.

So, given that we have this need, how do we fill it? Buddhist chants? Surrender to an all-powerful god? Why should we allow this basic part of our humanity to be separate from a basic part of our individual selves, our Jewishness? Rather, let us explore the meaning of a secular spirituality.

Max Rosenfeld, a founder and leading light of the Sholem Aleichem Club in Philadelphia, a contributing editor to *Jewish Currents,* and a teacher of Yiddish at Graetz College, talked about spirituality as "a state of mind that reinvigorates the spirits of Humanists" and said that spirituality serves to "acknowledge and express the connection between humans and the universe."

Sherwin Wine, rabbi of the Birmingham Temple and founder of the Society for Humanistic Judaism, describes spirituality as "the experience of intense beauty," giving examples of the experience of the majesty of nature. He quotes Santayana in maintaining that beauty gives meaning to our lives and is related to our survival and happiness. This feeling of overwhelming beauty, according to Wine, is the result of an interplay between the person and the object perceived as beautiful, and is thus an act of creation. (He gives the example of a concert of Yiddish music that moved him deeply but would have left an Irishman emotionally unaffected.)

Marilyn Rowens, ceremonial director of the Birmingham Temple and a certified Secular Humanistic Jewish Leader, describes spirituality as validating or touching a piece of the true self, a reaching inward.

These three conceptions of the religious or spiritual experience have one commonality, a feeling of congruence that can take place in three arenas: the self, the outside world, and the interface between the two.

The experience of congruence with self is that rare feeling of peace and self-knowledge at once. In the sixties and seventies, my friends used to chant or meditate or take drugs to induce that state, but the state of intense self-awareness can be attained in Jewish environments and practice as well. A Jewish spiritual home needs to provide the opportunity for people to reach that touching of the self, the congruence between what we are and what we seem.

The congruence with the unself-aware universe is another sort of spiritual experience. The sense of being part of a wondrous universe, the sense of awe at living in a world that has the Rocky Mountains or the Pacific Ocean or the perfect trillium, can be overwhelming. The sense of identity with a painting or piece of music or a poem is, perhaps, the same sort of experience, one that swells the heart with the perception of the beauty in the world.

The sense of being part of something greater than oneself is the third element in the triad of congruences that make up a secular spirituality. I grew up in a wonderful era of struggle. With my parents, my *kindershule,* and my friends, I went on civil rights marches, peace marches, women's, and gay rights marches. I sang with hundreds and with thousands and once with hundreds of thousands. Each time, I knew my voice was part of the chorus, and, though I couldn't hear its separate tones at all, I knew that without it, the sound would not be the same. It was a magnificent, joyful, and empowering feeling, a feeling of congruence with others that I cherish.

That same congruence with others exists in those rare moments of perfect oneness with a lover. It comes into being when we sing a song that was sung by our ancestors and we enter into the stream of our people's history and heritage.

This experience, universal as it seems, most clearly differentiates secular from religious spirituality. For the religious believer, the feeling of being part of something greater than the self means entering into the larger something that exists independent of the people who enter into it. For the Secular Humanist, it means entering into the larger something that is made up only of its participants and relies upon human beings for its existence.

How do we create these essential experiences for ourselves, our families, and our communities? The tools are available within our Jewish culture to create meaningful Jewish experiences. The second section of this book will give you some ideas of how to go about creating Jewish cultural experiences for holidays and life-cycle events.

II

RECLAIMING OUR JEWISH HOLIDAYS

4

The Elements of the Jewish Holidays

Why do so many cultures celebrate holidays of light on the winter solstice? Why do so many cultures have holidays during which they eat eggs and lamb in the spring? Why do so many cultures make loud noises of various sorts at important times of year? Why do so many cultures have the most important and portentous holiday at the beginning of the rainy season? Human holidays evolve to fit human needs: the need to have the sun come back, to encourage fertility in the earth and among the animals, to scare away the evil and frightening forces in the universe, to come together with those we love and trust. Holidays were not, for the most part, invented as outgrowths of the stories we tell about them now; they evolved from our basic human needs, and we told stories and made up explanations about them after the fact.

This doesn't mean that the holidays aren't meaningful and real and significant. Not at all. It makes them more meaningful, adding layers of history to the official stories. It makes them more real, tying them more firmly to our universal human needs. It makes them more significant, with not only religious but also historical, ethical, cultural, seasonal, and national components. It also allows us to use pieces of our tradition other than the religious tradition to understand and celebrate our holidays. And it puts us firmly in the long evolutionary line of Jewish tradition, encouraging us to add new meaning to the old holidays and to interpret them for our time.

JEWISH HOLIDAYS

Name	Season	Also called	Date
Rosh Hashanah	fall	New Year	1 Tishri
Yom Kippur	fall	Day of Atonement	10 Tishri
Sukkot	fall	Feast of Booths/Feast of Tabernacles	15 Tishri
Simchat Torah	fall	Feast of Rejoicing	23 Tishri
Hanukkah	winter	Holiday of Lights	25 Kislev
Tu b'Shvat	winter/spring	New Year of Trees	15 Shvat
Purim	spring	Feast of Lots	14 Adar
Pesach	spring	Passover	14 Nisan
Lag b'Omer	spring	Scholars' Holiday	18 Iyar
Shavuot	summer	Feast of Weeks/ Day of First Fruits	6 Sivan
Tisha b'Av	summer	Fast of Av	9 Av

NOTE: Jewish days begin at sunset, so all the Jewish holidays start at sundown of the day before the day listed on your calendar. We Jews like to say that we are among the earliest people who did not worship the sun and that is why we start our days at sunset. Just for the record, Druids also started their days at sunset.

All the holidays have at least some of six elements: primitive, religious, historical, ethical, national, and seasonal. The primitive element, referring to the ancient roots of the holiday, is best covered in Theodore Gaster's *Festivals of the Jewish Year* (1952), no longer in print but available in many libraries, both Jewish and public. Gaster describes how the earliest people dealt with the need met by each holiday. We think of this type of element as basically magical or religious, but it is perhaps more correct to think of it as technological, that is, the set of actions that are needed to bring about a desired result.

The seasonal component is most closely related to the primitive aspect of the holidays. Our seasonal holidays may refer back to the specific seasonal agricultural activity in ancient Israel at certain times of the year, or may be more universally seasonal in nature, celebrating the return of the sun or the renewal of life in the spring. These components also give us a chance to reflect on our relationship with the world we live in and our natural environment.

The religious component deals specifically with acts performed by the historic Jewish god for humankind in general, or for the Jewish People. This religious element is often imposed upon the previous primitive element. These explanations were attached to the holidays in historical, or close to historical times, by officials of a religious hierarchy. The religious component is the one most American Jewish children learn about in Hebrew school and the one most accessible to you if you go looking for information about the holidays. It's the official explanation, so it always includes the self-conscious power that's the Jewish god and often includes a mythological event that is presented as history. These explanations are not factual, but that doesn't mean that there isn't a certain truth to them, a truth about history, or nature, or the way human beings should behave.

The historical component deals with the actual historical event that is commemorated by a holiday and also includes other historical events that became associated with the holiday throughout the ages. Additionally, it includes the historical reasons that the holiday was accepted and gained prominence. Very few of the historical reasons given for holidays are corroborated by fact, but there are a few holidays, like Hanukkah, which, although originally primitive in nature, came to commemorate verifiable historical events. Many holidays also have picked up historic meaning because of other events that occurred on the holiday. The Warsaw Ghetto Uprising, for example, has become an important part of the Secular Pesach observance, because the uprising began on Pesach. We can gain insight into our history by looking at the process by which holidays became holidays and the political or societal reason for establishing a particular holiday, such as Purim, at a particular time.

The ethical component deals with relations between human beings and the proper way to behave. The stories that have grown up about the holidays teach lessons about human nature and the effects of our actions on ourselves, on each other, and on the world. These meanings are not necessarily the reason the stories were told, but the meanings can be used nonetheless. We don't have to accept the official ethical teaching given, but these official religious interpretations do pose interesting ethical questions for us to think about and to design our holiday observances to answer.

The national component acknowledges three different meanings to Jewish nationality. First, it looks back to the ancient Jewish nationality based in the tiny area of the Middle East where our people originated. We celebrate our earliest heritage and our earliest sovereignty and get an idea of what our nation was like in ancient times.

The second, recent, national meaning recognizes the renewal of Jewish sovereignty in Israel. Whether or not we agree with the particular policies of the Israeli government, we can celebrate self-determination and a place of safety for the Jewish People.

Third, we celebrate the Jewish nation as a self-definition. Even though all the Jews of the world do not look to one political homeland, we do have a feeling that, despite our political, religious, and cultural differences, we belong to one people, a "national-historical people," as Chaim Zhitlowsky called us. That we are all celebrating the same holiday at the same time is a powerful symbol of our national identity.

While not all Jewish holidays contain all these elements, most contain at least a few of them, and we can build our understanding of the holidays and our celebrations on whichever of these elements speak to us as individuals. Over time, as our interests and concerns change, we may find that different components of the holidays become more important to us or take on added significance. We can alter our observances year by year to reflect these changes in our own lives.

A General Model of Holiday Observances

How should we observe our holidays? We have four choices:

We can use the traditional religious models and just change the things that are objectionable to us. This is not an entirely bad method, since it ties us to the rest of the Jewish people throughout the world and through time. The use of traditional religious elements also makes our ceremonies more comfortable for those who came from religious backgrounds. It is, however, not satisfying. It's not enough. We have more to say.

We can invent our own ceremonies, unrelated to the traditional religious models, and use them every year. This solution, like the first, has the advantage of constancy. People know what to expect when they attend the observances and become comfortable with a tradition. The drawback of this solution is that it doesn't feel Jewish. Further, both this solution and the first are stagnant. Using *only* ritual, saying *only* the same words every time is comfortable but boring, and the words, no matter how true, how compelling, lose meaning through rote repetition.

We can invent new ceremonies every time, drawing on new material, Jewish and non-Jewish, for readings. This is an attractive and often-used solution. The observances are meaningful and have Jewish content. They are, however, inconsistent. Those attending don't know from event to event what they're coming to. They have no definition for what we are doing. Those of us who grew up in the Secularist community, at least, are used to this model. We understand the underlying coherence among all the ceremonies, but this understanding is not universal. Those who did not grow up in our particular part of the movement do not feel comfortable with wholly new observances each year. What makes this solution even more unrealistic, however, is how hard it is to write new ceremonies every year. Even for educated people with lots of resources, this model takes a lot of time.

Our final option is to create blended ceremonies, including traditional elements—those adapted from religious ritual and those from our own Secularist Jewish traditions—and fresh new readings. This solution combines the sense of comfort and connectedness of ritual with a meaningful set of new readings every year. Admittedly, it takes time and some education, but since the Jewish ritual portion is given, the resources needed to add the new readings do not have to be only those from the Jewish tradition, and are therefore more accessible to the average busy, worldly Jew.

This blended model has three elements: a fixed element, a menu element, and a changing element. The fixed element consists of rituals and customs associated with a holiday. The menu is a list of ideas or themes of the holiday. Each holiday has multiple, but not infinite, themes. Each year a different theme or set of themes may be chosen, or one theme may be used every year along with a changing theme each year. The changing element is the actual readings. The readings come from a vast set of sources, some specific for each holiday, some generally Jewish, and some from the non-Jewish world.

At a recent weekend seminar of the North American section of the International Institute for Secular Humanistic Judaism, I led a short session on using this model. We were asked to address the holiday of Hanukkah. First we listed the fixed elements of ritual and customs and came up with lighting candles, playing dreidel, nuts, Hanukkah gelt, and latkes. The themes we listed included heroism, cultural diversity, light in the dark times (of the year and of our lives, both individual and as a people), dedication (of a building or a person), nationalism, and self-defense. Some of the sources we thought we could use included mythologies, Yiddish poetry, secular English poetry, speeches by leaders of freedom movements, and the Books of Maccabees.

Using this model, we could choose one year, for example, to dedicate the candles to heroes of national self-determination. We would first read our fixed ritual candlelighting statement, such as the one found in *We Rejoice in Our Heritage: Home Rituals for Secular Humanistic Jews*. Then, as we dedicate each light, we could use readings from the Maccabees, from speeches of the early Zionists, from writings of Diaspora Nationalists, from speeches of Gandhi, Nelson Mandela, Sojourner Truth. Another year, we could dedicate the candles to those who have brought light into our dark moments. After the ritual statement, we might dedicate the candles to individuals who have helped us through hard times, or talk about those individuals who were lights for the Jewish People during our hard times, using excerpts from writings by or about those people. We can choose any of the listed themes and then look among our varied sources to find the readings that support the theme we have chosen.

This technique allows us to be creative and relevant while responding to the specific themes of each holiday. The constancy of a few fixed rituals and songs provides a sense of connection and homecoming for the participants. The combination of fixed ritual, a menu of themes, and a plethora of sources can produce emotionally satisfying, rich, varied, and meaningful Jewish holiday observances.

5

Fall Holidays

The fall holidays are really all one holiday, later separated into several distinct observances. The primitive roots of the holidays are intertwined and have to be discussed together. In addition, each holiday has its own set of components. Theodore Gaster's explanation has been nicely summarized and augmented by Hershl Hartman in a pamphlet entitled *The Jewish New Year Festival: A Guide for the Rest of Us* (available from the Congress of Secular Jewish Organizations), from which much of this explanation is adapted.

The entire fall holiday season is a combination of primitive and ancient needs for sustenance and for some measure of control over the environment. Like many cultures, we have a year-end "time out of time" period—now the ten days between Rosh Hashanah and Yom Kippur. This primitive concept was strengthened by the need to reconcile the lunar (pastoral) and solar (agricultural) years so that the harvest holiday actually occurred at the same time as the harvest, and the rainmaking ritual occurred close to the time the rains should begin to fall.

The harvest nature of the whole holiday season is seen in the use of dried sheaves of grain for the roof of the sukkah, in the fruit and vegetable decorations and foods, and in the echo of the fertility rites that we find in the weddinglike dancing, circling, and celebration on Simchat Torah. Our fall celebrations have a lot in common with celebrations in other northern hemisphere cultures, but we have taken the original universal primitive observances and given them a Jewish flavor. Both the universal and the particular are of value to us. Our humanity and our Jewishness complement rather than compete with each other.

Like many cultures, we make a lot of noise at the New Year. We use the shofar, a ram's horn, because as a herding people that's what we had handy in ancient times. Other cultures use bamboo sticks, gongs, drums, gunshots, or those little party blowers. It's all the same thing—we're making noise to scare off the evil spirits. Each culture, as it modernizes, comes up with new reasons to continue the folk traditions. As our culture progresses, we need to have new explanations and reasons for our folk traditions if we want to keep them. And why do we want to keep them? They appeal to our human instincts, and they connect us with our people throughout time and space. And they're just plain fun.

The fall holidays are all about the communal, or national, nature of Jewish life. Yom Kippur is a time of *communal* rather than individual stocktaking. The scapegoat, a real goat used in the time of the Temple, was made to take upon itself the sins of the entire community. At Sukkot, we try to ensure rainfall so that we'll have a good harvest year, so all can eat. If the rains don't come, we all starve.

Rosh Hashanah

Rosh Hashanah has seasonal, religious, and ethical components. In addition to the well-known religious belief that Rosh Hashanah is the anniversary of creation, there is an interesting religious meaning in the seasonal nature of the holiday. Rosh Hashanah, the Jewish New Year, is placed at a very odd time in the solar year. Many cultures celebrate the New Year as the winter solstice passes. Others celebrate the New Year in the spring, when the earth comes to life again. Few, if any, other cultures celebrate a New Year in the fall. This is no accident.

We know from the biblical numbering of the months, with the spring month the first, and Tishri, the month in which we celebrate

Rosh Hashanah, called the seventh month, that the ancient Jewish New Year was the spring, at the time of lambing and the appearance of wild foods. However, ever since the Jews became an agricultural, rather than herding people, we have celebrated the New Year in the fall. This spring versus fall New Year disjunction is the result of the tension in ancient Jewish life between farmers and herders. The more ancient nomadic herding economy gave way to an agricultural society about three thousand years ago as is well documented in the Bible. Elements of this duality remain in our holiday celebrations and halacha.

As agriculture overtook herding, the fall holiday of harvest and rainmaking became more important. Hundreds of years later, the priestly class took advantage of this change to make a religious point. This made it clear to their followers that they did not worship the sun or the earth. If the New Year were at the winter solstice, it could be seen as a celebration of the return of the sun. If it were in the spring, it could be seen as a celebration of the earth or of fertility. Both possibilities were idolatrous and could not be tolerated, so the religious establishment supported the celebration of the New Year in the fall when the sun is waning and the living things are dying.

The other seasonal components are largely incidental. The symbol of the holiday for European Jews is the apple, which is said to symbolize the roundness of the year. The apple harvest is in the fall, therefore apples were available. Raisins, which are baked into the holiday challah, are being used up, since the grape harvest is in the early fall. The tradition of buying or making new clothes for the New Year is reasonable because the season is changing and new winter clothes are needed for growing children.

Most important for Secular Humanistic Jews is the ethical component of Rosh Hashanah, the message that this is a good world and valuable in itself, not just as an anteroom to an afterworld. Since the culture that we live in is primarily one in which the theology denigrates the material world and desires the end of time, this ethical component serves to anchor our own opposing views. It also serves to give us an opportunity to renew our commitment to making the world a place we can and should celebrate.

Observances

Rosh Hashanah is a communal rather than a family holiday, although there are certain family traditions. Cassie, who is beginning to develop a Jewishness that suits her and her family, remembers with mixed fondness and disgust the traditional trip to the mall with her mother. Although it seems like a materialistic middle-class American tradition, previous immigrant generations also remember that new clothes were often bought or made for the children at this time of year.

A round challah with raisins in it is eaten along with apples dipped in honey, symbolizing the wish for a sweet year to come. During the time just before Rosh Hashanah some families visit the graves of their deceased.

The season actually begins in the month of Elul, the last month of the year, which is devoted to getting ready for the solemn accounting of the New Year season. The shofar is blown during the morning service every day during the month. There are particular penitential prayers that are recited beginning about a week before Rosh Hashanah.

A communal observance may include themes of the unity of the Jewish People as we all observe this holiday that has been observed for generations. Some discussion of awe at the beauty of the world (the holiday traditionally celebrates the creation) may lead to a commitment to preserve the earth and life on earth. The theme of awakening is traditional. The shofar is sounded as an alarm, or wake-up call. We try to become aware of our lives, how we are living them, and what effect our lives are having on others. We give ourselves ten days—until Yom Kippur—to bring ourselves to an understanding of what we must do to change for the better. This process is called *cheshbon ha'nefesh*—an accounting of the soul, or stocktaking.

Outside of Israel, Orthodox, Reconstructionist, and Conservative Jews celebrate Rosh Hashanah for two days. Reform Jews celebrate one day. In Israel the traditions vary. Secular and Humanistic Jews tend to celebrate one day, but some celebrate two, if it is their family tradition.

On the first day of Rosh Hashanah it is traditional to walk to a running body of water and empty bread crumbs out of the pockets and into the water to symbolize the casting off of one's sins. We may wish to think of the need to keep our water, air, and earth clean and beautiful for future generations.

If you have a shofar, listen to the three different traditional blasts. Anyone who can play a brass instrument can learn to sound the shofar with a few minutes' practice.

A Rosh Hashanah at Home

The weekend before the holiday, take a trip to a pick-your-own apple orchard or a farmers' market. Get lots of different kinds of apples. Pick up some you've never tried before—after all, Rosh Hashanah is about newness and fresh starts.

The day or night before the holiday, bake round sweet challahs. Sure you can! Bread is very forgiving—it's almost impossible to mess it up. Never baked before? Give it a try—remember, new beginnings!

Use the recipe in the Shabbes section, but while you're kneading it, add an extra quarter to half cup of sugar, an extra couple of eggs, and about a half stick of melted butter, and knead in some raisins or other dried fruit. When it's ready to braid, make long skinny braids and spiral them to make circles. Or just make nice round loaves. If you're feeling ambitious, make a honey cake, too.

How to Make Honey Cake

1 ¾ cups (180 ml) of honey
1 cup (230 ml) extra strong coffee
4 eggs
2 tablespoons oil
1 cup (200 g) sugar (white, brown, or a combination)
2 ½ cups (600 ml) sifted (or not sifted) unbleached white flour
1 cup (230 ml) rye or whole-wheat flour (or use all white, or change the proportions if you want to)
1 teaspoon baking soda
2 teaspoons baking powder
1 teaspoon cinnamon

½ teaspoon allspice
½ teaspoon cloves or nutmeg or some other sweet spice

First, boil the honey. Cool it and add the coffee. Set aside.
In a big bowl, beat the eggs until light. Add the oil and blend, then beat in the sugar.
In another bowl, mix the flour, baking soda, baking powder, cinnamon, allspice, and cloves.
Add the flour mixture and the honey-coffee mixture gradually to the egg mixture, beating well.
Pour into a greased 9 x 12 x 3 (22 x 30 x 4 cm) pan and cook at 300° F. (150° C.) for an hour. Check to see that a toothpick comes out dry.
When it's cool, cut it into the traditional diamond shapes.

On Rosh Hashanah, find a place where there's running water, if you can—a small lake or pond or stream is fine. If no body of water is handy, stay home or go to some other beautiful place outdoors. Set out candles, wine, apples, challah, and honey. Light the candles, using the Ashrei from *We Rejoice in Our Heritage: Home Rituals for Secular and Humanistic Jews* in English, Yiddish, or Hebrew, or use any other poem, saying, or song you like. (See resources at the end of the holiday section.) Ask everyone present to share a special light from the year past and a commitment to how they will share their own light in the year to come.

Next, pass around the glass of wine (or provide each person with his or her own glass). Say or sing the Ashrei or anything else you'd like. Ask everyone to share a happy time from the past year and a time they're looking forward to in the year to come.

Next comes the challah. It's round, to symbolize the continuity of life. Talk about the things you treasure that come around every year. Cut up the challah and dip the pieces into honey. Wish each other a sweet new year. Ooh and aah over how good it is and how impressed you are with the person who actually baked it. (This is very important! If you don't make a big fuss, the baker may never do it again.) If this is the first time you've ever made challah, say a Secular Shehecheyanu for that: "We rejoice in our heritage, which has given us the indomitable spirit that has preserved our people and sustained us and brought us forward to this moment." Or just say it because you are happy to be together with your friends and family on a holiday. Or because you have decided that just because you don't have a community is no reason not to celebrate—it takes a lot of that indomitable spirit to prepare for and celebrate a holiday all alone.

THE ASHREI FOR BREAD

We rejoice in our heritage, which teaches us to love our earth that gives us wheat and to honor the farmers who grow it and the workers who make it into bread.

Hebrew:
Ashreinu bi'yerushateinu   אַשְׁרֵינוּ בִּירֻשָׁתֵנוּ
she'morah lanu   שְׁמוֹרָה לָנוּ
le'ehuv et ha'adama   לֶאֱהוֹב אֶת הָאֲדָמָה
matsmichat dagan   מַצְמִיחַת דָּגָן
u'l'chabed et ha'ikar   וּלְכַבֵּד אֶת הָאִכָּר
ha'motisi lechem min ha'aretz   הַמּוֹצִיא לֶחֶם מִן הָאָרֶץ
v'et hapo'el ha'ofeh chalot   וְאֶת הַפּוֹעֵל הָאוֹפֶה חַלּוֹת

Yiddish:
Mir freyen zikh mit   מיר פרייען זיך מיט
undzer yerushah   אונדזער ירושה
vos hot undz oysgelernt   וואָס האָט אונדז אויסגעלערנט
az mir zoln leeb hobn   אז מיר זאָלן ליב האָבן
undzer erd   אונדזער ערד
vos git undz veytz,   וואָס גיט אונדז ווייץ
oon dermont   און דערמאָנט
undz opgebn koved   אונדז אָפגעבן כבד
di vos akern dos erd   די וואָס אקערן דאָס ערד
oon kooltivirn dem veytz,   און קולטיווירן דעם ווייץ
oon di arbeter vos bakn   און די אַרבעטער וואָס באַקן
far undz dos broit.   פאַר אונדז דאָס ברויט

Now there is time for a little reflection. Take a moment to think of the ways you want to change your life this year. Share with others, or just make this a time for quiet reflection.

When you're ready, it's time for *tashlich*. Walk over to the water and empty the crumbs from your pockets into it. Say to yourself or share with others what you're getting rid of—it can be a feeling, a habit, an old worry. Watch it float away from you. If you like, you can also throw flowers or flower petals into the water, as a symbol of sharing the good things about you with others, or to add beauty to the place where you just threw your junk.

The atmosphere turns festive again as you return to the table or picnic blanket for an apple tasting. Cut up all the different kinds of apples you bought and taste them all. Don't forget to dip them into honey! Use the honey cake to clear your palate.

Still have some energy? Hershl Hartman, education director of Sholem Community Organization in Los Angeles, suggests in *The Jewish New Year Festival: A Guide for the Rest of Us* that since we threw our junk into the water, we might want to think about cleaning it up. We can organize a river cleanup and spend some time fishing the litter out of the water and disposing of it properly. He also hopes that this energizes people further to "do something about the real sinners: the industrial polluters and the growth-blinded civic powers who use our waterways as sewers."

Yom Kippur

Among religious Jews, Yom Kippur is a time that is almost purely religious, dealing with divine forgiveness and divine judgment. In fact, secular Jews are often asked how we can observe Yom Kippur at all. The answer is that Yom Kippur has important national and ethical components that we want to observe.

The national component is found in the attitude of group responsibility for the problems in the world. The idea of justification (what Christians might think of as salvation) in Jewish life tends to reflect a communal rather than an individual orientation. Rewards and punishments are meted out to the Jewish People as a whole for community behavior. At Yom Kippur we remember that the whole Jewish People is responsible for one another and is judged by others as a whole, not as individuals. We remind ourselves that we have the obligation to improve not only ourselves, but the Jewish People as well.

The ethical component of Yom Kippur is tied to the idea that human beings are capable of change and worthy of a good life. At Yom Kippur we ask forgiveness of other people, implying that we are worthy of forgiveness. We forgive ourselves and we forgive others, showing that we respect others as we respect ourselves. We emphasize our beliefs that people can change for the better, that we as human beings are capable of goodness, that we are responsible as individuals and as groups for our own sins, and that we have the power and the responsibility to atone for them and to refrain from repeating them. This is an attitude cultural Jews share with many religious Jews, including Orthodox Rabbi Emmanuel Rackman, who was chancellor of Israel's Bar-Ilan University; he said Yom Kippur teaches people that "no matter how low [they have] sunk, [they] can rise again."

Because Yom Kippur is a holiday in which we celebrate our ability to change and grow and our responsibility for our own direction, it is, above all, for Secular Humanistic Jews, a holiday of self-respect.

Observances

Like Rosh Hashanah, Yom Kippur is a communal rather than a family holiday, although before the communal observance the individual makes an effort to reconcile herself or himself with those s/he has wronged or who have wronged her/him. We ask for forgiveness from others and are obliged to grant forgiveness if it is requested.

Religious Jews spend the day (beginning, of course, at sundown the night before, fasting and praying or meditating about their lives. (A full Jewish fast is a complete abstinence from both food and drink for twenty-five hours. You can brush your teeth, but you can't swallow any water.) In recent years some Secularists have found it meaningful to fast, either out of solidarity with the Jewish People, or to sensitize them to the condition of those who suffer hunger involuntarily, to bring them to an appreciation of the abundance in their own daily lives, or as a reminder to keep on task and not to be distracted from the business of Yom Kippur by tending to physical or other needs. Others find that fasting is counterproductive. They are distracted by the hunger and the dehydration headache and find it impossible to concentrate on the work at hand.

The service of the eve of Yom Kippur is called Kol Nidre after the prayer that is said. This prayer has been a problem for several hundred years to many rabbis and Jewish scholars because it absolves people of carrying out vows they may make between this Yom Kippur and the next. In fact, many Jewish leaders throughout the years have wanted to eliminate Kol Nidre entirely. The founder of Modern Orthodoxy, Rabbi Dr. Samson Raphael Hirsch, did not allow it to be sung in his synagogue.

There's a lot of folk etymology surrounding this prayer, but the origins are not really known. In fact, it's not even a prayer, since it is not addressed to any deity and is completely secular in nature.

The next day, services are held from the morning through the early afternoon. There's usually an afternoon break of two or three hours, and then the late-afternoon (including the reading of the Book of Jonah) and early evening services, Ne'ilah, are held.

Since Yom Kippur is a day of mourning, many religious Jews carry out traditional mourning customs. They do not wear leather clothes or shoes and some do not bathe until after they have broken their fast at the end of the holiday.

Yiskor, the remembrance of the dead, is also traditional at Yom Kippur. Although the Yiskor was originally a remembrance of the whole communities that were wiped out by Crusaders and pogroms, it has evolved into a personal remembrance as well. We can use the opportunity to remember those who died at the hands of genocidal monsters—Jews and Gypsies and Ibo and Cambodians and Tutsi and Hutu and Albanians and so many more. We also can use the opportunity for personal memories. Many Secularist and Humanist Jewish groups refer to this ceremony as *nizkor*, which means "we will remember" rather than as *yizkor*, which means "he [that is, God] will remember."

Fast-breaking parties are common. The first food eaten is an egg, symbolizing life. Then small portions of bland foods are eaten. Later, a full meal can be served.

A Community Yom Kipper

A small group or a large congregation can put together a meaningful Yom Kippur observance. It needn't take all night and all day, as religious observances typically do—a short observance on Kol

Nidre night and another during the afternoon on Yom Kippur works well. If you hold your afternoon observance during the break in your local religious services, you may find that there are people who will want to attend both. Set out a table near the entrance with *pushkehs*—containers for donations—for various charitable organizations, as was done in Eastern Europe. In Europe, the *pushkehs* were for the various community funds: dowries for orphans, matzah for the poor, etc. You can choose international, national, Jewish, or local groups, but put out several to give people a choice. You might put out one to respond to a current disaster (a flood or earthquake), one for the New Israel Fund, one for the Jewish Fund for Justice, and one for a local organization helping battered women. Whoever's setting up can throw a few dollars into the containers to prime the pump.

The community observances, whether on one day or broken up into a Kol Nidre and a Yom Kippur observance, may stress the four important themes of the holiday: recognition of one's behavior, repentance for wrong behavior, forgiveness, and commitment to change for the better.

During the observance, you can talk about our community responsibility, the responsibility of one Jew for the other, and of one human being for the other. Talk about how our individual and communal behavior can influence our communities and our world for good or bad. Give people an opportunity to remember how their behavior has affected others and to recognize that they haven't always behaved as they should. Quiet music or singing helps people to concentrate and keeps them from wondering if it's time to move on.

Zalman Schachter-Shalomi, writing in *The Jewish Holidays: A Guide and Commentary* (1985) by Michael Strassfeld, suggests asking those who attend to bring cards on which they have written (before the holiday, since Jewish law forbids on Yom Kippur any activity that's forbidden on Shabbes) the sins they have committed against themselves, against God, against others, and against the world. The cards are then collected and read in addition to the liturgical confessional.

Awareness of wrongful behavior leads directly to repentance for it. Give people permission to feel truly sorry for what they have done and to fully feel repentance for the way they've hurt others.

People tend to cry during this portion of the observance. That's okay—it's what we're supposed to be doing.

Only after fully feeling grief for our own actions are we ready to forgive ourselves and others. Set aside the next period during the observance to examine and to give up old grudges, to examine the pain others have caused us and to forgive them, and to examine the pain we have caused others and ourselves and to forgive ourselves. This is quite a lot of mental and emotional work. You might divide these tasks into time periods broken up by readings of poetry or the singing of songs.

Finally, it is time for the commitment to a change for the better. Talk about which values you wish to uphold and how you can uphold them. Remind yourself that sin is not a permanent human condition, but a straying from the right path. Spend a little time trying to set yourself on the right path, with your values as your compass.

You may want to include a *nizkor* ceremony before ending. Give people a chance to speak about those who died during the year and those who died earlier. Let them talk about what they want to remember about those people, the ways in which their lives influenced others, and the values that guided them.

Yom Kippur observances traditionally end with one long blast of the shofar. Shofars can be expensive, but your group can probably get a small one for a reasonable price. You use it only twice a year, on Rosh Hashanah and Yom Kippur, but it lasts forever.

Yom Kippur Alone

You might find yourself without a small group or community to spend Yom Kippur with, or you might want to experiment with a Yom Kippur alone. If so, you have two choices—you can go somewhere completely removed from your everyday life, or you can stay home. Either way, you can use the community activities, adapting them for solitude.

If you need to get away, find a place where the only distractions are natural. A woods or lake is ideal. You can find a place to sit or wander around, and just let your mind float. After a while, you'll stop thinking about the tasks you have to get done and whether you left the oven on, and you can think about the year past and the

year to come. You can make your resolutions, forgive grudges, remember loved ones who have died. You can choose to stay until
nightfall, or just until you feel finished.

If you stay home, try to avoid the activities of daily life. Don't
make that dentist appointment or wash the floor. Instead, spend
some time doing things you have been promising yourself all year.
Play a piece of music that moves you and sit down and really listen
to it. Collect all your scattered photographs of a loved one who has
died, write down notes or stories about your memories of him or
her and put them in a book for the younger members of your family. Write a letter to a friend you've lost touch with. Write or record
an ethical will, a traditional Jewish literary form in which you explain your philosophy of life to your children. What? You don't
have a philosophy of life? What better time than Yom Kippur to sit
down and think about what you really believe?

Sukkot/Succos

The seven-day holiday of Sukkot has seasonal, historical, national,
and ethical components. The holiday, which was originally called
the Feast of the Ingathering (of the harvest), is a seasonal harvest
festival, celebrating the fruit harvest. The sukkah, or temporary
shelter, is said to have been used by those who worked in the fields
for shelter from the sun during the hottest part of the day. Even
today, in the Middle East work starts early in the morning, breaks
for several hours in the afternoon, and starts again when the air begins to cool. Similar booths could have been used by those gathering at the Temple for the seasonal ingathering of the tribes.

The holiday ends with two additional holidays called Hoshanah
Rabbah and Shmini Atseret. Hoshanah Rabbah is an ancient rainmaking holiday and is probably the most important of the fall holidays in an agricultural world. If the rains come, everyone eats. If
they don't come, everyone starves. As Jews became more urban
and left the Middle East in greater numbers, this holiday shrank in
importance until almost all that is left of it is the prayers for rain
that are actually recited the next day, on Shmini Atseret.

The rabbinic authorities gave this harvest holiday religious significance by saying that the temporary shelter was like that used by

the Hebrew people in the forty years of wandering—never mind that the sukkah is made of trees and green branches, which are in short supply in a desert.

Although the sukkah was not used by any wandering tribes, and although we understand now that the period of slavery in Egypt, the exodus, and subsequent wandering were not experienced by all Israelites, we have adopted this story as part of our national sense of our history.

An additional religio-historical myth is that the Temples, both the first and the second, were dedicated at Sukkot. This could certainly be true, since this was a feast at which the people gathered at the Temple to sacrifice. This story is quite old, as we learn in the Books of Maccabees, dating from the first or second century BCE, which tells us that the Temple was rededicated in a celebration called "Sukkot in Kislev." (Kislev is the month is which Hanukkah occurs.)

Along with the story of the wandering and Temple dedication, we strengthen the national component with the tradition of symbolically inviting into the sukkah *ushpizin,* or guests, such as Abraham, Moses, and David, who are figures in our national development.

The first century Jewish philosopher and historian Philo of Alexandria and the medieval sage Maimonides stressed an important ethical component of Sukkot. They noted that all adult men, rich and poor, priest, noble, and layman, had to spend all seven days of the holiday in the sukkah. Rich and poor would be exposed to the same elements and be cold or wet all week. Maimonides said that this was established to teach "equality—the first principle . . . of justice."

The ethical component that is perhaps the most relevant to us today is the theme of food and shelter. Amid a harvest of plenty, there are those who are hungry, and the temporary shelter is a reminder of those who have no permanent shelter. Further, the flimsiness of the sukkah reminds us that our only home, the Earth, is fragile and needs care to preserve the environment.

In addition, the identification of the sukkah with the wandering in the desert makes it clear to us that the holiday is about being refugees, and should make us aware of the plight of those who, like Jews throughout the ages, have had to flee their homes and rely on the goodwill of strangers in strange lands.

An additional national and ethical message is often drawn from the *lulav* and *esrog*. The *lulav* is a wand made up of branches of the willow, which has no smell or fruit, myrtle, which has a pleasant odor but no fruit, and the date palm, which has no odor but bears fruit. The *esrog* is a citrus fruit with a pleasant odor. It is said that the willow is like a person with no learning and who does no good works, the myrtle is like a learned person who does no good works, the date palm is like the person who knows nothing but does good works, and the *esrog* is like a person who is learned *and* does good works. We are taught that all these people are represented among Jews and that we are all bound together, as is the *lulav*. We also learn that the myrtle, palm, and willow need each other to be whole, but the esrog stands alone, showing us that the true *mentsh* needs to learn and to act.

Observances

Sukkot is a family holiday. The family builds a temporary booth—a sukkah—in the yard. To be kosher, it has to be a certain size, have at least three walls, and have a half roof of branches, corn stalks, palm fronds, or the like. The roof has to provide more shade than light, but you should be able to see the stars through it.

YOUR OWN SUKKAH

How to make one:

Instructions: I found clear and easy instructions for a sukkah with lattice sides at http://bethelsdubury.org/sukkah. Instructions for another lattice sukkah, completely different in construction, were at http://www.pswtech.com/~stevenwfjewish/sukkah/sukkah2.html.

Both of these sukkahs use the sort of lattice you find at garden shops or home-supply stores. You attach the lattice to the lumber and hold them together with fasteners. You should be able to make a sukkah for about $100, and it'll last forever.

A Web search also yielded instructions for a bamboo sukkah, which looks hard to make (I haven't tried it), but it's lightweight and strong and easy to store. Just do a Web search for "sukkah" and you'll find lots of instructions for various sorts and sizes.

Where to buy one:

Sukkahs that you can buy fall into two main categories. Some places will sell you instructions and hardware and then you buy the lumber and whatever you want to use for the sides. Other places will sell you the whole shebang, including tools. These complete sukkahs are very sturdy; they look like permanent structures rather than flimsy temporary shelters. They are very durable and easy to put up, but they're expensive.

Your best bet for lumber and hardware is The Sukkah Project. They are at http://www.sukkot.com or 919/489–7325. Write them at Steve Henry Woodcraft, 4 Pine Tree Lane, Chapel Hill, NC 27514. You get hardware and instructions for an 8' x 8' or 12' x 8' sukkah. Lumber is not included in the kits. You can also order tarp walls or paintable parchment walls.

If you want to order the whole shebang, try Etrogim at http://etrogim.com or 516/292–7824. They sell modular wood or fiberglass-walled sukkahs of several sizes as well as canvas-walled sukkahs. They also have an extremely nifty canvas portable model that takes no tools at all to set up and *schach* (roofing material) is included.

It's not easy to build one the first year, but you use the same pieces from year to year and you get better at putting it up. (See pages 74-75 for a list of places you can buy prefab sukkahs of kosher dimensions and places to find instructions for making your own.) You can use permanent wooden sides or hang cloth every year. The sukkah is traditionally decorated with fruit, but may also be adorned with origami, paper chains, strung cranberries and popcorn, or dyed rigatoni.

Making the decorations is a nice family activity for Sukkot. Harlene Appelman, a prominent Jewish family educator, has linked the decorating of the sukkah to the decorating of a Christmas tree. In fact, she has said that getting to erect and decorate a sukkah Christmas-proofs Jewish kids, who don't need to ask for a Christmas tree when they have something beautiful of their very own.

In the sukkah there is often a table with candles to light. Edward Greenstein, writing in Strassfeld's *Jewish Holidays,* suggests lighting the sukkah with a "Yaakov lantern." What is it? Well, see, first you hollow out a pumpkin. Cut stars for the eyes, etc. Place a candle inside. Sound familiar?

On the table you can also set out challah or fruit desserts. People can eat in the sukkah if the weather permits. Some people even like to camp out and sleep in it.

Each night of Sukkot we can invite different *ushpizin* to our sukkah. As Secular Humanistic Jews we may invite in those who are important to the development of the Jewish People, the Secular Humanistic movement, or Humanism. We can invite in labor leaders, resisters of oppression, those who are being oppressed, the homeless and hungry, those in need of sanctuary, peacemakers, and environmentalists. Family members can take turns inviting a guest. We can also invite real people for a potluck dinner or just for dessert.

A *lulav* and *esrog* can be purchased at Jewish stores, on-line, or through synagogues, but they are expensive. You can use a lemon and make a lulav of three branches native to your own area if you want to, but it should include a branch from a tree or plant that has neither fruit nor a scent, one from a tree or plant with a scent but no fruit, and one from a tree or plant that has a fruit but no scent. Traditionally, the *lulav* is waved in all directions and up and down. The original symbolism of this activity is not known, but we can say that it means to us that we are part of the entire earth, that all things are interconnected, and that what affects one person or one eco-niche affects all people and the whole world.

On Hoshanah Rabbah the *lulav* is not only waved but also beaten on the ground, making a sort of rain sound in an ancient sympathetic magic. This is a great time to acknowledge our dependence on the earth and to make ecological resolutions.

Because Sukkot is the harvest holiday, it is an ideal time for the community to hold a food drive, to commit to a year of working at a soup kitchen to donate to the United Farm Workers. You might make a donation to Mazon, a Jewish organization combating hunger in America. (Send your check to Mazon, 12401 Wilshire Blvd., Suite 303, Los Angeles, CA 90025–1015.) We can also use the theme of temporary shelter as a focus for organizing a Habitat for Humanity chapter, helping to staff local shelters for the homeless, or lobbying for more governmental funding for affordable housing.

Sukkot Activities

If you have made a sukkah without permanent walls, you can use sheets or other large pieces of cloth as walls. During the holiday, you can decorate one of the sheets each year. Be sure to date the sheet. In several years, you'll have four lovely sukkah walls and a family artistic history. To decorate, try apple prints with tempera paint, or leaf prints with spray paint. Cut an apple through the equator, dunk it into paint, and press it onto the sheet. Or cut shapes from the apple and use them to paint with. You can cut fruit shapes or leaves or stars or flowers or anything else that suits you. For leaf prints, collect leaves of lots of sizes and shapes. Lay them on the sheet, weighing them down with little stones, and spray paint over them. When you pick them up, you'll see leaf shapes in negative. Or draw a tree trunk and branches onto the sheet with a crayon. Then decorate the branches with painted leaves of many colors and shapes. You can use crayons to draw fruit, too, or, if you're ambitious, supply bits of pretty fabric and appliqué or glue fruit shapes onto the walls.

Make decorations to hang from the sukkah along with your fruit. The youngest children can make paper chains. Older kids and grown-ups might like to make origami flowers or stars. Tissue-paper flowers are pretty, too. Use your imagination—anything that is pretty or symbolic of the harvest can be used to decorate your sukkah.

If you have a real *esrog,* plant a couple of its seeds in an indoor pot. You can put them in the ground on Tu b'Shvat, if you live in a warm enough climate.

For Hoshanah Rabbah and Shmini Atseret, you can make a rain stick. No, they are not at all traditionally Jewish or Middle Eastern, but they do make that rain noise, just like the *lulav,* and they're fun, and sometimes using another culture's symbolism for things we do, too, makes us realize how universal our needs and hopes really are.

To make a simple rain stick, use a cylindrical poster-mailer. You can get one for about a dollar from a poster store, packing shop, or stationery store. Or you can make a tube out of rolled-up newspaper and tape it up well all over. Decorate the outsides with glitter or paint or pretty pictures cut out of magazines. You can shellac it if you want to keep it nice for a long time. Mailing tubes come with bottoms and removable tops, but it you've made your own, cover one end with cloth held on by a rubber band or taped on. Use a long nail to make several holes through the cylinder, and insert sticks. Alternatively, you can just leave the nails in, if you like that sound better. Then put some beans of different kinds, or some seeds (birdseed works) or some tiny pebbles into the cylinder. Put on a cloth top held by a rubber band or taped, or snap the mailing tube top on. Voilà!

You might also like to make bird feeders, since Sukkot comes close to the start of winter. Take the inner cardboard cylinder from a toilet paper roll and punch a hole near one end. Smear the whole thing with peanut butter (or almond butter, if you have an allergic person in the household) and roll it in birdseed. During Sukkot, hang it inside the sukkah for decoration. When you take down your sukkah, hang the feeder on a tree for the birds to eat from all winter long.

Simchat Torah

Simchat Torah is the day after Sukkot ends. Although it has become part of the ancient and primitive fall holiday season, it didn't even appear until about a thousand years ago. Despite its relative newness, it has an important place in religious Jewish life.

Simchat Torah has national, religious, historical, and ethical components. At Simchat Torah religious Jews finish the yearly cycle of reading the Torah and begin again immediately. The Torah purports to be the ancient national history of the Jewish People and, as such, is a symbol of our existence as a nation. Nonetheless, the Torah is also a religious document, and the commandment to read the Torah year after year is celebrated by religious Jews on this day.

While the holiday itself does not commemorate any particular historical event, certain events have become attached to the holiday in recent times. The most important is that on this one day each year Jews in the former Soviet Union would gather openly. Young Jews would gather on the street in front of Moscow's Central Synagogue to sing and dance and to proclaim publicly their allegiance to their despised and even outlawed peoplehood. Hershl Hartman says, "Our celebration honors them and all people who resist efforts to forbid or defame their own languages, cultures, and traditions." Simchat Torah, then, becomes through its historical element, an ethical holiday honoring cultural diversity.

One other ethical component has to do with the actual study of the Torah. Like Lag b'Omer, Simchat Torah honors the act of studying. The repetitive study of the same document is analogous to the yearly retelling of the Pesach story. The fact that the document is ancient can remind us that old knowledge and insight can be as valuable as new and that old people have something to teach us. The act of studying Torah involves a process of extracting meaning from fragments and words, not just reading it. Judaism honors the interpretation of the text and imaginative, even fanciful, explanations for what's written there. As Secular Humanistic Jews, we can also interpret the text and learn about it. We can extract that which is meaningful for ourselves, and we can do it in a way that is traditionally Jewish.

Observances

Simchat Torah is a community holiday. Traditionally, on the eve of the holiday, Torahs are paraded around in the synagogue and the children march around with flags. The flags are sometimes topped with apples or other seasonal fruits and vegetables, sometimes hollowed out with candles burning in them. Even women are allowed to see the Torah. (This, until very recently, was an anomaly in Jewish life.) At the morning service, the very last bit of Deuteronomy is read and then, immediately, the very beginning of

Genesis. Congregations that own two Torah scrolls prepare one beforehand by rolling it all the way back to the beginning. Congregations with one Torah scroll roll it back during the service. Sometimes everyone sings during this process—it takes a while—or sometimes the rabbi or person doing the rolling will stop every now and then to point out special sections, like the Ten Commandments.

A Cultural Simchat Torah Celebration

Only a few Secularist Jewish communities in North America have evolved celebrations for Simchat Torah, among them Los Angeles's Sholem Community Organization. Their celebration focuses on the merrymaking and the connection with other harvest holidays around the world. The children in their Sunday school make decorated flags and parade with them. Each class picks a theme for decorations from among the following ideas, or others:

- Celebration of learning (symbols of knowledge; e.g., books, microscopes and telescopes, biblical scrolls, computers, scales of the law, etc.)
- Symbols of the New Year Festival (e.g., beehive, apple slices, shofar, Zodiac signs, peace dove, etc.)
- Holidays of the Jewish Year
- Flags of countries represented by neighbors in our communities and classmates in our weekday schools

Some Secular Humanistic Jewish organizations use this as a holiday about books and literature in general. Other organizations prefer to defer this theme to shavuot or Lag b'Omer. Some groups also try to borrow a nonkosher Torah to look at. These are sometimes available from a local Hillel or a congregation with many Torahs. Your group can invite a member or someone else who knows about it to do a show and tell about how the Torah is physically made—the ink, the way the letters are written, how the pages are sewn together, and what they are made of. One woman who grew up Orthodox and is now a member of a Secularist group was deeply touched to be able to see the Torah up close. "This is the closest I've ever been to a Torah," she said. "When I was

Orthodox, I never thought I could see and touch it." Even though it was no longer the word of God to her, it is still an ancient document that has influenced the Jewish People for three thousand years. Experiencing it as an artifact is powerful for religious and secular Jews, alike.

Since the Torah is both a national history (which was, like all histories, written by the victor), and a family story, we can use this holiday at home as a special time to tell stories from Jewish history and from the history of our families. Call up the oldest members of the family and ask them for their stories. Storyteller Laura Pershin says that you get stories by asking specific questions, so try some like these:

What was your favorite food when you were little?

What do you remember (or what did you hear from your parents) about the trip to America? What did you bring with you? How did you get to the boat?

Did you ever meet anyone famous? Did you ever know someone who should have been famous?

Who was your favorite teacher? Who was you favorite Hebrew school or *kindershule* teacher?

What were your nicknames? Who called you that?

These are simple questions, but they lead to specific memories, which can then lead on to more and more stories. Tape the person telling the story, or take really really good notes. You can make a book of your family stories and paste in pictures of the person who told each story. You can add to this book every year, when you bring it out at Simchat Torah.

If you have a family genealogy, try making up rhymes for each ancestor and see if that helps you memorize them way, way back. Find out whom you were named for. See if anyone had the same birthday as you. (This is hard to do beyond a couple of generations because many European Jews did not know their birthdays and if they did, it was not by the Gregorian calendar, but by the Jewish calendar.) Or find someone with your name in the Bible and see what you have in common.

6

Hanukkah

Hanukkah is rich in meaning; it has all six holiday components: primitive, seasonal, historical, religious, national, and ethical. The primitive and seasonal components have to do with the winter solstice. Like many cultures, the Jews make light when the sun is least in evidence. The Yule log, for example, is a primitive Germanic custom that dates from long before the Christianization of that part of Europe. It's sympathetic magic: By making bright lights, we hope to show the sun what we want it to do. We Jews have a tradition of making more and more light for a whole week, showing that we want the sun to come back and make longer and longer days. Don't laugh! It has worked so far!

Was this sun magic the original Hanukkah? We don't know for sure, and scholars have debated the issue. It seems probable that there was a holiday of lights at this time of year—although the ancient Hebrew tradition would have been bonfires, not oil lamps. If such a holiday existed, it was successfully reinterpreted, or Judaized, as many folk traditions have been over the ages.

The historical component, perhaps the most obvious, is the successful war fought by the first guerrillas in recorded history. On Hanukkah we celebrate the victory of the Maccabees over the Hellenized Syrians in 165 BCE. The contemporaneous record, the first two books of Maccabees (along with writings by the Greek historian Polybius), tell of a civil war waged between Hebrews who were allied with their Greek-Syrian rulers and a band of Hebrews who appear to be a combination of nationalists and religious fanatics who demanded that all acculturation to Greek ways be halted. These zealots wanted to stop Hebrews from worshiping Greek gods, wearing Greek clothes, giving children Greek names, and playing Greek sports, as well as studying all secular learning. If we look at this in modern terms, we see that the bad guys of the story—the assimilationists—are a lot like us. It is not clear at all just who are the real bad guys in this story.

Another viewpoint also has some historical truth. Ancient Israel was fought over by two Hellenized kingdoms, one based in Syria and the other in Egypt. It eventually came under the rule of the Syrians, who decided, in an effort to unify the empire, to establish the universal worship of their king. This worship was not to the exclusion of other gods, but in addition to the worship of other gods. The king, Antiochus, was said to be the personification of whatever god was being worshiped. This suited many ancient religions but was an anathema to the Hebrew priests. Finally, a band of zealots led by Mattathias of Modin and his sons (including Judah Maccabee) arose in rebellion—luckily for them, at a time when Syria was otherwise occupied with rebellions all over the empire— and were victorious.

They established the Hasmonean dynasty, which ruled, with the support of Rome, until Rome decided a few generations later that it would just take over. The land of Israel/Judah under the Maccabees (the Hasmoneans) eventually encompassed a huge territory. The Hasmoneans were no better or worse than other ruling powers, though. They were proud of their conquest of the lands of others and even forced conversion—including circumcision—on some who found themselves within their borders.

Throughout the years, the national significance of Hanukkah played a large role in the folk mind. Early Eastern European Zionists (in the 1800s) were responsible for reclaiming the holiday as a time of national aspiration rather than celebrating the folk and religious aspects. They began, against the loud protests of the religious establishment, to celebrate the holiday, which had been considered a minor one, as the holiday that embodied their central ideals. They also used it as a day to glorify physical prowess, fighting ability, and sports.

Also in the late 1800s the holiday was used to energize the Jewish militias that fought back against pogromchiks. The Yiddish Hanukkah songs from Eastern Europe often contain mournful statements about how hard it was to believe that Jews were once fighters and had their own land. Although the establishment of Israel has made those songs seem like quaint echoes of days gone by, the national longing is clear.

It is because of the national and historical components that the ethical component of Hanukkah is so important. We see in the Hanukkah story a phenomenon that has been repeated many times in the modern world: a tyrant so strong he can be overthrown only by fanatics. Just as the moderates never spoke out against the shah of Iran, the moderate Jews of the time did not speak out against Antiochus, the Greek-Syrian ruler. As the tyranny tightened, only those who were fanatics were willing to sacrifice all for the cause of overthrowing the tyrant. The fanatics began rebellions, and when it looked like they might win, the moderates joined them. The fanatics ended up taking over the government and becoming tyrants themselves, as fanatics are wont to do. We learn from this that it is necessary to speak out against injustice and tyranny immediately and not to acquiesce even to the first injustice.

We also learn from the holiday the need of people for their own heritage and culture and the lengths to which they will go to defend their national and cultural rights. We remember how we resented being deprived of our culture, and we speak out against instances in which others are being deprived of their culture. Progressive Jews were among those who protested, for instance, when the Bulgarians forced their ethnic Turkish minority to take Slavic names and give up their own ways, an instance closely related to the example of the Hanukkah story. And Jews must also remember the forced removal of Native American children to boarding schools outside their communities, schools in which they were forbidden to speak their own languages and engage in their own traditions.

The religious aspects of the holiday are a later overlay. They are a result of the antipathy of the rabbinic establishment to the idea of

Jews acting on their own and to the idea that there could be Jewish kings who were not of the Davidic line. At least two hundred years after the events of 168–165 BCE the rabbis invented the story of the miracle of the oil and gave God, rather than the freedom fighters, the credit for freeing the Jews from outside tyranny. They also succeeded in making the story one about religious rather than cultural oppression. By paying attention to the nonreligious aspects of the holiday, we are returning it to its true historic and ethical roots.

Observances

On the eight-day holiday of Hanukkah we light a menorah or Hanukkah-lamp each night, lighting one candle with the shammes (worker candle) the first night and adding a candle each night until the entire menorah is lit on the eighth night. *Menorah* is the word for candelabra and often refers to the Jewish symbol, the seven-branched candelabra. In Israel, the nine-branched Hanukkah menorah is called a *Chanukiyah* and in Yiddish a *Chanukah-lomp,* which means Hanukkah lamp. In America, most Jews just refer to the Hanukkah menorah as a *menorah.*

Menorahs can be obtained from Jewish stores, catalogs, synagogues, or made by hand. An easy menorah can be made by gluing ⅜-inch nuts (the hardware kind, not the kind that grows on trees) to a piece of 1-by-2. Even easier is poking nine holes in a large potato. An article on the jewishfamily.com Web page suggests making oil lamps out of glasses that held *yortseit* candles. You fill the glass halfway with water, then float a thin layer of olive oil on top. Place a floating wick (which you can buy from a candle shop) on top and light it. If you have kids, you might want to have a menorah and a separate box of candles for each of them.

On Hanukkah it is customary to eat fried food. This is presumably to honor the oil in the *ner tamid,* the eternal light, of the story of the light that burned for eight days. In Eastern communities, including Israel, the fried food is doughnuts. Among Ashkenazim, latkes (potato pancakes) are popular.

Among Jews living in predominantly Christian countries, gifts are often given at Hanukkah-time, since the holiday occurs near Christmas. The traditional gift, however, is a small amount of money, Hanukkah gelt, symbolic of the right to print coinage that was won with our national sovereignty. Some families now give gifts each night.

On Hanukkah it is traditional to play with the small spinning top called a dreidel, which can be obtained at Jewish stores or synagogues. The dreidel is a traditional Eastern and Central European toy with letters on its four sides. Each letter stands for a word telling you what to do, but this has been Judaized to stand for the words "a great miracle happened there." (In Israel, they've changed the letters so that they stand for "a great miracle happened *here*" and they had to change the game rules to accommodate the new letter!) You play a betting game based solely on luck. It's the measure of the goodness of a parent to play innumerable excruciatingly boring games of dreidel with his or her young children. It is traditional to bet with nuts, but M&M's or pennies can be substituted.

An Eight-Day Celebration

Hanukkah lasts eight days, and it's a challenge to find something special each night so the holiday doesn't become just the mechanical lighting of the candles and the clamoring for a toy. You can rescue the candlelighting ceremony by dedicating the candles differently each night. As we light the candles we honor those in all generations who have fought to sustain our heritage. You can choose a special person or movement for each night and dedicate the candles appropriately. Dedicate the candles to freedom fighters in our own country and in other lands, or to the people who influenced your own Jewishness. Dedicate the candles to cultural heroes (artists, musicians, writers) or to Jewish heroes throughout the ages.

Need ideas? Find a one-volume Jewish encyclopedia and open it at random. You'll probably find someone interesting whom you've never heard of before. Read the short article to everyone at the candlelighting. Or each night celebrate a different aspect of Jewish culture: Yiddish and Hebrew poetry and songs, art, language, food, and ethics are only a few of the possibilities. Each night at the candlelighting you can read a poem or short story, sing a song, show pictures of works by Chagall or Modigliani and try your hand at making a piece of artwork in their particular styles, tell a story about being different. Or tell how you, yourself, will increase the light in the world in the coming year and ask each family member to do the same.

What we all really want from each other is *time,* not *stuff.* Here are some ways to make Hanukkah a special time at your house without succumbing to the unfortunate noisy commercialism of the season:

> *Day 1:* Tell your kids or grandkids or the children of friends about Hanukkah when you were a child.
>
> *Day 2:* Have a latke taste test. Make some with a lot of onions and some with few. Or put some in the blender and grate some. Or use zucchini or sweet potatoes in some and just potatoes in others. Make your own applesauce—it makes the house smell great.

How to Make Latkes
The Three (or Maybe Four) Great Controversies

Latkes are not the kind of food you have an actual recipe for. They're more the kind of food your grandmother makes, and when you ask her how much flour to put in, she says, "enough." Luckily, it's really really hard to make a bad latke.

The first big controversy is whether to grate or to grind the potatoes. My family ground the potatoes in what I assumed was a potato grinder, but found out, when I was grown, was really a meat grinder. I like grated latkes better, but the easiest thing is to do them in a food processor. Makes the onions less tearful, too.

Grate or grind or food process at least one huge potato per person.

Now it is time to argue about how much onion to put in. My father argued for one onion per potato, but this is excessive, even for an onion lover. If you really like onions, put in one onion for every two potatoes. If you think of onions as a condiment, rather than as the staff of life, put in one for every three or four potatoes.

Grate or grind or food process the onions along with the potatoes. This will keep the potatoes from turning an unpleasant black color. You can drain off the liquid that gathers at the bottom of the bowl.

Add a little bit of salt. No, a little more than that. Okay, that's good.

Add one egg. Yes, one egg. My father always claimed that no matter how many potatoes you use, you need one egg. Out of filial respect, I always add only one egg to my latkes. Sometimes they fall apart, though, and I'm sure it would be okay if you added more.

Add a handful of flour or matzah meal. Stir it up, and if it looks too liquidy, add some more. Better to have too little than too much, though; you don't want floury latkes.

Put at least a quarter inch of oil into a heavy frying pan and heat it well. Lift out a large spoonful (or handful) of latke batter and squeeze it out in your hand. Plop it into the pan and shmush *it flat, so that at least half of its height is covered with oil.* (Oh, no! another controversy! My editor insists that she does *not shmush* her latkes!) *When the bottom is brown, turn it over. After browning the other side, drain it well on paper towels and eat it with sour cream or applesauce.* Which to use? The third—or maybe fourth— great Hanukkah controversy! Galitzianers (those from an area of southern Poland) like sweet food and use applesauce. Litvaks (those from Lithuania) use sour cream. I suggest trying a little *shatnetz* (the mixing of unlike things, which is forbidden by Jewish law) and eating some of each on the same plate, or even both on each latke.

Day 3: Sing a Jewish folk song or dance a Jewish folk dance. (A Yiddish Hanukkah song says

לאָמיר אַלע זינגען אוּן . . . לאָמיר אַלע טאַנצן)

(*Lomir alleh zingen oon . . . lomir alleh tantzn.* Let's all sing and . . . let's all dance.)

Don't know any? Call an older relative and ask for a song. Get a Jewish songbook and learn one. Play a recording of Jewish music—any kind: klezmer, Israeli, Yiddish folk songs, or something from the Jews of Bukhara or India. Put on some

Jewish dance music and just dance—after all, you're the folk in folk dance so whatever dance you do is folk dance.

Day 4: Ask each person to tell what she or he can do to keep Jewish culture alive and growing. Will you learn some new Yiddish or Hebrew words? Learn a new song? Tell stories of our heritage? There are lots of ways in which we can all enter into the stream of our civilization and enrich it.

Day 5: Give Hanukkah gelt. You can give real money or the chocolate coins that you can buy in the grocery store or from Jewish organizations.

Day 6: Give *tzedakah.* Let everyone decide together on an organization to make a donation to. Or shop for toys or clothes for an organization like Toys for Tots that gives Christmas presents to kids who wouldn't otherwise have anything.

Day 7: Play dreidel.

HOW TO PLAY *DREIDEL*

The dreidel has four sides, each with a Hebrew letter on it. The letters stand for the word in Yiddish that tells you what to do when the dreidel falls with that letter up. (Be careful— two of the letters look a lot alike. The only difference is that one has a notch in the base.)

First, ante up! Everyone puts in a nut (or several nuts). Then the youngest person spins the dreidel and follows the directions on it. Play continues around the circle. When you're out of nuts, you're out of the game, which goes on until one person has all the nuts. This can take just about forever!

Like everything else in Jewish life, dreidel is not standardized. There are two different sets of meanings for a couple of the letters. I'll give you both and you can decide which you like best.

נ This letter is called *nun.* In one version, it means *nisht,* or *not,* and means that the player neither takes nor gives any nuts. In the other version, it means *nem,* or *take,* and means the person gets all the nuts in the middle.

ג This letter is called *gimmel*. In one version it means *gantz* or *all*, and means that the player takes all the nuts in the middle. In the other version, it means *gornisht*, or *nothing*, and means that the player neither takes nor gives any nuts.

ה This letter is called *hey*. It stands for *halb*, which means half. The player takes half of the nuts in the middle.

ש This letter is called *shin*. It stands for *shtel*, which means put. The player puts one nut into the middle (or however many nuts the ante was—sometimes in an attempt to make the game go faster, adults suggest that the ante be five or more nuts).

Day 8: Read a Hanukkah story or poem from Jewish literature. There are lots of Hanukkah books for kids, and there are translated stories by great Yiddish writers like Sholem Aleichem, I. L. Peretz, and Isaac Bashevis Singer. Don't forget modern Jewish writers like Cynthia Ozick and Grace Paley.

For those who have time and are adventurous, how about dipping candles? You can get candle-making wax, wicks, and instructions at craft shops. Or melt down old candle stubs, adding crayon chunks for color. (Don't, however, plan on using that pot for food ever again!)

The December Dilemma

"My friends say that Hanukkah is the Jewish Christmas. How come I don't get a lot of presents? How come we don't have a tree?" These are familiar questions to many Jewish parents, and they're not easy to answer. Well, they are in a sense easy to answer, but the answers are not always readily accepted by kids.

"Is Hanukkah the Jewish Christmas?" No, of course not. What Hanukkah *is*, historically, is a holiday about it being okay to be different from the majority culture. Hanukkah celebrates cultural diversity and takes a stand against the homogenization of society. Hanukkah and Christmas do seem to be linked in the public mind, though, and we professional Jews seem to spend a lot of time trying to unlink them. "Hanukkah is not like Christmas," we say over and over, to very little avail. Why can't we seem to convince anyone? Perhaps, because in a very important way, Hanukkah *is* like Christmas.

Ask any Christian on the street what is the most important and lasting memory he or she has about Christmas and it's not likely to be the presents or the religious ceremony. The most common answer I have heard from my Christian friends and relatives is that the most important thing about Christmas is that it's a special happy family time.

Now ask any Jew on the street the same question about Hanukkah. You'll hear the same answer. Hanukkah is a time for us to get together with our families. There seems to be something about the cold winter that makes us reach for the warmth of our loved ones. It's a sign of our common human condition, and one that we should celebrate instead of condemn.

"How come you don't get a lot of presents?" This is a harder question, since some Jewish kids do, in fact, get a lot of presents. But for those of us who come from families that don't give presents at Hanukkah, the answer is just that Hanukkah isn't a holiday that's about presents like toys and games. It's a holiday that's about the gifts of Jewish culture. You can use each night of Hanukkah to celebrate one of those gifts (see above).

"How come we don't have a tree?" Because we have a sukkah, that's why. (Okay, I know that's a flippant answer, but it is true.)

It's true that Christmas is an official holiday in America and Jews are off work with nothing to do but go to the movies and eat Chinese food, while Christians go to church and gather at the tree and open presents and have a family dinner. Even without a tree, however, American Jews can actually have a Christmas tradition. Lots of organizations need volunteers on this day—to serve dinners or help in hospitals, for example. Every Jewish volunteer frees a Christian volunteer to be with his or her family on Christmas. It's a gift we can give to our Christian neighbors on their holiday as we fulfill our Jewish obligation for community service.

Some of our kids have the opposite viewpoint from the one at the start of this section. They don't envy Christmas at all; rather, they resent it. They point out Christmas decorations everywhere and grumble about how "all that Christian stuff" is being imposed on them. This isn't really any better than the complaints about not getting to celebrate Christmas. We want our kids to be happy living in a diverse community, and we want them to be able to maintain their own identities as free of envy as they are of coercion. It's important to express your support for the value and the fun of living in a multicultural society. "Christmas lights on people's houses are pretty," I used to tell my daughter when she would complain. "We are lucky to live in a country where there are all kinds of people and we can enjoy everyone's decorations for their own holidays." This emphasizes both the value of an open society and the value of each culture maintaining its own traditions.

Hanukkah Is Important

The Jewish establishment, in its effort to differentiate Hanukkah from Christmas, spends a lot of time trying to explain that Hanukkah is really a minor holiday and that we shouldn't make such a big deal over it. But, in fact, in America, Hanukkah is an important holiday, mostly because of its proximity to Christmas. Hanukkah gets set up as a competitor holiday. (Kids compare presents and weigh whether it's better to get a lot of presents on one day or one present every night.) But it's really the juxtaposition with Christmas that makes Hanukkah meaningful for kids—and not because of the presents.

Hanukkah is important because it is the first instance in which the child distinguishes herself as a Jew from her friends and neighbors who are Christian. Hanukkah is important because it is the first symbol kids identify with that differentiates them from non-Jews. Everything else we do as Jews is extra. We get Thanksgiving and the Fourth of July and school vacations *and* Purim and Pesach and Tu b'Shvat. We don't get Christmas but we *do* get Hanukkah. "We celebrate Hanukkah" affirms the child's Jewish identity at the youngest age and allows the child to celebrate her Jewishness instead of bemoaning her lack of Christianess.

What If You Do Both?

Lots of families have both Jewish and non-Jewish members. In most of these cases, the non-Jew is at least nominally Christian, even though he or she may no longer subscribe to Christian doctrine. These Christians grew up celebrating Christmas, and to them it's a special family time. They typically have great memories of Christmas and they would like their kids to have the same fun and family feeling that they had. There are lots of different ways to handle this attachment to Christmas. Each family has to experiment and find the way that's right for it.

Michael Goldblum was brought up Jewish, and his wife, Charlene, is the daughter of a retired Methodist minister. The Goldblums have solved the Christmas problem by visiting the Christian grandparents at Christmas. In their own home, they don't celebrate Christmas, but they take their kids to Grandma and Grandpa's house to help decorate their tree and to have a big dinner and open presents. Grandma and Grandpa go off to church after dinner, and the Goldblums clean up the kitchen. The Goldblum kids are Jewish, but they enjoy helping Grandma and Grandpa celebrate their holiday. They know it's important for their grandparents to have them there at Christmas, and they enjoy the family and the presents. The grandparents are not entirely happy that the children are not Christian, but they appreciate that they are able to share the holiday with them.

The Sapersteins solved the problem differently. Janet Saperstein made a commitment to raising her children Jewish, even though she was raised a Catholic. To her, this means that they don't celebrate Christmas. When their kids were born, Janet made it clear to her parents that they should not give the children Christmas presents and should not expect the family to celebrate with them. But she makes sure that the kids call Grandma and Grandpa on their holiday because she knows it's important to her parents to have family contact on Christmas and she wants her children to respect their grandparents' needs and holidays.

Joe Fitzpatrick and Emily Klein have taken a third, more controversial, route. Joe has no living family but he has fond memories of Christmas and did not want to give up his own cultural heritage just because his wife and children are Jewish. Joe has a Christmas tree and he invites his wife and kids to help him decorate it. The whole family enjoys daddy's tree, and it doesn't seem to confuse his kids at all.

The Wellbourne kids, however, are a little confused. "We're

Jewish, but we celebrate Christmas. Like, we have a tree and every-thing. I guess we're not really too Jewish," says Amy Wellbourne, who is seven. Her mother, Cheryl, who is Jewish, and her father, James, a "cultural Christian" in his own words, have had a tree every year since they were married.

"We blended our family traditions," explains Cheryl. "We cele-brate all the Jewish holidays and all the Christian holidays to-gether. We don't want religion to keep us apart, and, anyway, the way we celebrate Christmas isn't even religious." Cheryl is con-cerned that Amy thinks she might not be Jewish enough, but be-lieves that Amy will come to appreciate her blended culture and understand it better as she grows older. It doesn't matter to Cheryl and James whether Amy and her younger brother Ben choose Christianity or Judaism when they grow up. Both, they feel, are part of the cultural heritage of their children, and they don't want to deprive them of either half of their heritage.

Some families have even invented a sort of blended holiday, putting Hanukkah symbols on the tree or putting the menorah among Christmas decorations. It seems to work for them, although it strikes me as insulting to both traditions.

Which way is right for your family? Consider whether you want your children to identify as Christian, Jewish, "half-Jewish," or "My dad's Christian and my mom's Jewish and I'm mixed," or "We're Jewish but my mom's family is Christian," or some other permutation. That'll give you a basis for deciding whether you want to have Christmas in your home, either as one parent's holi-day or as the family holiday, if you want to visit someone for "their" holiday, or if you want to ignore Christmas altogether.

You might try one way one year and another way another year until you find the way that fits your family best. Or you can switch methods at a certain point, perhaps visiting relatives before you have kids and while they are young, but staying home after the kids are old enough to understand the holiday. Although no decision needs to be permanent, bear in mind that families who start out celebrating Christmas have a particular problem if they change their minds. Through the years of her marriage to a Jewish man, Janine has gradually become Jewish. She did celebrate Christmas with her kids for many years. Eventually she lost interest in cele-brating it at all. Her two raised-Jewish kids, now fourteen and nine, really love the holiday. Even though they identify strongly as Jews, they don't want to give up the tree and the presents. "It's fun!" says Michael, their older child. "I like celebrating both holidays—you get twice as many presents!" Janine is trying to downplay the holiday gradually, but she's getting a lot of resistance from the kids.

There's no one right way for every family, and sometimes there's no one right way for each family. There might be some wrong ways, though. You just have to keep consulting your own feelings each year about the holidays, about your family, and about what being Jewish really means to you.

7

Spring Holidays

Unlike the fall holidays, which are all related, the three spring holidays are distinct and have separate roots, although, as is natural for springtime celebrations throughout the world, there's at least an element of fecundity present in all of them. They occur at almost exactly one-month intervals at the three full moons of the spring, and are followed at about one-month intervals by the early summer holidays. From February on you can always be preparing for (or recovering from!) a Jewish holiday

Tu b'Shvat

Just as my ancestors planted for me, so will I plant for my children.—Talmud Ta'anit 23a

Tu b'Shvat, the New Year of the Trees, has historical, primitive, seasonal, national, and ethical components. Historically, it is a tax date: Trees that had flowered before that date were taxed for the year before; if the tree had not flowered by the fifteenth of the month of Shvat, taxes were deferred until the following year. Taxes, at the time, meant offerings brought to the Temple to support the priests.

Why was this date chosen? Almost certainly the holiday is the remnant of a religion worshiping Asheret, the goddess to whom groves of trees were dedicated in biblical times. As we learn from the Bible, it was almost impossible for the religious authorities of the Temple to wipe out this religion, even among the Hebrew people. So they adopted a date that was already a holiday—the first full moon of the early spring—and added the Temple offering to it. This is one of the effective techniques of religions that survive; the Catholic church also used this technique when it adopted the local gods of various lands and made them into Catholic saints. As Jews became urbanized, and this form of nature worship died out in the Middle East, and after the Jewish state was finally destroyed in 73 CE, Temple Judaism ceased to exist, so this tax date was no longer observed. It was preserved only in one text and was not revived until modern times.

The month of Shvat occurs in January or February, a time of year when it is still frigid in much of Europe and North America. In Israel, however, Shvat is the month the sap rises and the trees flower. It is the time for the planting of some kinds of trees. This connection with the land of Israel is the national component—even hundreds of years and thousands of miles from the Land of Israel, we still celebrate the holiday during the season appropriate for our national homeland.

The ethical lessons of Tu b'Shvat are those that relate to ecology and to our responsibility to the earth. The fact that we have responsibility to the earth is a profoundly Jewish belief harking back to the idea that we are partners in creation. In recent times, new Jewish ecological groups have grown up around the country, and Jews have begun to talk about eco-kashrut. Kashrut is the practice of keeping kosher, and has to do with what things are fitting, or allowable. If a product is eco-kosher, it has been produced without harming the Earth or the workers who produce it. Companies that use harmful pesticides that pollute land, air, and water do not produce eco-kosher goods. Neither do industries that exploit the workers or force them to work in unsafe or unsanitary conditions. California grapes were declared not kosher by the Boston *Beit Din* (Jewish religious court), and the Congress of Secular Jewish Organizations took a stand supporting the grape boycott. These are only a few of the actions taken by Jewish groups to help preserve the environment. To learn more about eco-kashrut, check out writings by Elisheva Kaufman, Lynn Gottlieb, Arthur Waskow, Zalman Schachter-Shalomi, and the Coalition on the Environment and Jewish Law.

What Is Our Relationship to the Earth?

Traditional Western religious thought sees humans as stewards of the earth, the overseer of God's holdings. Humans are to understand that the earth is not ours, but God's, and we are to take care of it and preserve it for him.

Postmodern thought sees humans as enemies of the earth, threats to its existence and well-being. Humans are to understand that the earth is not ours, but belongs to its own self, and we cannot impose ourselves upon it.

Neither of these outlooks is particularly satisfying to the Secular Humanist because each supposes a nonhuman self-conscious personality, either God or Gaia, with whom we must interact. A more rational and perhaps more emotionally satisfying view is that we are part of the earth, just as we are part of our families and our communities. We cannot take unfair advantage of our families and communities; we cannot exploit them for our own purposes or impoverish or harm them, but we can take advantage of the resources of our families and communities, understanding that we are just as responsible for them as they are for us. We can take, but we must also give.

This family/community model can serve as a framework for thinking about our relationship with the earth. We cannot take unfair advantage of the earth; we cannot impoverish or harm it, but we can take advantage of the resources of the earth, understanding that we are just as responsible for its well-being as it is for our very lives. We belong to the same system as the earth, its plants, seas, and animals. We're all in this together, our selves, our families, our communities, and the earth.

The other important ethical teaching of Tu b'Shvat is that the earth is a good place. Many theologies, including our culture's dominant Christian theologies, tend to view the world as a place of evil and corruption, in contrast to the afterlife, which is pure and good. Jews tend to believe that the earth is good, as it says in the

Torah, and that we should enjoy physical pleasures, including the ritual foods of the holiday and the beauty of nature.

Observances

Tu b'Shvat is a fairly minor holiday best celebrated in the home. It is traditional to plant a tree on the holiday, and it's the perfect time to plant the seedling that has grown from your Sukkot *esrog* seeds, but in areas in which this is not feasible (it's still frozen in much of North America) it has become customary to plant parsley, which will be ready in time for the Pesach plate. You plant the parsley in pots and grow it indoors. Another possibility is giving money to plant a tree in Israel or contributing to a reforestation organization like Larry Bush's reforestation campaign for North Vietnam, which you can contact at The Shalom Center, P.O. Box 380, Accord, NY 12404 (or Shalomcter@aol.com). Other organizations are groups concerned with saving the rain forest, preserving heritage species, etc.

We can also engage in recycling activities and other environmental concerns. A wonderful book for this holiday is Dr. Seuss's *The Lorax*. It's not just for kids!

On Tu b'Shvat it is customary to eat the fruits of trees found in Israel: carob, figs, dates, olives, oranges, almonds, etc. Some groups have adopted the new custom of having a Tu B'shvat seder at which the fruits are tasted and four glasses of wine, ranging from white through red, are drunk. The various movements have materials and ready-made seders that you can draw from. If you put together a seder for your family or group, be sure to ask members to submit poetry and pictures to you for inclusion in the booklet.

A Tu b'Shvat Workshop for Kids

Before the kids arrive, set up your stations. If you have a whole lot of kids, you can divide them into groups and have several activities going at once, letting the groups rotate. If there are mixed ages, ask the older kids to help the younger ones. Here are some ideas to start you off the first year—use any or all of them:

Station 1: Planting. Collect tiny planters or yogurt cartons. Provide materials to decorate the pots or cartons: glitter, paints, yarn, glue, or anything else you can think of. Let the kids decorate the pots before you put in the potting soil. Then pat parsley seeds into place just below the surface of the soil. They will grow in time for Pesach.

Station 2: The Lorax. Rent the movie or get the book from the library. Watch or read the story aloud.

Station 3: Ecology tree. Cut a huge tree trunk and branches out of brown paper and tack it to the wall. Provide green, red, orange, yellow, and brown paper and plenty of colored markers. Each child can cut out a leaf shape and make a New Year of the Trees ecology resolution and write it—or ask an older child to write it—on the leaf. Tape all the leaves up into the tree. Just as this tree is diverse and has lots of different kinds of leaves, the Jewish people, too, is diverse, with many expressions of Jewish life.

Station 4: Fruit tasting. Show pictures of the various kinds of trees that grow in Israel and let the kids taste carob, figs, dates, olives, oranges, almonds, and anything else you can find that can be grown in the Middle East. Kids may say "eeewwwww" at figs, especially fresh ones, and refuse to eat them. That's okay. Not everyone likes everything. That's another lesson about the diversity of the Jewish people!

Station 5: Singing and dancing. If you know some songs about trees or ecology—songs in English are fine!—teach and sing them. Or find an easy Hebrew or Yiddish song like "Ezey Zeitim Omdim." If you know Israeli folk dances, teach an easy one. Little kids can't grapevine, so just let them run. If you don't know any dances, dance anyway. Put on some Israeli music and do interpretive movements about being newly planted trees with the littlest kids. Help them wiggle their toes and feel their roots digging deep into the ground. Let them stretch their arms high into the air like branches and wiggle their fingers like blowing leaves.

Station 6: Paper making. This is messy and will ruin your blender, but it's a lot of fun. Your best bet is to call your local ecology center and see if they run paper-making programs for kids. They'll come out and, best of all, they bring their own blenders and they clean up.

Station 7: Seed mosaics. Get lots of different sizes and colors of seeds. You can use sunflower and alfalfa, if you like, not just seeds from trees. Draw pictures on pieces of cardboard and glue on the seeds.

Purim

First and foremost, Purim is fun. All else is commentary!

Purim, which celebrates the story chronicled in the Book of Esther, has primitive, seasonal, national, historical, and ethical components. The primitive aspects appear in the folk customs of wild celebration and drunken revelry at the full moon of the spring. In addition, the naming of a new queen in the Esther story is paralleled in many primitive spring celebrations, like the May Queen; and the ancient cultures of Egypt, Babylonia, and Greece included spring festival ritual marriages by kings and religious figures.

Although the story purports to be historical, it was written several hundred years after the events it talks about would have taken place. There is no evidence in any other record, either Jewish or otherwise, that the events ever happened or that the characters ever existed. In fact, the historical record directly contradicts the main plot ideas, and the characters appear to be named for Babylonian gods. The story, itself, is what we would now call a fairy tale. Still, we have adopted this episode into our national history, and it serves to remind us European Jews that there are also Eastern Jews, like the people in the Purim story, who have a history and a place in the Jewish People. This strengthens our national identity.

A further national component arises from the fact that it was all Jews that Haman wanted to kill, not just the one who annoyed him. The fate of the Jewish People is a collective fate.

Although the story itself is not historical, there is an actual historical holiday on the day that came to be the Fast of Esther (a minor sunup-to-sundown fast), the day before Purim. That was a holiday celebrating the victory of Judah Maccabee over Nicanor, a Syrian general. The rabbinic establishment so hated the Hasmoneans (because they had declared themselves not only High Priests—although they were not of the correct lineage—but also kings, a position reserved only for the House of David, a line that had died out) that the rabbis, when they came to full power near the end of the first century C.E. deliberately made a fast on the day that had been a holiday. Since the folk tradition was already to have a festival, they used merry-making for their Purim holiday.

The story, found in the Book of Esther, tells about a Persian king, Ahasuerus, who marries Esther, a Jewish woman, without knowing she is Jewish. The woman's cousin, Mordechai, overhears and foils a plot to kill the king. Meanwhile, Mordechai also antagonizes the evil prime minister, Haman, who retaliates with a plan to kill all the Jews. The king hears about Mordechai's help against the traitors and rewards him, causing Haman to hate him even more. Esther invites the king to a dinner party at which she risks her life by telling him that she is Jewish. The king becomes angry with Haman and allows the Jews to fight back on the day that was named for their destruction.

The theme of the whole story is profoundly secular in nature— it is really about the role of luck or chance in human history. Mordechai happens to notice the contest to become queen; Esther happens to win it. Mordechai happens to overhear a plot. The king happens to be unable to sleep and the portion of the record read to him when he can't sleep just happens to be about Mordechai saving his life. That we live in a random universe is a statement with profound ethical import. We cannot control nature or chance, but we can plan for contingencies and, most important, we can control our responses to happenstance. There's no sense praying for rain; we have to irrigate and store food and then, if there's a drought, share with others.

The other ethical issues of Purim are more problematic. The story brings up the question of dual loyalties, which has plagued Jews in many times and places. It demands attention to the question of intermarriage and to the idea of hiding one's Jewish identity. These questions are interesting and important, but there's something more ethically troubling in the text.

Purim is a nice holiday commemorating the saving of the Jews by Queen Esther, who is good and sweet and feeds her husband before she asks any favors. That's the story most of us remember from Jewish school. But that's not what it says in the Book of Esther!

What the Book of Esther really says is that Ahasuerus refuses to countermand his own order that the Jews be massacred and their possessions plundered. His excuse is that a king's order cannot be annulled. (This echoes the Orthodox belief that no part of the Jewish law—given by God, who is often called in the Hebrew prayers the king of kings—can be annulled.) Instead, after the famous dinner with Queen Esther, the king issues another order allowing the Jews to gather and fight in their own defense on the day appointed for their destruction.

What do you suppose the Jews were thinking and doing before this second edict was issued? Do you imagine that before Ahasuerus gave permission to fight back, all the Jews in all the 127 provinces were really waiting passively to be murdered?

Once given permission to fight, the Jews really go at it. According to the Book of Esther, they kill five hundred men in the capital city of Shushan. When Esther hears this, she asks Ahasuerus to allow the Jews another day of murder. He grants her wish and the Jews kill three hundred more Shushanites on the next day. The rest of the Jews in the 127 provinces ruled by Ahasuerus also rise up and they kill seventy-five thousand people.

I always liked the story I was told as a child, and I wasn't too happy when I read the Book of Esther for myself. I love Purim and prefer to be proud rather than ashamed of the history of my people. Knowing that the story isn't true doesn't help, either, because the authors of the story and those who included it in the Bible appear to have approved wholeheartedly of the slaughter. And they don't seem to condemn the supposed passivity of the Jews before the king's proclamation allowing them to fight back.

The Purim story deals with themes that appear again and again in Jewish history. All through our history, whenever we are powerless, from the time of Jeremiah to the time of Akiva to the time of Abba Kovner, we struggle with the issue of whether to fight the oppressor. According to the Purim legend, had the Jewish People not arisen to fight back, the Jews of Persia would have been annihilated. Individual Jews, Mordechai and Esther, could not save the Jewish People. The Jewish People had to act collectively to save themselves. We learn from this story not to rely on heroes, but to understand that the people are responsible for the course of history. We don't have to be heroes to influence history, but we do need to be willing to act in concert with others.

But there's another element to the story. All through history, whenever we are powerful, from the time of King David to the time of John Hyrcanus to the time of Ariel Sharon, we struggle with the issue of a just use of power and a just defense. How much fighting back is too much? Do you just make the oppressor stop or do you wipe him out? Should Jews keep other people subject in order to protect our own safety? Must we choose between being oppressed and being the oppressor? Isn't there a middle road?

Observances

Purim is a holiday of fun and making fun.

On Purim, communities read the Book of Esther or tell the story of the holiday, and every time the name of Haman, the villain, is heard, a noise is made to blot it out. You can write Haman's name on the bottom of your shoes and stamp when you hear the name, or you can buy or make any kinds of noisemakers to use. In some synagogues, they write Haman's name on balloons and then pop a balloon each time his name is read.

Sometimes the reader tries to read all of the ten names of Haman's sons in one breath. If she or he accomplishes this, be sure to cheer loudly! Or try it yourself. Here are the names: Parshandata, Dalfon, Aspata, Porata, Adalya, Aridata, Parmashta, Arisay, Ariday, and Vayzata.

The story can be straight from the Book of Esther or can be a Purim *shpiel,* a traditional Purim play, including as much foolishness and making fun of authority—both civil and religious—as you can dream up. You can make a play out of it, changing it to reflect what's going on in the news, using men to play women's characters and vice versa, and making it as funny as you can.

Jews traditionally dress up on Purim, often cross-dressing or dressing as characters in the story. There is drinking and reveling and all sorts of merrymaking. Purim often comes close, both in time and custom, to Mardi Gras.

Children are a big part of the holiday. They love to dress up for costume parades, which can be a lot of fun, if you're careful. Let me share an experience that impressed upon me how not to run a costume parade. There were about thirty children dressed up in the synagogue I was visiting, listening to the Book of Esther. Afterward, they paraded through the aisles to loud music, showing off their costumes and enjoying themselves greatly. Then prizes were given for the best boy's costume and the best girl's costume. Twenty-eight children were soon in tears, and the evening's fun was ruined for them.

Here's how to make a costume parade work: Get lots and lots of small prizes—a candy bar or handheld puzzle is fine. Then each child gets a prize for what is distinctive about his or her costume. Here are some ideas: The costume with the most jewelry. The pinkest costume. The most colorful costume. The meanest Haman. The sweetest Haman. The oldest Haman. The youngest Haman. The giggliest Haman. The Esther with the most missing teeth. The best use of bed linen. The most creative use of paper. They can be as silly as you like—after all, laughter is imperative on Purim—but the important thing is that everyone gets a prize.

Kids also enjoy putting on their costumes to deliver *shalach-manot* to neighbors and friends. *Shalach-manot?* Purim is sort of like a reverse Halloween. You dress up and then knock on the doors of your friends and neighbors and deliver, rather than demand, goodies. Just as many Christians make and share Christmas cookies, Jews make and share special treats at Purim-time. You can organize your neighbors and friends, each making a different sort of cookie, or you can just make whatever you like and exchange them potluck. For many years, I was the only one of my friends who delivered *shalach-manot.* I'd make hamantashen with a half-dozen different fillings. I'd make lemon bars and brownies and ginger cookie crowns. Over ten or twelve years, people got the idea, and now a dozen or more households are carrying *shalach-manot* each year. They all make hamantashen, but some add nuts and some add fruit and some make other cookies, too. The evening of the holiday, my family sits down and taste tests the hamantashen, comparing pastry and fillings.

Hamantashen? Hamantashen are the Eastern European traditional treat for Purim. They are shaped like a three-cornered hat, with cookie dough folded around a filling. The word means "Haman pockets," because they are like little pockets. The association with Purim is the word Haman, the villain, but the word probably came from *mun,* which means poppy seeds, one of the traditional fillings. Hamantashen are easy to make and can be filled with just about anything. Canned fillings are quite good. You can also make your own fillings, use cherry pie filling, or even chocolate chips.

How to Make Hamantashen

Use your favorite sugar-cookie recipe, but be sure it is stiff enough to roll. Or use this recipe from my oldest son's nursery-school teacher:

1 cup (230 ml) sugar
½ cup (120 ml) shortening
2 eggs
2 tablespoons sour cream
1 teaspoon vanilla
2 ½ cups (600 ml) flour
½ teaspoon salt (optional)
½ teaspoon baking soda
Mix well, knead, and refrigerate for several hours.

Roll out the dough to ⅛-inch to ¼-inch (.3 cm to .6 cm) thick and cut it with the top of a drinking glass. It should be about three inches in diameter. (Once you have emptied a can of Solo brand filling, you can use the can as a cookie cutter—it's the perfect size.)

Use a teaspoon—not a measuring spoon—and put a lump of filling in the middle. You'll have to experiment a little to find the right amount. If the filling is stiff, you can use more than if it is runny.

Now fold it up. Lift one edge of the circle of dough and deposit it almost in the middle of the lump of filling. Now look at the remaining round part of the circle. Put one finger halfway between the edges, where the circle part meets the folded part. With your other hand, pick up an edge halfway between your finger and where the circle meets the fold. Deposit that edge in the middle of the filling. Now lift the middle of the remaining rounded part and put it in the middle. You should have a triangle with a lump in it. Pinch the edges together and bake for about ten minutes in a 400° F. (250° C.) oven, until the dough is slightly browned.

They're best very fresh, so deliver them the same day or the next morning.

Sephardic Jews make *orejas de Haman,* or "Haman's ears" for a Purim treat. You can find a recipe for these delicious pastries in many Jewish cookbooks.

Purim, like many Jewish holidays, is also supposed to be an occasion for donation to worthy causes. We like to donate to organizations that protect women and women's rights, since a woman is the hero of this story. We can donate to or volunteer our services to a shelter, safe house, or crisis line. Chicago's Shalva House (Shalva, 1744 W. Devon, Box 53, Chicago, IL. 60660), a shelter for abused Jewish women, is a great choice, as is the New Israel Fund (New Israel Fund, 1625 K St. NW, Suite 500, Washington, D.C. 20006), which supports Israel's only battered-women shelter.

Pesach

Pesach is rich in symbolism and meaning, having all six of the holiday components: primitive, seasonal, religious, national, historical, and ethical. Its earliest roots are in the ancient New Year. While the fall is the most important time for agriculture in the Middle East, spring is the most important time for both herding and hunter-gatherer societies. Spring is when the food begins to appear again and when the lambs are born. By the time the Bible was written down, spring was no longer the political New Year; that had shifted to fall. But at that time, the first month of the year was still the spring month in which Pesach occurs, so Rosh Hashanah is said to be in the seventh month. We still often list the Jewish months starting in Nisan.

The seasonal significance is tied to the primitive. It is most clearly seen on the seder plate, with its greens and egg symbolizing the waking of the world and the new life of spring. The shank bone of the lamb is also a springtime element, as lambs are available only in the spring.

"How do you do Pesach without God?" the university students who sometimes teach at Ann Arbor's Jewish Cultural school used to ask me.

I'd always answer, "I can't figure out how they put God into the story." The central myth of our national identity, the leaving of Egypt, was told for centuries not as a story about people rising up and leaving oppression, but about the acts of a supernatural god who deliberately allowed his people to be enslaved, who caused miracles, and who hardened the heart of the pharaoh. This is meant to show the power of the Hebrew god, one who can control not only events in his own territory, as was typical of primitive gods, but events all over the world and people who didn't even know he was a god. How much more inspiring is the human story, the story of a man who sparked a slave's rebellion, the story of a people who organized themselves to escape oppression.

The historical component is the escape from slavery in Egypt. This event is largely mythical, but there is historical evidence that Semites did enter and rule in Egypt for about two hundred and fifty years, after which they were overthrown. There were undoubtedly Semites left in Egypt after the overthrow (although one has to assume there was a great deal of mixing during such a long period of time). One theory holds that a small number of them did leave Egypt and became the Levites, who entered the land of Israel quite late in the conquest, and gradually made their way northward. They were worshipers of the mountain god YHVH and brought the worship of YHVH to Israel, where he eventually became the god of the Jews. Although the Hebrews who left Egypt were a small number, and, if enslaved, were certainly not enslaved in the way we think of it—they left Egypt with their herds of cattle and their gold and jewelry!—their exodus from Egypt has become the central myth of our national story. Although they were probably only a small part of the Jewish people, their story belongs to all of us, as do the stories of all the Jewish people everywhere.

Though the events told in the Pesach story are not historically accurate, we do have truly historical events that occurred on Pesach. The Warsaw Ghetto Uprising began on Pesach and has become a powerful symbol of Jewish defiance in the face of overwhelming odds. Just as the Hebrews of the Pesach story were pursued by a large and powerful band of soldiers, so were the starved few left in the ghetto faced with a huge and powerful army. Surely the mythical escape of the Hebrews was inspiring to the young secular socialists who led the uprising against Hitler's overwhelming forces.

The ethical component is complex and involves the necessity of organizing response to tyranny, remembering history lest it be repeated, and recognizing that others throughout the world are enslaved and oppressed. A further ethical element is contained in the story: Joseph was welcomed by the pharaoh who ruled in his time. Later a non-Semitic tribe, the ancestors of the modern Egyptians, invaded and took over Egypt. It was the pharaoh of this group who "knew not Joseph" and enslaved the Hebrews. Pesach seems, therefore, a time to dwell on race relations as well as on the struggle against oppression.

Observances

Pesach is a home-centered holiday, but a seder may be held for a group, as well. The seder consists of the reading of the Haggadah and a festive meal.

"When I was a kid," Marc remembers, "the Haggadah was read all in Hebrew, and all the men would be reading as fast as they could, to prove who was the best Jew. The women were in the kitchen, and the kids were bored silly. And we never ate until ten o'clock so we were hungry, too. I hated Passover." It doesn't have to be that way. The Haggadah can be totally in English, short enough to keep everyone's interest, and can contain real meaning.

The Haggadah traditionally has several components, the most important being the telling of the story of the Exodus from Egypt. While the religious Haggadah is a set of prayers of praise to God, Secular Humanistic Haggadahs tend to concentrate on human effort. We remember that we were delivered (that we delivered ourselves) from bondage, and we talk about those who still need to be delivered or who were not delivered from bondage.

The Four Questions

The most important job for the children is the asking of the four questions, which you can find in any Haggadah.

The answer to these questions is the explanation of the ritual foods and the story of the Exodus, which we tell incorporating myth and legend in a longer or shorter version, depending on the hour and the number of young children at the table. Here's a short example:

This night is different from all other nights because on this night we celebrate the liberation of the Jews from slavery. Once we were slaves in Egypt, but today we are free.

Once we were slaves in Egypt. Matzah is the bread we ate in the wandering.

Once we were slaves in Egypt. Our children cried bitter, salty tears. We worked with mortar and bricks. This is why we dip our food and eat bitter herbs.

Once we were slaves in Egypt and had no time to rest. We recline with our family and friends because this is a sign of being free and our ancestors became free on this night.

Our legend tells us that after the Jews were enslaved the pharaoh wanted to reduce their numbers, and he decreed that all the newborn boys should be killed. Then he made the work even harder. There arose a man of the tribe of Levi, a man named Moses, who had been saved from the pharaoh's cruel decree by Shifra and Puah, and by the bravery of his sister, Miriam, and his mother, Yocheved, and by the daughter of the pharaoh, who colluded with them and who raised Moses as a prince. Moses could not stand to see the cruelty with which the Israelites were treated. Because he had been raised as a free man, he could envision freedom for his people, and he became their leader. Moses and his brother Aaron went to the pharaoh demanding the immediate release of all Jews from bondage. The pharaoh responded, as do all tyrants, by tightening, rather than loosening, the bonds of oppression. He was unmoved by pleas for justice.

With no recourse left, the people planned for their escape. One spring night, when the prince of Egypt had suddenly died of an epidemic, and the whole land was in turmoil, our ancestors arose, abandoned their homes, and fled to the desert.

If our ancestors had not fled ancient Egypt, they would have died as slaves of the pharaoh and we would not be here today. Therefore, our sages ordained that from year to year we should remember the exodus of our people from Egypt and celebrate this feast of Pesach in the season we became free.

The Ritual Foods

A second important component of the Haggadah is the explanation of the items on the seder plate, which is set in the middle of the table and holds most of the ritual items. Most of the foods can be tasted at the time of the explanation. This helps to hold the attention of the kids, and it keeps everyone's stomach from rumbling with hunger during the ceremony.

The roasted shank bone is a symbol of the pascal lamb. In biblical times, each household in Israel would come to the Temple in Jerusalem three times a year, at Pesach, Sukkot, and Shavuot. At the full moon of the spring each would bring a lamb as an offering to support the priests who worked there, just as in the fall (Sukkot) they brought fruit and in the summer (Shavuot), grain. A modern vegetarian alternative is a beet.

Charoses (Charoset, in Israeli Hebrew) is a pasty mixture of chopped local fruits and wine. Those of Eastern European heritage make it from apples and nuts; Jews from the Middle East use dates, figs, and other local fruits and spices. *Charoses* symbolizes the mortar that the Hebrews in the Pesach story used in their work as builders. When we taste the *Charoses,* we remember that the work was hard but it made us strong.

How to Make Charoses

Ashkenazic *charoses:* Grate or chop one apple for every four people. Add a couple tablespoonsful of chopped walnuts or almonds for each apple. Pour in enough of that sweet Pesach wine to make a paste. Add a little cinnamon, if you like, or a little ginger, and some lemon juice. Next year, vary the type of apple you use, and the kind and amount of nuts. Chop it coarsely or make a smooth paste in a food processor. It's all Charoses and it's all delicious!

Yemenite *charoses:* Chop up dates and dried figs, about a quarter cup per person. Use more dates than figs for a sweeter *Charoses.* Add a couple of tablespoons of toasted sesame seeds for each cup of date/fig mix. Add enough red wine to make a paste. Add a little bit of ginger (fresh or ground), ground coriander, and a sprinkling of dried red chilis, if you like hot food.

Your own *charoses:*   Use any of the ingredients of Ashkenazic or Eastern recipes above. Add some pine nuts, bananas, chocolate chips, raisins, or whatever you have around that will make a sweet mixture. Add enough wine to make a paste and some honey or sugar, and spices, sweet and savory. If it's too strong, you can cut it with a little matzah meal.

Moror is usually translated as "bitter herbs." Horseradish is the most common *moror,* and it can be bought in jars in many grocery stores. If you're lucky, you can find a fresh horseradish to grate at home the day of the seder. Be sure not to wipe your eyes before washing your hands! And save a little chunk of it to plant. Master gardener Yonassan Gershom, who lives in Minnesota, says that a chunk of horseradish planted in the ground will grow, even in his cold climate. But put it somewhere remote, he warns, because it becomes huge. You dig out the root just before the seder the next year.

The bitter herbs remind us of the bitterness of the slavery that our people endured in ancient Egypt and of the bitterness of the lives of all oppressed people. It's traditional to eat enough horseradish to make your eyes water.

The greens, typically parsley (use the parsley you planted at Tu b'Shvat) or celery, symbolize new growth and the ever-fresh hope and desire of all people for freedom. The saltwater reminds us of the tears we shed in slavery and the tears of all enslaved people. You can dip the greens into the saltwater and eat them.

The seder plate also includes a roasted egg, but if you are going to eat the eggs, hard-boil them. Roasted egg tastes awful. The egg reminds us of the new life of spring and the new life the Jews made for themselves when they left slavery that spring so long ago.

A new addition to the seder plate is an orange. Over several years the story of the orange has changed, but it began with a statement that a woman belongs on the *bimah* (the platform at the front of the synagogue) like bread belongs on a seder plate. Later, it was told that someone said that a lesbian belongs in Judaism like bread belongs on a seder plate, and this evolved into the orange on the seder plate as a statement of inclusion of the gay community. Bread is forbidden at Pesach, but an orange is permitted, although not historically traditional, on the seder plate. By including the orange on our seder plate, we say that all Jews are welcome in our community—not just tolerated, but actively welcomed as enriching the whole.

In all times, though we Jews have suffered adversities and persecutions, we have always been optimistic about the future of our people and our ideals. Symbolic of this mixture of sorrow and hope, we combine the bitter herbs and the sweet charoses on matzah, as did the sage, Hillel, in the time of the second Temple. The lives of all who are enslaved are sweetened by the hope of freedom. All over the world, people have looked to the story of the Exodus for hope. At many of our seders, we sing songs of hope drawn from our tradition and sung by slaves in America, songs like "Let My People Go."

In the matzah cover are three matzahs. Two of these symbolize the two loaves of bread Jews traditionally bake for holidays and festivals. The third matzah is the bread of poverty. It reminds us of how our ancestors left ancient Egypt in great haste. It reminds us of how they lived in the desert. Thus, the matzah is a reminder of life's necessities: bread and freedom.

The middle matzah is broken and one half is hidden before the seder. The hidden half, the *afikomen,* symbolizes all whose lives are broken by fear and poverty. At the seder, all the children hunt for the *afikomen,* and the seder cannot end until it is found. This shows that everyone must participate in redeeming those who suffer and that they can be freed from oppression only if we help them.

On a practical note, finding the *afikomen* helps to keep children awake until the end of the seder. At many seders, the children bargain to ransom the matzah for a prize, often candy or money. The ransom can be just about anything. (In our family, we award "stay up a half an hour late tonight" certificates for use at a later time.)

Everyone has a wineglass, but there's also an extra glass on the table. This glass is Elijah the Prophet's. Elijah, a powerful voice against the domination of the ruling elite in the ninth century BCE, is said to visit every single seder in the world. (We figure that by the time he tastes all that wine, he's so drunk he thinks it's Purim!)

Elijah's cup is set as an invitation to all those who are strangers in our land, in need of a home, of a family, during this festival time. At one point during the seder, the door is opened either as a symbol that everyone is welcome, or to let in Elijah. Some families pour a glass of wine for Elijah, and when the children leave the table to open the door, someone quickly drains the glass, proving that Elijah—the spirit of bettering the world—has been at the table. Our tradition, which follows Rabbi Naftali of Ropshitz, is to pass Elijah's cup around the table. Each person pours in a little of the wine from his or her own cup, showing that we all have to contribute to Elijah's message. Since we have several wines on the table, the result is usually a disgusting combination that my husband has to down quickly as the kids open the door. Each year he begs for someone else to be "Elijah," but each year he is overruled. It's tradition!

The Four Glasses of Wine

Another traditional element is the four glasses of wine. We drink four glasses of wine that we dedicate in any way that seems appropriate for us, and these dedications can change from year to year. In the religious ceremony, ten drops are taken from the second glass in memory of the ten plagues that struck the Egyptians. We Secularists often list ten contemporary plagues, such as homelessness, nuclear proliferation, sexism/heterosexism, racism, disease.

Here is an example of a dedication from the Ann Arbor Jewish Cultural Society Haggadah. You can find others in the many Haggadahs written by other organizations and people. See the resource list for some other Haggadahs.

Traditionally we dip ten drops from our second cup to mourn the victims of the ten plagues visited upon the Egyptians and in memory of the Egyptian soldiers who were killed as the Red Sea closed over them. Though they were our enemies, they were human, too, and must have suffered terribly. We dip from our own cup of happiness the sorrow of others. Let us now dip ten drops symbolizing these ten ancient and ten contemporary plagues:

The ancient plagues:

- Rivers of blood
- Frogs
- Lice
- Wild beasts
- Pestilence
- Boils
- Hailstones
- Locusts
- Darkness
- Death of the firstborn

Contemporary plagues:

- Poverty
- Sickness
- Disrespect for the Earth
- War
- Bigotry
- Indifference
- Violence
- Slave labor
- Greed
- Contempt for Justice

We drink this second cup of wine as a rededication to the principles of freedom and justice. Let us pledge to eradicate these plagues so that future generations will be able to drink a full second cup.

Keeping Kosher for Pesach

Pesach has particular dietary laws that stem from biblical times but that have evolved over the centuries in different places. Ashkenazic (Central and Eastern European) Jews have more restrictions than Sephardic (Spanish) and Eastern Jews. (Ashkenazim don't eat rice and beans during Pesach, but Sephardim do.) These additional restrictions were added in the 1500s, making them fairly recent in Jewish historical terms. The basic idea is not to eat "chametz," which translates as "vinegar" but really means anything fermented and, by extension, anything that can be fermented. The law, in practical terms, however, does not really—even for the most orthodox—prohibit eating anything that *might* be fermented; rather, it prohibits only those things that can be practically eliminated from the diet. For example, even the most orthodox eat potatoes during Pesach, although their fermentability is evidenced in every bottle of vodka. Potatoes were a staple in modern Europe and parts of the Middle East, but they were introduced to these areas after the Shulchan Aruch was written. Since they were unknown, they were not forbidden, which was a good thing, because the poor Eastern European Jews had very little else to eat.

Not only *chametz* is forbidden, but so is anything that has come into contact with it. Many Jewish families have special Pesach plates, silverware, and cooking utensils that they bring out only for the holiday each year. They *kasher* (make kosher) their countertops, stoves, sinks, and anything else that comes into contact with food. Zalman Schachter-Shalomi, writing in Strassfeld's *The Jewish Holidays,* goes so far as to recommend *kashering* utensils in a bathtub full of Drano, which strikes me as excessive, even for Orthodoxy.

In America, many Jews do not restrict their diets but instead add matzah to their meals during the holiday. Others refrain from eating bread, but don't obey the other dietary laws. Some religious Jews clean all the *chametz* out of their houses for Pesach. Some "sell" the *chametz* in a legal fiction involving locking up the food and temporarily deeding it to the rabbi, who then sells it temporarily to a non-Jew. After the holiday, the *chametz* is bought back. Some progressive synagogues have taken this opportunity for *tzedakah.* Members bring in all their unopened containers of non-kosher-for-Pesach food, which is then donated to a local food bank.

Macaroons are a traditional Pesach dessert because they don't use any flour. Chocolate and almond macaroons are common, but my favorites are coconut macaroons.

How to Make Macaroons

3 egg whites
1 cup (230 ml) white sugar
1 tablespoon cornstarch (Use potato starch if you keep Ashkenazic kosher for Pesach.)
Dash of salt
2 cups (460 ml) unsweetened shredded or ground coconut*

Beat the egg whites stiff. Beat them in the top of a double boiler so you don't have to get an extra bowl dirty. Add the sugar and cornstarch. Cook this over boiling water for 20 minutes stirring constantly.

After 20 minutes, remove from heat and add the salt and coconut.

Spoon out with a teaspoon or roll balls about one inch in

diameter and put on a greased cookie sheet. Bake in a slow oven—about 300°F. (150°C.)—for about 15 or 20 minutes, until the tops of the macaroons are just brown. After you taste a real homemade macaroon, you'll never eat another canned macaroon again.

* You can get unsweetened coconut at your food co-op or health food store. If you can't find unsweetened, you'll need to fool around with the recipe to avoid having the macaroons come out way too sweet.

A Different Kind of Haggadah

You can get a wonderful secular Haggadah in a beautifully illustrated book from Philadelphia's Sholem Aleichem Club. Almost all of the organizations in the CSJO have Haggadahs they'll share, too. Even if you start with someone else's Haggadah, you will want to add your own readings and dedications and explanations. You can use the exodus theme as a chance to retell your own family's immigration story. You might want to dedicate candles to those you know of who worked for freedom and dignity. You could also change the songs to some that are more meaningful for you.

Several years ago I got tired of being responsible for writing the Haggadah each year and went on strike. Instead of writing a new Haggadah, or rewriting and changing an old one, I decided to make the people at the seder responsible for the Haggadah. Instead of a Haggadah, I passed out two pages with an introduction and a few Ashreis, a list of questions, and a song sheet. Once your family or group has attended a good number of seders, you can try something like this. You will be amazed at the responses. I particularly liked my youngest son's answer to the question about the *afikomen*. He said we hide the *afikomen* to show that we need the next generation to clean up the messes that the current generation has made.

8

Summer Holidays

Lag b'Omer

Lag b'Omer, the Scholars' Holiday, is the thirty-third day of the counting of the Omer, the seven weeks between Pesach and Shavuot (the thirty-fourth day for Sephardim). During this period, ancient Israelis brought sheaves of wheat each day to the Temple. In the late Middle Ages, this whole fifty-day period became a time of half mourning, similar to Lent, during which many religious Jews do not cut their hair, wear new clothes, marry, or attend any public entertainment. Only on the thirty-third day is this half mourning lifted.

The holiday has primitive, seasonal, mythical-historical, and ethical components. Gaster describes the holiday as the equivalent of the European May Day, a strictly seasonal, rustic celebration, and also notes that the spring holiday bonfires in other cultures have a parallel in the Lag b'Omer bonfires lit in Israel.

The historical events said to have taken place at this holiday are a later overlay. Various stories are told about events that occurred on this day, and it is commonly associated with the period of time in which the Romans, having destroyed the Temple, forbade the formal study of Jewish texts. The legends hold that famous rabbis took their students to the woods to study where the Roman soldiers couldn't find them. If the Romans appeared, the students took up bows and arrows and pretended to be hunting. Of course, this is improbable, since hunted meat is not kosher, but it created the idea of the Scholars' Holiday instead of a pagan celebration, and so served the purposes of the rabbinic establishment. The bow and arrows are also reminiscent of the weapons used in the failed Bar Kochba Rebellion against Rome in 135 CE.

The ethical component appears when we remember that we Jews have known many periods of history when it has been uncomfortable to study our history and culture, but this study has been so important to us that we have been willing to risk lives, at times even taking up arms, to continue it. The Scholars' Holiday celebrates all those throughout the ages who kept Jewish history and learning alive and who fought to preserve our heritage. Just as Pesach celebrates saving our physical lives, Lag b'Omer celebrates saving our cultural lives.

Observances

Lag b'Omer is by its nature a community holiday. Among some Orthodox communities, it is traditional to have ceremonies for the first haircuts of three-year-old boys. Weddings are also held on this day. In Israel, many religious Jews visit the grave of Rabbi Shimon Bar Yohai, who lived in Roman times and was said to have died on the eighteenth of Iyar, which is Lag b'Omer. (Shimon Bar Yohai is beloved of mystics, since he is the purported author of the Zohar, a Jewish mystical book actually written in Spain by Moses DeLeon in the Middle Ages.) There is singing and dancing at Rabbi Shimon's gravesite and people light bonfires. Picnics and archery games are common, through a tortuous series of connections among Shimon Bar Yohai, Noah, rainbows, and archery bows.

Lag b'Omer occurs in very early summer, about the first time most of North America is warm enough to do something outdoors. Picnics and archery games are fun. You can also run races and play New Games and other sorts of field games. Your family or youth group might like to go camping the weekend of Lag b'Omer. You can light a campfire in many campsites. It's smaller than a real bonfire, of course, but it's pretty and ties to the tradition. And it's an excuse to make s'mores.

Although the holiday is mostly about celebrating being comfortable outside again, you might note that we are honoring scholars and all those who contributed to the richness of our culture throughout the ages. Talk about what's worth defying authority for—younger children can talk about under what circumstances they would break a rule—and which principles are worth dying for (as the Jewish martyrs did in Roman times). This is pretty good fireside conversation and can lead to a fascinating expression of values.

Shavuot

Shavuot has primitive, seasonal, religious, national, and ethical components. Shavout marks the festival at which the product of the grain harvest was brought to the Temple. The reason that the Book of Ruth is read on the holiday is that part of the story of Ruth takes place at the time of the barley harvest. Jews decorate their houses with sheaves of wheat and other grains, or with branches, flowers, (or paper cuts of flowers), and leaves. Other cultures also have summer holidays in which flowers and green twigs are carried and used for decoration; many European Christian churches are decked out in wreaths and flowers at Whitsun. In fact, according to Abraham Chill's *The Minhagim,* the Vilna Gaon discouraged the use of flowers and branches at Shavout because he recognized the custom as having pagan origins.

Shavout is traditionally a dairy holiday for European Jews. Although this has been explained in various Torah-based ways, Gaster's *Festivals of the Jewish Year* notes that many ancient and modern cultures have a dairy-eating holiday this time of year. He mentions, among others, that dairy dishes are tradition for Beltane in Scotland and that the Sunday before Lent is known as Cheese Sunday in Macedonia. Although explanations for this vary from culture to culture, the reason appears to be that milk is available. The young cattle born earlier in the spring are just being weaned and the mother animals are uncomfortably full of milk.

The religious meaning comes from the legend that the Torah was given on Mount Sinai on Shavuot. Although this idea does not appear in the Bible, it was inconceivable to the rabbis that a Jewish holiday should be totally pagan, so, probably sometime in the early Middle Ages, they began to teach this.

The national component is one that most speaks to Secular Humanistic Jews, since this is the component that makes Secular Humanistic Judaism possible. According to religious tradition, Shavuot is the time of the giving of the Ten Commandments, and by extension, all of the written and oral Torah. While we believe that the Jewish law evolved rather than being revealed and is a creation of the Jewish People, we agree that the existence of law and the Jewish national narrative is of primary importance to our People. For us, the existence of Torah (by which we mean both oral and written law and the stories that are told along with the law) represents the transformation of a tribal religion ruled by its god into a civilization ruled by its laws. The fact that the Jewish People are ruled by law and carry forth a literary culture makes us a nation, a People, a civilization, rather than just a religion. It allows the existence of Jewish Secularism.

The ethical component is made up both of what is in the Torah and the other stories and customs concerning the holiday. The Torah itself is full of stories and ideas. It contains the concepts of *mentchlichkeit* (behaving like a decent human being), of social justice, of *tikkun olam* (the completion of the creation of a just world), of a defiance of the status quo, of the dignity of each individual), and of *tzedakah* (the just economic ordering of society). In fact, the story of Ruth includes an important scene demonstrating the importance of this just economic order. Ruth goes to glean in the fields of her husband's relative, Boaz, who has, in accordance with Jewish law, left unharvested the corners of his fields for those who were too poor to buy food and had no land to grow their own.

Talmudic stories of the giving of the Torah include a statement that all Jewish souls, born and yet unborn, were present at Mount Sinai. This reminds us of the absolute equality of every Jew to understand and interpret Jewish law, history, and culture. This is the meaning of the phrase "a nation of priests," and it signifies that Jewish learning and literature belong to all of us, no matter our religious perspective.

Ruth, the hero of the story we read on Shavuot, was not born a Jew. She converted by the simple expedient of saying she would be Jewish. She didn't go to any *mikveh,* she didn't promise to follow 613 commandments, and no three male rabbis ruled on her fitness.

She chose to be Jewish and she was Jewish. She married a Jew, and the story has it that her great-grandson became king of Israel. We learn from this that a sincere attachment to the Jewish People is a sufficient conversion (despite the Orthodox insistence that Ruth had a halachically correct conversion that wasn't included in the book) and that converts have the same standing and value as born Jews.

Observances

Shavuot is celebrated in both the community and the home. The Book of Ruth is read in a community setting during the morning service. It should be noted that although the book is profoundly antiracist, it has offensively ageist, sexist, and heterosexist elements that cannot be ignored.

Some Jews follow the tradition of staying up all night before the ceremony and studying sacred texts in the synagogue. It's a good time for a youth group all-nighter with some learning interspersed with fun activities and, of course, plenty of food. You can also make a fund-raiser out of it; youth group members can get sponsors to donate a certain amount for every study hour.

Reform Jews often conduct the ceremony of confirmation for sixteen-year-olds at Shavuot. New Jews (converts) may be welcomed with a ceremony at Shavuot, the holiday at which we note Ruth's conversion to Judaism. It's also a good time to think about what your commitment to Jewish life is and to write your own "ten commandments."

SOME JEWISH AFFIRMATIONS FROM HOWARD BOGOT

Professor Howard Bogot wrote these eleven affirmations. They are reprinted here with his permission.

1. I have the responsibility to safeguard the gifts of creation and celebrate life. I can learn to differentiate the sacred from the ordinary.

2. As the world grows older, I grow older. I can grow to act in more mature ways. I can affect the maturity of the world, its environment, and humanity.

3. I have the capacity to determine my own character and reputation. I can judge, improve, and redeem myself.

4. I need others. I am aware that nature, chance, and change have an impact on my life. I realize that life is fragile and am humbled by that awareness. I can and will seek opportunities to express thanksgiving.

5. I possess a treasure. TaNaCH (the Bible, and, by extension, all of Jewish learning) communicates demands on my thoughts and behavior. I can discover unparalleled meaning in TaNaCH and accept both implicit and explicit obligations in its prose and poetry that represent the perennial values of Jewish identity. I am a missionary for TaNaCH and its messages of prophetic idealism.

6. I am proud to be a Jew. I can and will assert the values of Jewish identity. The Jewish People deserve my loyalty. I can be a light to others, using Jewish teaching to guide them on the path of brave self-esteem.

7. My Jewish identity may make others uncomfortable. My Jewish values are often controversial. However, I must and will defend my beliefs.

8. I am free. I will not tolerate slavery for myself or others.

9. I am a realist. Suffering is a possible aspect of my Jewish identity. Yet I am an optimist. I am confident that the future can be better. I can help build a beautiful tomorrow.

10. I can and will experience the State of Israel both as a model of the TaNaCH's prophetic idealism and a national example of the social, political, intellectual, economic, and cultural style required for secure survival in the "global village." I will contribute to the fulfillment of these goals.

11. I can make choices. I recognize in the commandments of our Torah a valuable resource for personal and interpersonal discipline and decision-making.

Secular and Humanistic Jews sometimes use the holiday of Shavuot as Max Rosenfeld suggested in his *Festivals, Folklore, and*

Philosophy: A Secularist Revisits Jewish Traditions, as a first fruits holiday in which the community celebrates the accomplishments of its members. It's a good time to honor those who have graduated or earned advanced degrees or published during the year. You can exhibit artwork created during the year, or read poetry written that year, or demonstrate any new skill learned during the year. And don't forget to show off the new babies!

At home you can decorate the house with paper cuts, branches, and flowers and enjoy a dairy meal. Blintzes are most commonly prepared for Shavout (see recipe below) and are often accompanied by challah, borscht, and gefilte fish. Cheesecake is the traditional dessert.

Bobeh Celia's Blintzes

My grandmother was a cook of the *"meh shit arayn"* (you just pour it in) school. Consequently, we could never get a real recipe for anything. Finally, my mother and aunt plotted to figure out how my Bobeh Celia made blintzes. They went to her house when she was ready to make them. My mother stood by with pencil and paper. My Aunt Millie, holding a cup measure and a teaspoon, intercepted every ingredient before it hit the bowl and called out the amounts to my mom. Here's the result:

First, make the batter for the *bletlech*, the crepes.

3 egg whites (save the yolks for the insides)
4 whole eggs
½ teaspoon salt
½ teaspoon baking soda
2 cups (460 ml) flour
2 cups (460 ml) water

Mix all ingredients well. Make sure the batter is not lumpy. You can add up to ¼ cup (60 ml) more of water if the batter is too thick.

Now make the insides.

3 egg yolks
½ teaspoon salt
4 teaspoons sugar
1 cup (460ml) sour cream (low-fat or nonfat versions are fine.)
3 pounds (1.3 Kg) hoop cheese, farmer cheese, or a mixture of the two.

(Okay, so you've probably never heard of hoop cheese and can't find farmer cheese anywhere. Use ricotta and a little dry cottage cheese. It's not as tasty, but it'll do.)
Mix well.
Now it's time to cook the *bletlech* and assemble the blintzes. Find a crepe pan, which is a frying pan with a rounded bottom. An 8-inch (20-centimeter) diameter pan makes a nice-sized blintze. Turn a burner on high. Use a piece of paper napkin or waxed paper to wipe a little oil onto the pan. Get it hot, then ladle in some batter. Swirl it around quickly so it covers the pan and dump the excess batter back into the bowl. Put the pan back on the heat. Within a few seconds the edges will curl up and you can just dump the crepe out onto a clean cloth or oiled plate. Quickly oil the pan and start a new crepe. While it's cooking, dump a spoonful of filling into the crepe on the cloth and roll up the crepe. Just before it's all the way rolled up, tuck the ends in neatly. Set aside. The crepe that's cooking should be just done. The recipe will make about three dozen.
When you're all done making the blintzes, or even while you are making them, fry them in a little butter until they are brown. Be careful turning them so they don't break open. Serve with sour cream or jam.

A Jewish Book Festival

Shavuot, the traditional time to celebrate the giving of our germinal Jewish literature, the Torah, is also a great time to celebrate all of Jewish literary culture. Have a gathering of adults and children, read the Book of Ruth, eat blintzes, and have your own book festival. Here are some ideas for your festival:

1. Kids can write their own books. Ask them to write or dictate a story about a Jewish holiday or event. Let them illustrate the pages, then sew them together into a book.

2. Kids are good poets, too, but they need to be given a framework. Use the acrostic method—write the name of a holiday or some other Jewish symbol, one letter on each line. Then ask the kids to write a line starting with each letter—it doesn't have to rhyme. They can work separately or cooperatively. You'll end up with something like this:

Plenty of hamantashen for everyone
Under my costume, I'm nice and warm
Riding a horse, like Mordechai did, is fun
I like Purim
More than any other holiday.

3. Ask members of your book club, if you have one, or anyone who reads a lot, to review recent Jewish fiction. You can actually use this occasion to form a book club, and have the first meeting on Shavuot. Or you can have several people discussing the common themes and content of different current Jewish books.

4. Have an informal discussion on the books—whether Jewish or not—that have most influenced your lives.

5. Invite a local Jewish author or poet to read and discuss his or her work.

6. Ask several people to bring in their favorite pieces of poetry to read and discuss.

7. Ask everyone to bring in an old book for a grab bag.

8. Ask everyone to bring in a new kids' book to donate to your local shelter or an organization that gives books to kids.

9. Be sure to have flyers from your local literacy volunteer group available. Being a literacy volunteer is a great contribution to the lives of others and to the entire society.

10. Invite a storyteller, or have someone reading Jewish kids' books aloud.

11. Invite classes of kids to act out scenes from their favorite Jewish stories.

12. Call the CSJO or SHJ and get a selection of the books they sell. (CSJO, the Congress of Secular Jewish Organizations publishes books and also carries works published by the Sholom Aleichem Club of Philadelphia, Kopinvant Secular Press, and others.) Set them out and let people buy them or order them.

13. Make bookmarks out of leather and tooling devices or out of heavy paper. Decorate the paper with glitter or paints or crayons and laminate the bookmarks with a laminating machine. (You can rent them.)

Tisha b'Av

Tisha b'Av has historical, primitive, religious, national, and ethical components. The historical, or quasi-historical, element is the most prominent. Tisha b'Av is a fast day commemorating the destruction of the first and second Temples in Jerusalem, first at the hands of the Babylonians and then the Romans, as well as other disasters that befell the Jewish People. The fast was already established by the time of the prophet Zechariah, although there is no indication of it in any writing before that. We date the institution, then, from the Babylonian exile of the sixth and fifth centuries BCE and can see that the historical events that are mourned on this day were added to the already existing fast, although no evidence exists that these events actually occurred on the Ninth of Av. In fact, historical and biblical evidence tend to show that these events did not occur on that date. The ancient rabbis seemed to have understood that these misfortunes did not really fall on the date of Tisha b'Av, but deliberately assigned only one day in the year for mourning our historical defeats.

That the holiday dates from the Babylonian exile shows its primitive roots. Gaster refers to a Babylonian Ninth of Av on which dead heroes were said to walk the Earth. He mentions also, that Professor Julian Morgenstern believed that the Ninth of Av fast was a pre-midsummer fast. It is common in many cultures to have a Lenten period before a holiday, and Professor Morgenstern felt that this was the case with Tisha b'Av.

Because of the lack of sovereignty over our own land, Jews had nowhere to go when they were persecuted in other countries. Had we had a sovereign Israel, Jews would have been able to escape the vicious anti-Jewish riots and pogroms of Europe, the humiliating position of second-class noncitizens in the Middle East and northern Africa and, of course, the annihilation of the Jews during the Second World War. Tisha b'Av must remind us of the necessity of a national Jewish homeland.

The ethical component of the holiday lies in the idea that there must be some destruction of an old order for growth to occur. If all the trees of the forest stood forever, there would be no humus to nurture them, and they would block the light from the struggling young. Along with the destruction of the Temples came the end of animal sacrifice, the end of a hereditary ruling group, the end of Judaism as a national religion. The destruction of the Temples allowed for the primacy of congregational Judaism, advancement by knowledge rather than by inheritance of position, an emphasis on scholarship and interpretation, and a new understanding of personal responsibility for actions. It marked the beginning of the Jews as an international people and is responsible for the richness and diversity of worldwide Jewish culture.

A further ethical message comes from the (somewhat erratic) wisdom of the ancient rabbis, who decreed only one mourning day for the entire list of tribulations that have afflicted the Jewish People. If we had a mourning day for every disaster, we would spend all our time mourning, not rejoicing. We would think of ourselves as a sorrowful rather than a joyful People. We would lose heart and not want to be Jews. Instead, we can mourn intensely one day a year and be free to build our culture for the rest of the year. (We might think of this message on the new holiday of Yom HaShoah, or Holocaust Day.)

Observances

The central observance of Tisha b'Av, besides the fast, is the reading of the Book of Lamentations in the synagogue. Among the Sephardim, parts of the book of Job are also read. Lamentations, popularly ascribed to the prophet Jeremiah, is a series of five dirges about the destruction of the Temple in Jerusalem by the Babylonians in 586 BCE. The poems are very old and appear to date back to the generation of the destruction or the first generation after. Four of the poems are in the literary form of the acrostic, with the letters of the Hebrew alphabet each beginning a verse. The book is very similar in form to an ancient Sumerian text mourning the destruction of Ur, at least five hundred years before the Babylonian conquest of Jerusalem. Other Babylonian texts follow the same patterns. This gives additional credence to the idea that the holiday originated in Babylonia.

Because it is a day of mourning, many religious Jews follow some traditional mourning customs on Tisha b'Av; they do not sit on chairs or wear leather shoes. Some go so far as to sleep on the floor. Some also visit the graves of their ancestors. Among some religious Jews, a period of half mourning is observed from the first of Av until the fast, itself, on the ninth.

What are modern Secular Humanistic Jews to think and do on this date? We cannot mourn the dispersion of the Jews, which has resulted in a rich and diverse Jewish culture all over the world. We don't mourn for the Temple, with its hereditary leadership and animal sacrifices. We don't mourn for a religio-monarchical government. But we can mourn for those whose lives were lost, whose homes were destroyed, who were exiled. We can weep for those millions through the ages, victims of the Crusades and the Inquisition and Hitler, who might have been saved had Israel been a Jewish state. We can recognize that destruction and rebirth go hand in hand, and that every end can be a new beginning.

And we should take to heart the rabbis' idea that it is more important to rejoice than to weep, that we should contain our mourning to one day and spend the rest of the year celebrating and building Jewish culture.

9

Shabbes

Shabbes has national, religious, historical, and ethical components. While a day of rest exists in other cultures, the Jewish
Sabbath is so regular, frequent, and universally celebrated that it
has become a hallmark of the Jewish community and thus, has national significance. Furthermore, the religious practice of meeting
together as a community on Shabbes demands that Jews live in a
community with other Jews, which helps to create a sense of ourselves as members of a community and a conviction that it is almost impossible to be a Jew alone.

The strand of the Bible that shows the Jewish god as the creator
of the entire world is a late biblical work, dating from the fifth and
sixth century BCE. This strand is the basis of the religious rationale
for the already-existing holiday, which is *imitateo dei,* the imitation
of God. As God rested on the seventh day, so, too, do people rest,
abstaining from any creative work except procreation. This religious reason became dominant, and observing the Sabbath was
considered of equal importance with circumcision. It was so important, in fact, that the rabbis decreed the death penalty for anyone who broke the Sabbath rules.

The historical rationale for the holiday is one that underpins
many Jewish ideals, the remembrance of the slavery in Egypt that is
part of our national historical memory. Typically, slaves are not al-

lowed a day of rest, so resting on the Sabbath reminds us of the Exodus from Egypt. That has also been used as a religious reason for the holiday for those who believe that the Jewish god freed the Hebrews from slavery and therefore should be loved, feared, and worshiped.

The ethical component of Shabbes is the most important. Shabbes reminds us that even though we work for others, we are not slaves; we retain rights of our own. As such, Shabbes is the quintessential workers' holiday. It specifically elucidates the right of workers, even beasts of burden, to rest. Understanding that workers have this right leads us to question what other rights workers might have, such as the rights to medical care, job security, and fair treatment.

Furthermore, our bodies belong to ourselves, not to our employers; we are free people. As we appreciate, celebrate, and savor our freedom, we are forced to acknowledge that all people would appreciate, celebrate, and savor freedom.

And if our bodies do not belong to our employers, how much less do they belong to the state. We are reminded that the government has no right to violate our bodily integrity, whether to require blood donations, pass sodomy laws, or regulate reproduction.

Shabbes, as a day of rest, also reminds us that work is not the only occupation we should engage in. We should also cultivate our minds and spirits and we may, indeed, *must,* enjoy physical, intellectual, and emotional pleasures. Shabbes is more than a reminder that we are free; it is a reminder that we are human.

Observances

Shabbes is full of both prohibitions and traditions. Halachically, observant Jews do not travel, cook, write, or shop on Shabbes, or do anything that comes under a closely defined category of work. Others choose different ways to express the idea of resting. Some do not do paying work on Shabbes, but will do work they enjoy, such as woodworking, gardening, or going for a drive. My own longtime method of resting on Shabbes is to refuse to make any appointments on Saturdays. I will work, but I do so on my own schedule.

Many Orthodox men will go to the *mikveh,* the ritual bath, before going to services early Friday evening. They come home to a festive meal, introduced with candlelighting, wine, and braided challah, all with their own particular prayers. There are special blessings for the children as well, in which the father says to his sons "May God make you like Ephraim and Menashe" and to his daughters "May God make you like Sarah, Rebecca, Rachel, and Leah." The man may also recite the section of Proverbs called "Woman of Valor" to his wife.

Reform synagogues and some of the other movements tend to have Friday evening services after dinner. These are family events, and many congregations try to include the children in leading the special Shabbes songs.

There are religious services on Saturday morning, as there are every morning, but the Saturday service (like the Monday and Thursday in Orthodox congregations) includes the reading of the weekly Torah portion and can be quite long, sometimes running over three hours, especially if there is a Bar Mitzvah. Many service-goers do not arrive for the preliminary psalms and prayers but time their arrival for just before the reading of the Torah. The Torah is broken up into weekly portions and is read in its entirety every year. Each Torah portion also has attached to it a *haftarah,* which is a section of one of the other books of the Bible. These were chosen in Talmudic times or shortly thereafter. Sometimes the connection between the Torah and *haftarah* is obvious, but sometimes it is almost entirely unclear.

The afternoon is spent studying, visiting friends and family, or taking the traditional Shabbes nap. The third feast—Saturday night dinner—is a meal that is either cold or has been prepared on Friday and kept warm in a very slow oven (or Crock-Pot). The traditional dish for Saturday after services is *cholent* (from the French *chaud,* meaning *hot),* which is a casserole of meat, beans, and vegetables. The evening meal is prolonged with stories and singing, so that the Sabbath lasts as long as possible. After sunset, the Havdalah, or separation, ceremony is conducted. A special braided candle is lit, wine is shared, and sweet spices are smelled, to bring the sweetness of the Sabbath into the week to come.

A Secular Shabbes

A Secular shabbes can be full of ritual or completely free-form. The only requirement is to do whatever it is you do self-consciously, with the idea that you are doing it because it is Shabbes.

You might like to observe a Sabbath, but you probably don't want to do it by following prohibitions. Rather, you'd like to make it a positive, enriching experience. How to start? First, make a list of the activities you value but rarely make time to do. Next, make a list of the activities that are onerous or tedious or based on someone else's agenda. Siegel, Strassfeld, and Strassfeld's *The First Jewish Catalog* says, "Figure out who is master and who is the slave. Does your telephone (mail, work, study, office, house, car) control you or do you control it?"

Choose one—just one—from the value list and one of the onerous list. Next Shabbes, deliberately make time for the one and avoid the other. The following week, choose another pair. Find what makes you happy and comfortable and make it a regular part of your Friday night or Saturday. It's not the actual things you choose to do or not do that make a Shabbes; it's the choosing, itself.

Do you want a festive meal on Friday night? Maybe you choose to eat out or to order in pizza on Friday to start your break from the ordinary week. Or maybe you like to cook and love the smell of baking challah. If you have kids, they might like to cook on Friday nights. Perhaps you like to get together with your family or friends for a potluck dinner. Choose what Shabbes means to you and make it a regular part of your week.

How to Make Challah

The important thing is not to be afraid. That's what the Hebrew song "Gesher" says, and it's good advice when it comes to baking challah. It seems scary, but bread is really very forgiving. It's hard to make bad bread. And don't worry, you will not turn into the sorcerer's apprentice; the yeast will not cause the bread to rise and rise and take over your kitchen. And it doesn't take all day, either. In fact, in the warmer months, you can make challah in an evening, if you put the sponge on as soon as you get home from work.

2 tablespoons yeast
2 ½ cups (600 ml) warm water
¼ cup (60 ml) sugar
4 eggs
8 cups (1.9 l) flour, plus some for kneading
¾ cup (180 l) vegetable oil
1 tablespoon salt (or a little more, if you like)

In a big bowl, mix the yeast, warm water, sugar, and three of the eggs. Beat well. Stir in three cups of the flour and beat with a wire wisk at least a hundred times. This is called the sponge. Cover the bowl lightly with a kitchen towel. The batter should double in about half an hour and you'll be ready for the next step.

Now, as you add ingredients, be careful not to cut the dough. Use a large flat wooden spoon and stir from the edges, folding over the dough to the middle. Pour the vegetable oil around the sides of the bowl, sprinkle the salt over the top, and fold in. Gradually fold in about five more cups of flour, mixing each one in before adding another. Turn the dough out onto a floured board and knead.

How to knead: Grab the far edge of the dough and fold it over to the near edge. Put the heels of your hand against the doubled edge and push away, into the dough. Turn the lump a quarter turn and repeat. Keep turning and folding and pushing for about 10 minutes. You'll notice the dough will come alive and rise back.

Clean out the bowl and put a little oil in the bottom. Put the lump of dough back in the bowl and turn it to cover it with oil. This will keep a crust from forming. Put the towel back over the bowl and wait for the dough to double again. This could take anywhere from an hour to three hours, so keep an eye on it.

Once the dough doubles, punch it down, then turn it out on a floured board. This recipe will make two large or three medium challahs, which you can bake on cookie sheets or in loaf pans. Cut—don't tear—the dough into either two or three pieces. Then cut each piece into three or four pieces. Braid the pieces in regular triple braids or in braids with four strands. If you like, you can braid three of the four pieces, then cut the last quarter into thirds and braid that. Place the little braid on top of the big braid as a crown. If you are planning on passing the challah around and letting people tear off pieces, you don't need to braid it. Just make balls about an inch and a half (38 mm) in diameter and fill a loaf pan with them. They will bake into an easily torn apart loaf that looks as fancy as a braided challah.

Let the challahs rise in the loaf pans or on the cookie sheets for about half an hour. Then brush them with a beaten egg and sprinkle sesame seeds or poppy seeds on top.

Bake the challahs for 10 minutes at 250° F. (120° C.) before turning the oven up to 350° F. (177° C.) for 35 to 45 minutes (depending on the size of the challahs). Starting them at a low temperature will allow them to rise without cracking.

I usually make three challahs, one to eat, one to freeze for next week, and one to give away. There's usually not any left over, but on the rare occasions that there is, it makes really great Saturday morning French toast.

Whether your Friday night dinner is pizza or pheasant under glass, what makes the occasion special is the attention paid to the enjoyment and significance of the Sabbath. Before dinner, you might like to signal the beginning of the holiday by emptying your change into your *tzedakah* box. Since giving *tzedakah* is traditional on holidays, and since it is also traditional to free yourself from dealing with money on Shabbes, this is a great start to the observance of the day. *Tzedakah,* from the Hebrew root for righteousness, is the word that most embodies Jewish ideas of social justice. *Tzedakah* is not charity, because it is not a gift from the donor; it is, rather, the right of the recipient. Many Jewish families have special boxes in which they deposit their change. In the last generation, many of these boxes were from *Keren Ami* (My People's Fund) and the money was used to buy land and trees in Israel. Now, many Jews contribute to the United Jewish Appeal, the New Israel Fund, or other agencies. You can make a *tzedakah* box out of an old baking-soda can or the round cardboard box that Parmesan cheese comes in. Decorate it and put it in a prominent place in your house.

Light candles, make a little ceremony of sharing challah and tasting the wine. Sing a few songs. They don't have to be official Shabbes songs, either. Once when I asked "What song shall we sing?" my husband, who was tired and cranky, made a sarcastic recommendation of "Old MacDonald Had A Farm." My youngest son immediately began singing, "Old MacDonald had a Shabbes— E I E I O—and on that Shabbes he had some candles . . ." We all joined in, giving Old MacDonald candles, challah, and wine (with a hiccup here and a hiccup there). By the time we'd finished, we were all laughing and my husband was cheerful again.

A lovely custom from the religious tradition is blessing the children by saying "May you be like . . ." You can name anyone you'd like your children to be like, perhaps choosing people who have been especially kind during the week, or perhaps choosing someone extraordinary you've read or heard about on the news. You can say, "May you have the bravery of . . ." or "May you be as kind as the person who . . ." You can wish for your children to be like relatives or someone from Jewish history, too, but don't forget, most of all we want them to be like themselves!

At the dinner, talk about the week—your triumphs and disappointments and the moments you want to remember. Each person can take a turn to thank each other person at the table for something nice he or she did during the week. When your *tzedakah* box is full, spend a Friday night dinner deciding where to donate the money.

If you share your child with a parent who doesn't live in your household, you may need to make your Shabbes dinner and activities on a different day. Go ahead and do that. You will not be struck by lightning if you have challah on a Wednesday or a Sunday. Whenever you are with your child can be your Shabbes, a day for family and rest and enjoyment. But that doesn't mean you don't get the standard Shabbes—you do. Make an arrangement with another single parent or friends with or without kids to rotate Friday night dinners. Make them potlucks, order out, or the host can cook each time. Miriam Weinstein, in an on-line article entitled "When Parents Are Divorced: Three Perspectives" (http://www. jewishfamily.com) suggests that even if you are with your child on Friday night, you might like to join with others, since sometimes just one parent and a child or two doesn't seem like enough family.

She suggests finding other single parents to celebrate with, but you can join with two-parent families or with adults only. The important thing is that the people you are with feel like family.

On Saturday, we can make it a point to spend time with families and friends, to read, to sing, to attend cultural events. Torah study is a Sabbath custom. Secularist Jews, too, can read the Torah to see what's really in there. There are some amazing stories and some perfectly dreadful examples of how to behave, as well as lots of rules and descriptions that teach us about how people lived in ancient times. It's a fascinating document, especially if, as you read it, you also learn a little bit about the history of the time. Richard Elliott Friedman's *Who Wrote the Bible?* is a terrific source. It reads like a mystery novel but it's really good political history.

TORAH STUDY DISCUSSION QUESTIONS

When you read Torah portions, you may want to discuss them to understand them better. Here are some questions suitable for both kids and adults:

Who behaved well and who behaved badly in this story? (Remember that God is a character in the story and may behave well or badly.)

Was this rule a good one? Would it be good now? Why or why not?

What other stories do you know that have this theme or this moral?

Who benefits if we follow the rules or the morals in this story? Who benefited in ancient times?

Are there any phrases in this portion that would be good mottoes? How about words to a song?

What surprised you?

What do you see that tells you about life in ancient times? What did the people wear, eat, do for a living? What sorts of materials did they use for clothing, jewelry, housewares, and homes? Was there a social hierarchy?

Torah study isn't the only Jewish study, of course. We can read Jewish history, literature, or anything we normally don't have time to pay attention to. We can read stories and poetry out loud to the family in the evening, instead of watching television or going off to play computer games. Our favorite Shabbes stories come from Yiddish literature in translation. Some of the books we read from are not in print anymore, but you can still get the terrific collection called *Pushcarts and Dreamers,* translated by Max Rosenfeld, from the Sholem Aleichem Club Press (443 E. Wadsworth Ave., Philadelphia, PA 19119), CSJO, or order it from your bookstore.

How about learning a little Yiddish or Hebrew? If one family member (or one of the set of friends you celebrate Shabbes with) knows one of the Jewish languages, why not teach the others? Or call up a family member or friend who knows a language and get a weekly lesson. Introduce a word of the week in Yiddish or Hebrew for each family member to use as often as possible all week. Make a chart to keep track of how often everyone uses the word.

You can also make Saturday your get-in-touch-with-family day. Most of us have out-of-town family these days, and it's a lovely Shabbes tradition to call them or write to them. Everyone in the family can write to a different relative each Shabbes, or you can each write to the same one and send a big packet of letters and drawings. Or you can make a family newsletter and send it to everyone.

Shabbes is also a good day to devote some time to your favorite community service. Perhaps you have adopted a creek or roadside to clean up. Maybe you like to visit someone in a nursing home, or sort donated clothes for a charitable organization. Or spend one Saturday a month preparing and distributing flyers in your neighborhood, letting the neighbors know you'll be picking up donations for the local food pantry or animal shelter or safe house the next weekend. Then, the next weekend, drive around the neighborhood and pick up the donations and drop them off.

Shabbes is also a good time to organize and look at all those family photos that are lying around in shoe boxes. Or make or update your family Shabbes tablecloth. Tovah Lazaroff (who did *not* suggest doing this on Shabbes since it involves activities that are not permitted on Shabbes by Jewish law) suggests making the painted handprints of family members around the borders of a cloth ("How to Create a Personalized Shabbes Tablecloth" http://www.jewishfamily.com). Be sure to sign and date the print in markers. Later you can embroider the signatures. You can also paint, stencil, or applique Shabbes or other Jewish symbols onto the cloth. The author suggests writing favorite Torah quotes, but you can also write or embroider favorite quotes or sayings from other sources.

Most Americans have Saturday and Sunday off work, and many of us spend Saturday mowing the lawn, doing the grocery shopping, and cleaning house, so that Sunday seems more like a day of rest to us. So it does seem odd to make Havdalah, marking the end of Shabbes, on Saturday night. If you make Havdalah and then continue to rest, you're just observing a form with no meaning. But it would feel funny to make Havdalah on Sunday night. The only way you can make Havdalah is if you make Shabbes, that is, if you make Shabbes a special Jewish day.

Havdalah is a short ceremony centered on the lighting and dousing of a special braided candle, a glass of wine, and the smelling of sweet spices. As you pass around the spice box, you can each tell what sweetness of Shabbes you will try to bring into the week to come. Maybe it's the joy of being with family; maybe it's the sense of peace and unhurriedness; or maybe it's the great feeling you got when you were doing community service.

In an on-line article called "Herbs for Havdalah" ("Herbs for Havdalah," http://www.jewishfamily.com), Michael Brown suggests you grow your own herbs. He mentions lemon balm, some of the exotic basils, and geraniums. (If you have geraniums you know that it's the leaves that smell, not the flowers.) Maybe you can plant the seeds at Tu b'Shvat and spend some of your Shabbes gardening.

No matter how you choose to spend your Shabbes, make it your choice rather than allowing it to be dictated by outside forces. And enjoy it!

III

RECLAIMING
LIFE-CYCLE
OBSERVANCES

10

Baby Naming

You have three names: the name your parents bestow on you, the name by which others call you, and the name you earn for yourself through your conduct.—Sanhedrin 44a

Every culture has a way to welcome its newborns and to initiate them into the community. These ceremonies are performed by parents, community heads, or religious leaders, but they all serve to formalize the baby's place in society.

Judaism, like many other cultures, has evolved two separate ceremonies for boy babies and girl babies. Boys are circumcised in a ceremony on their eighth day of life. This ceremony, the *brit milah*, or covenant, is usually held at home and attended by the family and friends of the parents. The *brit milah* (or *bris*, in the Yiddish and Ashkenazic Hebrew pronunciation), is a highly formalized ritual during which the child is held and carried by several people whom the family wishes to honor. Specific prayers are recited and the baby's name is announced. The ceremony is an occasion for a large and sometimes elaborate party that relatives from even great distances make every effort to attend.

The story is entirely different for girls. Although many Sephardic and Eastern Jews name daughters in a small celebration at home, in most traditional Ashkenazic congregations, girl babies are named in the synagogue on the Saturday morning after their births. The father is called up for an *aliya* (the honor of saying the blessing before and after a section of Torah reading) and to make a special blessing after which the child's Jewish name is announced. Typically, neither the baby nor the mother is in attendance.

"I didn't even know Jessica's Hebrew name," confides Leah, who was brought up Orthodox but is now a member of a Secular congregation. "My dad had her named in shul, and I didn't even know it. It seems unfair that boys get made so much of and girls are treated like nothing."

In response to this inequality, both religious and cultural Jews are making attempts to elevate the naming of the daughter to a position equal to the *brit milah* ceremony and naming of the son. While various physical rituals (ranging from the ritual rupturing of the hymen to immersion in the *mikveh)* have been suggested in the religious Jewish community, it is most common to hold a home ceremony followed by a reception. During the ceremony, the child's name is announced and the parents or a rabbi recite prayers parallel to the prayers said at the *brit milah.*

The Secular Humanistic Jewish movement has taken the position that boys and girls should have the same ceremony. If a boy baby is to be circumcised, that procedure is performed by a doctor in a medical facility. Both boys and girls are welcomed into the community with naming ceremonies either at home or wherever the community meets.

Don't You *Have* to Have a *Bris?*

Can you get away with not having a *bris?* Many cultural Jews come from religious families who expect a *brit milah* conducted by a rabbi and a *mohel* (a ritual circumciser). It's an ancient ceremony, first mentioned in the Bible, and one of the few Jewish rituals that has a clear biblical history. To many religious Jews, the ceremony is one that makes the child a member of the Jewish community. You might have to contend with a lot of pressure from your family to hire a *mohel* and allow him (yes, they are all men) to conduct a religious ceremony. But, yes, you can probably get away with having your son circumcised in the hospital (if you decide to have him circumcised) if your naming ceremony has the ritual feel of a *bris.*

The issue of circumcision is a touchy one within the Jewish community. It has been explored in several Jewish publications, including *Humanistic Judaism,* the quarterly put out by the Society for Humanistic Judaism. There are also several Web sites devoted to this question.

The jury is out on whether circumcision is medically desirable. Some studies indicate fewer urinary tract infections and rates of STDs and cancers among circumcised men. Others show that wives of circumcised men have a lower incidence of cervical cancer, but others suspect that this has more to do with the genetics of Jewish women than the penises of Jewish men. If you're interested in researching this, start on the Web. Australian researcher Dr. Brian Morris maintains a Web site with links to about a hundred medical and demographic studies (http://www.physio.su.oz.au/brianm/circumsicion.html). Or just search for "circumcision."

The medical aspects, however, do not carry the emotional weight of the cultural and religious aspects of the question. Even if you don't believe that there's a god who demands the foreskin of every Jewish boy child, there is a powerful cultural imperative. Parents of Jewish boy babies may feel that if they don't circumcise their baby, they will be forever reading him out of the Jewish People. Although there are a few citations both in ancient and modern Jewish history of boys who were not circumcised (usually because they were too sick as newborns), the cultural norm is that Jewish boys are circumcised.

Some psychologists also make the argument that it is important for boys to look like their fathers, if not like their peers. Throughout most of history, Christians have not engaged in circumcision. There was a brief period in recent history when circumcision became generally popular in America, but that trend is beginning to reverse. Dr. Morris says that between the 1940s and the 1990s over 90 percent of newborn boys in the United States were circumcised, although the percentage has been decreasing in recent years. His statistics show that the Australian figure is now under 20 percent. Since fewer baby boys are now being circumcised, your uncircumcised child will most likely not have problems in the locker room, unless that locker room is at the Jewish Community Center Health Club.

If you choose to have your son circumcised, you have to decide whether to make this procedure public or private. New father Carl Brown (not his real name) recently agonized over whether he had failed to protect his eight-day-old son. It had never occurred to him that he might not have a *bris* for the baby, but he was struck by the repugnance the ceremony elicited in him, particularly when his non-Jewish father-in-law commented on how barbaric it seemed to mutilate a child publicly and then celebrate with cakes and wine. Carl regrets the public nature of the ceremony. If he has another son, he says, he would consider not circumcising him at all, even though he would then look different from both Carl and his own brother. If he opts for circumcision, Carl says he would choose a procedure before the baby is released from the hospital and then celebrate a naming shortly afterward.

How to Put Together a Baby-Naming Ceremony

First, decide on a Jewish name for your baby (see "Choosing a Jewish Name," page 149).

Next, choose a time. If it is important to you and your family that the ceremony resemble a religious *bris,* you will want to hold it on the baby's eighth day of life. If this particular tradition is not important, plan to hold the ceremony when you are recovered from the birth and when it is possible for relatives and friends to attend. Before the birth, make a list of people you want to invite, along with their phone numbers. Give this list to two or three relatives or friends. Then, when you decide when to hold the ceremony, you just have to call these two or three people and they'll make the phone calls letting everyone know when and where the naming is to be held.

If your child is adopted, you can have the ceremony as soon as you are comfortable. An older child will need more time to become accustomed to you before you'll want to subject him or her to a large gathering, but a baby can be named as soon as you can put together the ceremony.

The Ceremony

A naming ceremony is an opportunity to introduce the child to her or his community, and the community to the child. It is a chance to express the support and responsibilities of the community toward the child. It is an occasion for celebrating both the child and the people or qualities the child is named for. It is a time for dedications and benedictions.

If you want your ceremony to resemble a *bris,* you will want to perform certain rituals. While the baby is usually held by a parent, you may want to honor friends or family members as is done at a *bris,* by asking them to carry the baby, hold it at certain points in the ceremony, or read parts of the ceremony. You will also want to place a drop of wine in the baby's mouth, as is done at a *bris.*

Other children in the family can also be involved in the ceremony. A small child can carry the glass of wine from person to person or present the baby with a flower or toy. An older child can read a special benediction or even help to hold the baby.

Start with someone welcoming the guests and introducing the idea of a naming. You can explain that naming a child recognizes his or her individuality. Jews give the child her or his own name, but we also give her or him a Hebrew name. In this way we recognize the child's individuality but also her or his place in the Jewish community. Then you can say something about your love for the child. In her introduction to naming her own child, one mother spoke movingly about how improbable it may seem that a parent can love a second child as much as the first.

You might also like to explain why the ceremony includes the guests. You can ask people for their support in helping the parents teach the child to be a good member of society. You can ask them to share their wisdom with you so that you can guide your child to reach his or her full potential and to come to an understanding of his or her place in the world and in the Jewish community. If the child has a non-Jewish parent, you can add "while honoring the heritages of both parents." You can also provide the guests with a program including a group reading.

Next it is time to name your baby. Here are a couple of real-life examples:

> We give you the name Kira Rachel. *Kira* is related to the Hebrew words for *to spring forth* and *hearth.* You have sprung forth into our world and we welcome you. We hope you may always have the capacity for renewal and regeneration your name

implies. We wish for you also to be the kind of person who so generates warmth that people gather around you as around a hearth. *Rachel* is our foremother who was so loyal and steadfast that she waited many years for her husband to earn the right to marry her. May you be as loyal and steadfast as she was.

We give you the Hebrew name Edna Rachel. The Hebrew name *Edna* means *delight* or *desired*. We hope for you that you will always know how desired and how welcome you are in our lives and how we delight in your presence. Edna was also the name of my grandmother, a woman who was warm, friendly, happy, and giving, a woman who always made everyone around her feel special. May you inherit these qualities along with her name.

After the naming, you can drink from a glass of wine, saying:
We rejoice in our heritage, which has given us the cup of wine as a symbol of our rejoicing.

אַשְׁרֵינוּ בִּירֻשָׁתֵנוּ שֶׁמָסְרָה לָנוּ כּוֹס
פְּרִי הַגֶּפֶן
לְמוֹעֲדִים וּלְשִׂמְחָה כִּי שָׂמַחְנוּ בְּחַגֵּינוּ.

Ashreinu b'yerushateynu shemasrah lanu kos pri hagafen l'mo'adim u'l'simcha ki samachnu b'chageynu.

or:
This cup is the vessel of our hopes. It is filled with the new wine of a life just begun. The sweetness of its taste is the joy *(baby's name)* has brought. *(Len Cherlin)*
Put a drop of wine in the baby's mouth and drink some yourself. You can pass the cup around, or ask a child to do so. Invite the guests to tell their hopes for the baby's future as they sip from the cup. Or ask people to read things you have written or collected from books of essays or poetry. The traditional Jewish blessing is, "May you go forth into a life of learning, love, and good deeds, *Torah, chuppah oon g'milus chesed.*"
Len Cherlin, the leader of a Secular Humanistic Jewish group on Long Island, wrote, "May your name endure with honor as long as the rivers run to the sea, as long as the sun casts the shadow of the mountains over the slopes, and heaven shows the fire of the stars."
Algernon Black, in his book of readings *Without Burnt Offer-*

ings, provides a loving benediction, wishing the child the appreciation of the beauties of nature, the joys of comradeship, and "the meaning of generosity and compassion, the love of many and the love of one above all others."

End with a poem or other reading from secular or religious sources, or a secular shehecheyanu like this one:

We rejoice in our heritage that has given us the indomitable spirit that has preserved our people and sustained us and brought us forward to celebrate this joyous occasion.

אַשְׁרֵינוּ בִּירֻשָׁתֵנוּ הַכּוֹחַ שֶׁהֶחֱיָנוּ
וְקִיְמָנוּ וְהִגִּיעָנוּ לַזְּמַן הַזֶּה.

Ashreinu b'yerushateynu ha-ko'ach she'hecheyanu v'kimanu v'higiyanu lazman ha'zeh.

Choosing a Jewish Name

How you choose your child's Jewish name—or your own, if you are becoming Jewish and want to take a Jewish name—depends on your family traditions and your own personal preferences. Sephardim and Eastern Jews commonly name children after living family members. Among Ashkenazim, this practice is uncommon. Various Ashkenazic Jewish superstitions held that if a child was named for a living person the Angel of Death might mistake the younger for the older when the time came for the older to die, or that the soul with that name would flee from the older to the younger, thus causing the death of the older. The custom became so enshrined that even now most Ashkenazim observe the tradition of naming only for deceased relatives, even if they have no such superstitious beliefs.

In addition, a Jewish name includes the name of your father, or of both parents. This is done by including *bat* (daughter of) or *ben* (son of) along with the Jewish name of your father or parents. Most Orthodox use only the father's name. Conservative Jews have begun to use both, as do Reconstructionist, Secular Humanistic, and most Reform. If one parent is not Jewish, this can have an unexpectedly funny sound. "Devorah, bat Yehudis Chanah v'Mario" could be good for a laugh, but this can help everyone to understand that when Jews and non-Jews form families together, everyone gets to be part of both cultures. At a baby naming, you might want to announce the child's name not only with his or her parents' names, but also with the names of grandparents and siblings, like this: "Ruth, daughter of Etl and Shmil Rivn, grandchild of Yossl, Regina, Tsivia, and Shloimeh, sister of Judith and Deborah."

Religious converts to Judaism are traditionally named Abraham or Ruth because neither biblical figure was born Jewish. If you are undergoing a religious conversion, this name will be given to you. You can sometimes choose another name, but that will be up to the rabbi performing the conversion ceremony. Another religious tradition is to give you your own name, but to give you new parents—Abraham and Sarah, the mythical ancestors of the Jewish people. Your name then becomes "Your name *bat* (or *ben)* Avraham v'Sarah." Instead, you might add their names to the names of your real parents, rather than replacing your parents with Abraham and Sarah.

If you were born Jewish but were never given a Jewish name, or are becoming Jewish in a nontheistic way (see chapter on conversion) you may want to choose your own Jewish name, which you can announce in a ceremony. Any of the ways to choose a name for a baby is also a good way to choose your own Jewish name.

Naming for a relative is a common practice. You can give your baby the Jewish name of a relative and an English name related to that name. If you choose a related name, you can use the English equivalent name (Rebecca for Rivka, Samuel for Shmuel), or you can translate the name. Shoshana would become Lily, for example. Many parents choose a name starting with the same letter as the Jewish name, because they don't care for the English equivalent, and the translation doesn't render a usable name. (Ilan, for example, translates as Oak Tree.) Using this convention, Reyzl doesn't have to become Rosy; she can be Renée. Malka doesn't have to be Regina; she can be Melissa. Of course, you can give your child names that are unrelated in Hebrew and English. Brian Scott can be named for his grandfather, Shloimeh Moishe.

If you don't want to name your child for a relative, you can choose to name your child for a historical figure you admire or for a dear friend. You can also give your child a Jewish name that means something, perhaps a quality you admire. Shlomo (Shloimeh) and Shulamit mean peace, for example. Nadav means someone who is generous. Tikva means hope. Ask someone who knows Hebrew to help you make a name out of a Hebrew word, or check out a list of Jewish names in one of the many Jewish baby books.

If your child is non-white or comes from another non-Jewish ethnic culture, you need to decide how to honor the child's entire heritage. You may wish to translate the birth name of an adopted child into Hebrew, or to incorporate his or her ethnic birth name into the Jewish naming ceremony. If your birth-child is ethnically mixed, or non-white, you may also want to honor all the child's ethnic heritages in this way. Perhaps you will choose a Jewish name and a Yoruba name or a Jewish name and a Korean name. Or perhaps, if your child has African-American heritage, you'll choose one of the many biblical names that have been important to both traditions.

Does it have to be Hebrew? Certainly not. Hebrew is just one of the many languages Jews have spoken throughout history and is only one of at least six languages spoken only by Jews. You can give your child an Aramaic name, a Ladino name, or (most commonly) a Yiddish name.

Whatever name you choose and however you choose to bestow it, a Jewish name helps to welcome a child into the community and provides a Jewish identification for him or her throughout his or her life. It is the name by which she or he is called up as Bat or Bar Mitzvah, it is the name on the *ketubah* (marriage certificate), and it is the name under which she or he will be buried. And it is the name that will be carried by future children who will be named for him or her.

11

Bar/Bat Mitzvah

"**H**ow're they going to top this at the wedding?" one guest wondered at a recent Bat Mitzvah party. The Bat Mitzvah girl, barely pubescent, was dressed in her second new dress of the day, a tight-fitting black strapless affair and chunky-heeled strappy sandals. Her face was made up like a fashion model's, and her hair had been freshly recoiffed, also for the second time that day. The flowers were everywhere. There was an hors d'oeuvres table, a sweet table, and a sit-down dinner. There were two bands—one for the kids and one for the adults. Every child went home with a video of him- or herself dancing in front of wildly flickering strobe lights and a sweatshirt proclaiming "I was at Heather's Bat Mitzvah." Every adult went home with a gold engraved pen. It was just a normal Bat Mitzvah party in Boca Raton, or Short Hills or Highland Park or Encino.

How did a religious coming-of-age ceremony turn into this sort of extravaganza?

How the Modern Extravaganza Was Born

Bar and Bat Mitzvah students at most Secular Jewish schools prepare several academic papers during their two-year preparation.

Robert Lincoln Kutzik, a student at Philadelphia's Jewish Children's Folkshule, wrote a paper with his father, Alfred J. Kutzik (who was writing a book on the history of Jewish Secularism at the time of his death in 1994) on the history of the Bar Mitzah in 1972. Here's some of that paper, reprinted with permission.

    The term—or even the idea—of the Bar Mitzvah does not appear in the Bible. In fact, the Bible implies in Exodus and Leviticus that the age of legal responsibility was twenty years or older. Exodus talks about a census that was taken in which only those aged twenty or older were to be counted. The Talmud also is silent with regard to Bar Mitzvah at the age of thirteen. However, it mentions the term Bar Mitzvah twice. Both times the reference is to a person of any age who observes the commandments or laws of the Jews.

    The Talmud, when referring to a boy of thirteen, does not use the word Bar Mitzvah but *Bar Onshin,* which means one who is punishable; for at thirteen the child becomes legally responsible for any wrongdoing he may commit. But the Talmud also says that a man must be twenty years or older to serve as a judge or to inherit real estate. The Talmud comments on a verse of Genesis saying that Jacob and Esau both went to school until the age of thirteen. Afterward Jacob continued school but Esau became a dropout. Also, Talmudic legal rulings hold that a man is responsible for his son's education until the son is thirteen. However, this reference makes no mention of a Bar Mitzvah ceremony or the assumption of new responsibilities by the thirteen-year-old.

    Although one part of the Talmud, called Ethics of the Fathers, states, "At thirteen, the age is reached for the fulfillment of mitzvos," boys observed the various mitzvos that are associated today with Bar Mitzvah well before the age of thirteen. The Talmud says a minor—of any age—may be called to the Torah for an *aliyah,* which means the honor of being called to make a blessing at the time that the Torah is read. In 1100 CE, six hundred years after the Talmud was written, Maimonides indicated that when a boy is mature enough to understand the significance, he may be called to the Torah, put on tefillin, etc., whatever his age. On the other hand, when a boy was thirteen he had to assume the responsibilities of citizenship in the Jewish community, including paying taxes and voting for the elected officials who were members of the town council that governed the Jewish community. Unless the thirteen-year-old was one of the few who continued in school, he was expected to go to work and—pretty soon—to get married. This new status as a full-fledged citizen of the adult Jewish community is the real meaning of becoming Bar Mitzvah.

The first recorded use of the term Bar Mitzvah in its modern-day sense is that of Rabbi Mordechai ben Hillel, a German legal authority of the thirteenth century. All other references to the Bar Mitzvah appear after this date. From them we know that it had become the custom that on the Sabbath after the boy's thirteenth birthday a Bar Mitzvah celebration took place. The boy was called to the Torah for the first time, usually for the *maftir aliyah,* which means he had the additional honor of chanting a portion from the Prophets. When the boy finished, his father would rise up and say, "Blessed be He who has freed me from this responsibility." After the service, the parents provided a *seudah,* or meal, for relatives and friends in their home. The meal was often followed by a speech by the Bar Mitzvah boy, in which he showed how well he knew the Talmud. Soon the *seudah*—banquet or party—became very elaborate. In fact, such parties became so elaborate that in 1595 in Crakow, Poland, a communal tax was placed on it in order to discourage extravagance. These are the origins of the Bar Mitzvah as we know it today.

. . . In spite of contemporary criticism of the Bar Mitzvah banquet, the fact that it is the main part of the Bar Mitzvah celebration is brought out by the recently published *Encyclopedia of the Jewish Religion,* which states that the banquet is a *Seudat Mitzvah,* which means a feast celebrating the fulfillment of a religious commandment, and that the participation of the rabbi in addressing the Bar Mitzvah boy in the synagogue is "of comparatively recent origin."

So, we've been fighting the extravaganza battle for almost as long as the Bar Mitzvah ceremony has been in existence. That doesn't mean we have to give in!

Alternatives

That's the background leading up to Heather's sixty-thousand-dollar celebration. But what, exactly, was being celebrated? Heather had done a nice job leading services. She had a pretty voice and didn't falter over her well-rehearsed Torah reading. Her speech was nicely phrased and delivered in her sweet, earnest tone. She had correctly quoted Maimonides and Albert Einstein, clearly not understanding the context from which either had spoken. She had thanked her teachers and her parents and the assistant rabbi for helping her. She had demonstrated nearly everything she had learned at the congregation's Hebrew school.

Heather had been to Hebrew school for five years and had learned to decode the Hebrew letters. She had learned the *brachot* (blessings) for the Torah reading and for making Shabbes. She had learned to lead part of the Saturday morning service. She had learned some Bible stories and something about the Holocaust and a little about the geography of Israel. She had been exposed to the concept of *tzedakah*, which she understood to be charity. She had read a digest of the rabbinic commentary and tried to make some sense of her Torah portion while not challenging the basic assumptions in the text.

Heather's Bat Mitzvah suited her and her family and their particular way of being Jewish. But Heather's Bat Mitzvah ceremony and the preparation for it wasn't at all meaningful for Ruth, Heather's mom's cousin, who had wondered at the extravagance of the party. Ruth's own daughter, Ariella, was already eight years old, and Ruth knew that it was time for Ariella to go to Hebrew school so she, too, could have a Bat Mitzvah ceremony in four or five years. (Ruth and Ariella, as well as Stuart—whom you'll meet later in the chapter—are composite characters. Their story was told to me by many people over many years. The stories were startlingly similar, so many people may see themselves in these characters. Ariella's projects are also composites. All the projects were done by students at Secular and Humanistic Jewish schools.) Ruth had been considering joining the temple her cousin belonged to and was suddenly faced with the realization that this was not the sort of ceremony she wanted for her daughter, and not the sort of preparation that made sense for Ruth's way of being Jewish.

Ruth wanted Ariella to understand and participate in more than the religious expressions of Jewish culture. She wanted Ariella to know that Jewish history didn't just stop between the destruction of the second Temple in 70 CE and the Holocaust. And most of all, she wanted Ariella to understand that *tzedakah* meant social justice, and she wanted Ariella to become a part of making the world a better place. Ruth wasn't quite sure she was ready to give up what she had always considered a traditional Saturday morning service ceremony, but she knew she wanted a different way of preparing for the occasion. She went looking for alternatives and, because she lives in a large eastern city, she was able to find them.

Most large cities in the U.S. have Secular or Humanistic Jewish congregations that support an alternative Bar or Bat Mitzvah preparation and ceremony.

Bar/Bat Mitsvah Programs

Here are some of the Bar/Bat Mitzvah programs in use.

Rifke Feinstein, Executive Director of the Congress of Secular Jewish Organizations (csjo@csjo.org) provided this outline from an Israeli kibbutz. In addition to a community-service project, students choose four of the following topics to study. They may use many means of presentation, including written reports, oral reports (with written outline), multimedia (including tape, films, and music), artwork (including maps, graphs, and charts), drama, or creative writing.

1. *Diaspora:* Students study the reasons for the Jewish diaspora and the development of Jewish culture in non-Jewish countries.
2. *Present-day diaspora:* Students examine contemporary Jewish life in Russia, France, Spain, South America, Africa, U.S.A., Mexico, and the Arab countries, focusing on the treatment of Jews, politics, economics, and the degree of ghettoisation.
3. *Literature:* Students study a Yiddish or Hebrew writer's life and literature.
4. *Hasidism:* Students learn about the development of the

Hasidic movement, its place in the history of Judaism, and its present revival.

5. *Kabbalah:* Students become acquainted with the mystical manifestations of Judaism, including *gematria,* Jewish numerology.

6. *Biography:* Students write a biography including the life, work, and philosophy of a Jew who has made a substantial contribution to literature, graphic arts, music, journalism, science, social service, sports, etc.

7. *Pirke Avot* (a part of the Mishnah): Students choose five sayings and show their relevance to society, examining whether the sayings are meaningful, and why, and showing the need for society to set an ethical structure.

8. *History of Zionism*

9. *Secularism:* Students examine the socialism of the late nineteenth century, the labor movement in the U.S. in the early twentieth century, the history of Jewish Secularism, and the Labor Zionist movement. They are asked to trace the historical threads leading to the formation of Secular Judaism and study specific people, movements, and organizations within Secular Humanistic Judaism.

10. *Effect of Judaism on other societies:* Students discuss the tenets of Jewish law incorporated into Anglo jurisprudence.

11. *Tzedakah:* Students learn Maimonides' eight steps and discuss their application to modern life. They also discuss aspects of "Am I My Brother's/Sister's Keeper?"

12. *Women's role in Secular Jewish life.*

13. *Family history:* Students research several generations of their ancestors, including issues of economics, politics, and immigration.

14. *Comparative study of major types of Judaism:* Students learn the differences and similarities among the movements.

The Ann Arbor Jewish Cultural Society has similar requirements. Students choose three topics that interest them, one from each of three historical periods. At least one project must be historical and at least one must be cultural. A fourth project is an exploration of the child's Torah portion. The students are asked to examine the literary techniques and political ramifications, and to make a thoughtful response to the ethical issues raised. They ask questions like "Who behaved well in this story, and who behaved badly?" "Do you agree with the rules set down?" "Which groups would benefit from these rules?" "Would they work in modern society?" "Are we different from the people who lived then, and do we need different rules?" "What can we learn about the daily lives of the people from descriptions of food, clothes, and possessions?" These projects are presented at gatherings of that class with their parents. Both parents and students ask questions of the presenter and often the discussions take on lives of their own, with parents sharing personal histories and psychological insights.

In addition to the projects, students in Ann Arbor are required to perform at least thirty hours of community service, working on some issue that they care about. Students have worked with agencies helping the homeless, with ecological organizations, with tutoring programs, and humane societies, among others.

The Bar and Bat Mitzvah ceremonies are done as a group, with up to five participants, or they can be done individually. Typically, there is a lot of group singing, both in Yiddish and Hebrew. Families often use songs from Kopinvant Press's *Kumzits! A Festivity of Instant Jewish Songs* because it includes lots of songs with very few words, a must if many of the guests are unfamiliar with Secular Humanistic Jewish music. The students generally read one or more of their papers and also demonstrate a cultural aspect of Jewish life by playing a piece of music, acting out a short scene from Jewish literature, or even teaching the guests a folk dance. In a group ceremony, the students often interact with a scripted dialogue or a musical piece played together. Very often the parents or other family members speak to the B'ney Mitzvah, describing their qualities and the pride their families feel. Students often recite the Ashreis (rejoicings that take the place of blessings) found in *We Rejoice in our Heritage: Home Rituals for Secular and Humanistic Jews*. When it is important to the extended family, students occasionally recite religious blessings over bread and wine, but this decision is left up to the students who, having reached the age of moral development, must decide if they believe what is in the blessings, and, if not, whether other considerations make it possible for them to say what they do not believe.

Vancouver's Peretz School includes many of the same academic topics as the others and also requires a short report on the coming-of-age ceremonies of some other cultural group. Every class begins with music, and students study Jewish literature. They perform forty hours of community service and write a paper on some aspect of Jewish culture. The unique feature of this class is that each student must bring a Jewish joke to every class. Shane Dyson, who developed and teaches this program, says, "A lot of Jewish culture and history can be discovered within a simple joke."

Both the Sholem Community Organization in Los Angeles and the Jewish Children's Folkshule of Philadelphia provide an advisor for each child, but the process also includes the parents in a major preparatory role. The process is, like in most Secular groups, much more important than the product. In fact, in Philadelphia, as in Ann Arbor and other places, the Bar/Bat Mitzvah ceremony is optional. Some students go through the Sunday school and do not choose to celebrate their coming of age.

Each Sholem student prepares one major presentation, which can be an essay or dramatic or artistic production, but this is the result of a year's worth of research, interviews, and sometimes a related social-action project. The ceremony is always a community event. Sholem ceremonies usually celebrate two or three students becoming B'ney Mitzvah; Folkshule ceremonies are individual and written by the parents and student, with help from the B'ney Mitzvah coordinator. During the ceremony, the students present their projects and Sholem families give them five nonmaterial gifts representing their hopes for the future of the new B'ney Mitzvah. Folkshule students often include a candlelighting ceremony and a remembrance. Like most Secularist B'ney Mitzvah celebrations, both Sholem and Folkshule ceremonies include lots of singing. In 1997, Sholem instituted guidelines to deal with the problems of extravagant celebrations. These guidelines discourage differences in style associated with economic differences and insist that the celebrations following the ceremony be financially modest. Full dinners are not expected; in fact, Sholem encourages potlucks or just small receptions.

Preparation and Ceremony

Ruth chose to join the Secular Jewish organization in her city. Her daughter, Ariella, attended Sunday school for four years. She wrote a paper on Jews in the Civil Rights movement, a paper on the Jews who went to Turkey after the expulsion from Spain in 1492, and one on the battle between Hasidim and Misnagdim in Eastern Europe. She also researched her family history, describing the conditions in Europe that lead to her great-grandparents coming to America and their lives as immigrants on New York's Lower East Side. She tackled her Torah portion with an understanding that the Bible is a political, legal, social, religious, and literary document, and explored the meanings and morals from her own viewpoint. In addition, Ariella worked with children at the local homeless shelter after school twice a week for her entire seventh grade year. She helped them with homework, read to them, and played with them while their parents went out on job interviews.

Ruth was a little worried about what her family would think of the ceremony. They kept asking her if it was going to be a real Bat Mitzvah, by which they meant that Ariella would read from the Torah. Ruth told them that it would, indeed, be a real Bat Mitzvah, but that Ariella would do other things. The relatives, whose experience was limited to religious Bar and Bat Mitzvah ceremonies, were skeptical, but the family is close, and all of them agreed to attend.

At her ceremony, which she chose to perform individually, rather than in a small group, Ariella wove all her papers into one historical narrative about the diversity of the Jewish people. She played a Sephardic melody on her violin when she talked about the Spanish Inquisition, a Hasidic *nigun* when she discussed that part of history, and a frenetic klezmer tune, accompanied by her best friend on piano, when she described the lives of her immigrant ancestors. And she described her community-service experience, ending with the most important lessons she had learned. "I learned that one person really can make a difference. And I learned that those kids are just like me, just like all of us. They're not different just because they're poor." After the final singing of "Siman tov u'mazel tov" a beaming Ruth was gratified to hear from several relatives that this was the most meaningful Bar or Bat Mitzvah ceremony that they had ever attended.

Ruth was lucky to live in a city with a Secular Humanistic congregation to support this sort of preparation and ceremony. Stuart was not that lucky. He lives with his family—his wife Sarah who was brought up an Episcopalian, and two kids who are the only Jewish kids in the semirural school not far from the college where both their parents teach. When Josh, the oldest son, was eleven, Stuart suddenly realized that he needed his son to have a Bar Mitzvah ceremony. Thanks to the Internet, he was able to find Olam Katan, an e-mail listserv for Jews in small communities. (To inquire about Olam Katan, go to olamkatan@shamash.org) Stuart privately asked several other subscribers for help in formulating a study program and ceremony for Josh. A rabbi about six hours away from Stuart offered to tutor Josh if Stuart could bring Josh to the city one Sunday a month. Stuart also collected ideas from other subscribers, and he and Josh researched Jewish sites on the Internet because their access to Jewish books was limited. Stuart was worried that he could not adequately direct Josh's preparation, since he, himself, had not had any Jewish education since his own Bar Mitzvah, close to thirty years before, but he found that the on-line community helped him formulate a reasonable set of study goals. Stuart and Josh studied together, accessing sites and ordering books recommended by on-line friends, and Stuart now says that he learned more in the two years he studied with Josh than he did in six years of three-day-a-week Hebrew school as a child.

Then there was the question of where to have the ceremony. Josh could go to the congregation six hours away. He could go to his grandparents' congregation in Florida. He could try to borrow a Torah and have the ceremony at their own home, or forgo a Torah and have the ceremony at home. Each choice came with its own set of problems. The local congregation was Reform and, although Stuart was grateful for the rabbi's help and openness, the services were a little alien to one who had grown up in a very conservative Conservative congregation. Stuart's parents' congregation in Florida was a large Conservative synagogue and every Saturday morning of Josh's thirteenth year had been reserved four years ago. If they had the ceremony at home, it would need to be in the warm weather, when both sets of grandparents could travel to the northern state where the family lives. Borrowing a Torah is a big responsibility and not having a Torah at all was just not what Stuart's family would expect.

Stuart and Sarah are agnostics, with a great sense of spiritual connection to the Earth. Though they celebrate Jewish holidays, they have been influenced by the Native American culture around them and have a more Earth-centered spirituality than either of them was brought up with. They taught their children very little about any supernatural self-conscious gods, preferring to help them to discover a sense of awe at the universe around them and a sense of goodness within themselves. Still, it never occurred to them that Josh's Bar Mitzvah could be anything but a traditional Saturday morning service with a Torah reading. It was what they knew, what Stuart's parents expected, what was done. It took Josh, himself, to bring home the discrepancy to them. While he had enjoyed studying Jewish history and holidays with his father, he balked at the traditional ceremony, refusing to engage in what he called hypocrisy. The family did not attend services, did not believe in a god who meddles in human history and who responds to prayers—why should he perform a service and recite those prayers for his Bar Mitzvah? In vain, Stuart tried to convince his son of the value of tradition and of making his grandparents proud. Josh insisted that what he had been learning for the last two years had taught him that there's no such thing as "The Tradition" but that there are many Jewish traditions, and that his grandparents would be proud of him for standing up for what he believed.

In the end, Josh and Stuart both compromised. The ceremony was held at home, several months after Josh's thirteenth birthday, so it would be convenient for family members from all over to come. Josh described his studies and said the religious *brachot* (blessings) before and after reading a part of his Torah portion from a Soncino *chumash,* a book containing the text, rather than from a Torah scroll. Josh and his parents had come to the decision that the blessings meant more than just the plain meaning of the words, which they did not believe. Performing a traditional ritual was Josh's symbol for his connection with his grandparents and with Jews who had said those blessings throughout centuries. His grandfather blessed the wine, and as each family member took a sip, he or she made a personal blessing for Josh, wishing him long life, a happy marriage, engaging and important work. Josh's parents were able to express their own sense of spirituality in that personal blessing as well. The ceremony was authentic, accessible to both the Jewish and non-Jewish family members, and traditional in the finest sense of connecting Josh with his heritage and his people.

What Are Your Choices?

What are your choices if you have a child who would like a Bar/Bat Mitzvah ceremony, or if you, as an adult, would like one, yourself?

If you live in a place with or near a Secular or Humanistic organization, give them a call. If they don't have a Bar/Bat Mitzvah program, they'll be ecstatic to have you join and formulate one. Help is available from the umbrella organizations, the Congress of Secular Jewish Organizations, and the Society for Humanistic Judaism, too.

You might, however, have to contend with family pressures to have a religious ceremony in a synagogue on a Saturday morning. If this doesn't suit you, try explaining that Bar or Bat Mitzvah is a status that doesn't require any ceremony. A Jew is automatically Bar or Bat Mitzvah at thirteen or twelve. Chances are that won't get you very far, and you'll have to choose whether to compromise your principles (and your pocketbook) or risk offending your family. As Ruth found out, many religious Jews do appreciate the Secular Humanistic Bar and Bat Mitzvah ceremony, but some, despite Jewish law and historical evidence, still feel that it isn't a real Bar or Bat Mitzvah. If you find you have to have a synagogue ceremony, you still have some choices. You can allow your child to learn to conduct services as well as to read his or her Torah and Haftarah portion, or you can insist on only allowing your child to read, but not to conduct services. If your child does read the Torah and Haftarah, he or she will also have to make the blessings before and after.

Whether you opt for a maximal or minimal synagogue ceremony, you can still add cultural and historical aspects. Your child can still carry on independent study of Jewish history and culture, and can do independent community service. The Bar or Bat Mitzvah speech can reflect these studies and experiences, and not just be a sermon based on the Torah portion. Or your child can speak at a gathering immediately following the religious ceremony. This is actually very like the older tradition, in which the child did not speak at the ceremony, but gave a *d'var Torah* at the meal following the service. In this way, you can combine the religious ceremony with a Secular Humanistic ceremony of your own making.

What if there is no Secular Humanistic congregation where you live and you don't need to accommodate family members with a synagogue ceremony? You still have a couple of choices. You can go it alone—join CSJO or SHJ as an individual member and get guidance from the national staffs of either organization—or you can do some organizing. Unless you are living in an area with no other Jews, you will probably find a few families very much like yours. Your child will be friends with theirs, or you'll know them from political organizations, work, or school. You might get their names from the CSJO or SHJ, if they are on a mailing list, or from *Jewish Currents,* the Secular Jewish magazine. Or put an ad in the local newspaper. Broach the idea of having the kids (or adults) study together for a Bar or Bat Mitzvah. It's likely that the people you talk to have given up the idea of having a Bar or Bat Mitzvah but will be interested in the idea of being able to craft a course of study and a ceremony that suits their own worldview and spirituality and that has authentic culturally Jewish underpinnings. In America, it's not considered quite nice to talk about religion, so approaching others may be difficult. If you're brave enough to suggest the idea, though, you might find that the people you talk to are grateful, and you might even produce the beginnings of a community for yourself, a place to express your own Jewishness with others of like mind.

Where can you hold a non-synagogue ceremony? At home, if your place is large enough. At the Jewish Community Center or the Hillel Foundation at a local campus, or even in the social hall of a local synagogue or temple. At a union or professional hall, a fraternal organization hall, conference center, or hotel. At a nondenominational chapel used for weddings, or one at a hospital or university or private school. The only necessity is enough room and a place to feed people. You don't have to read Torah at a Bar or Bat Mitzvah, but it's hard to imagine an authentically Jewish ceremony without food!

12

Weddings

*Go eat your bread with gladness and drink your wine with a
joyous heart.*—Kohelet

"Oh, look, it's the real thing!" my Great-Uncle Charlie boomed
out as I placed the wrapped wineglass at the feet of my sister and her new husband. The laughter of the hundred guests was
eclipsed by the loud "Mazel tov"s and applause, but the point had
been made. If you break a glass, it's a Jewish wedding. If you don't,
it's not.

Of course, it's not really that simple—there are lots of factors
that enter into a wedding celebration—but the story illustrates the
power of folkways to define our cultural heritage. And it brings
home the point that it is the cultural symbolism, not necessarily the
religious words, that create a Jewish wedding. You can have a completely secular and humanistic ceremony that is also completely
Jewish.

You can also, of course, have a wedding that has secular and humanistic aspects and religious aspects, or both Jewish and non-
Jewish aspects. Your wedding should reflect your own cultures,
heritages, traditions, and values and should honor the people who
have been invited to witness and participate in it. There is, therefore, only one rule for a truly authentic wedding of any sort: three
people have to believe every word that is said—the speaker and the
two who are marrying.

Finding an Officiator

Although many couples first arrange for a place, a caterer, a florist, a photographer, a videographer, a dress, a band, and a cake baker, the key to having your wedding the way you want it is to find an agreeable officiator. Who is allowed to perform weddings? Any ordained clergy, a mayor, a judge, or a ship's captain in the high seas. Leaving the last as improbable, you still have lots of choices. If you live in a small city, the mayor will most likely be delighted to perform your wedding and will also probably be delighted to have you supply the ceremony. She or he generally will not, however, be able to help you craft the ceremony.

If you opt to have a judge perform your ceremony, you will probably have to do it at his or her convenience, typically during a weekday lunch break. The judge will be less likely to use your words for the ceremony, and you may be only one of a number of couples being married at the same time. You can, of course, choose to have a judge officiate a noontime legal ceremony and then perform a later ceremony yourself, with or without a nonlegal officiator, in front of your friends and family. This ceremony can be your own, but it may leave some guests feeling that they were not at the real thing. It's a reasonable option, though, if you'd like a public ceremony at a time convenient to your family and friends, and you can't find an officiator you like.

Clergy are the most common wedding officiators. If there's a Secular Humanistic Jewish leader where you live, that will probably solve your problem. If not, you can find someone from the Leadership Conference of Secular Humanistic Jews by calling CSJO or SHJ and asking for the nearest officiator who is willing to travel. You can also ask non-Jewish clergy to officiate. You can reach the American Humanist Association at 800/743–6646. E-mail humanism@juno.com. The AHA licenses Counselors who can perform legal weddings. Unitarian ministers are often Humanists and may agree to perform a nontheistic ceremony with Jewish cultural elements. Smaller groups, such as Scientology, also can provide officiators who may be willing to accommodate your preferences.

What about a rabbi from a religious Jewish movement? If you are both halachically Jewish you can be married by Orthodox or

Conservative rabbis or cantors (as long as you are not a same-sex couple). They will sometimes add readings you have chosen to their religious ceremonies, but will not remove anything. Of course, most of the words will be in Hebrew or Aramaic, so you can pretend you don't know that most of them are about exalting God and promising to pay back all the sheep if you divorce your wife. The man will be required to sign the *ketubah* (marriage contract), which also requires the signatures of two adult observant Jewish men. Some Conservative rabbis also allow the woman to sign the *ketubah*.

A Reconstructionist rabbi may officiate at a same-sex wedding but not at an intermarriage. She or he will be likely to include readings you choose, but, again, will probably not delete anything from the wedding ceremony. It will, however, be egalitarian, and the woman will be allowed to sign the *ketubah*.

Reform rabbis and cantors are forbidden to officiate at intermarriages, but many of them do, anyway. Some will also perform same-sex weddings. They are very likely to allow you to add readings and may limit their praying, but probably not eliminate it entirely. A *ketubah* is optional at a Reform ceremony.

Secular Humanistic rabbis, leaders, and senior leaders will officiate at intermarriages and at same-sex marriages. Some require the couple to write the entire ceremony (with adequate help, ideas, and support, of course) and some will write the ceremony by themselves or accept input from the couple. Secular Humanistic clergy do not use god-language, but may, if they choose, allow others to do so at the wedding. Some actively encourage you to include many participants; others prefer to conduct the ceremony themselves. If you have a preference, ask about this during your initial phone call.

How Do You Make It Jewish?

While not all Jewish wedding customs are secular or humanistic, a number of beautiful elements can signal the Jewish nature of the ceremony.

The Chuppah

First, consider a *chuppah,* or wedding canopy. The *chuppah* can be freestanding or can be held by four friends or family members. The poles can be any light material and can be covered with fabric and wrapped with foliage. The cover can be any flowers or any fabric. If you prefer a flower chuppah, a florist can probably provide it. If you have a Jewish officiator, she or he may be able to provide a chuppah. If not, get four one-inch dowels, drive a nail into the top of each one to attach the fabric to, and either drive the ends into the ground or ask friends to hold them.

A fabric top can be made of a family tallis, a shawl, or tablecloth brought over with an immigrant ancestor, a new cloth, tablecloth, or bedspread, or something made for the occasion. A lovely new tradition of quilt-*chuppahs* has emerged in the past several years. Send each invited guest a twelve- to fifteen-inch square of fabric and ask to have it decorated and returned by a month before the wedding. Your friends and family will create beautiful personalized squares that you or a friend can sew together into a *chuppah.* If it is large enough, it can become a bedspread. If not, it makes an interesting wall hanging or furniture throw.

The symbolism of the *chuppah* is myriad and can be explained during the ceremony or in a handed-out program. Or you can just have a *chuppah* with no explanation at all. You can explain about the *chuppah* in the following ways or you can invent a symbolism of your own.

"The four poles of the *chuppah* symbolize the four pillars on which our marriage is built: family, friendship, love, and heritage." You can substitute any four values here—honesty, comfort, respect, and laughter are all good examples.

"The *chuppah*'s flimsiness reminds the lovers beneath it that the only thing real about a home is the people in it, who love and choose to be together, to be a family" (adapted from Sharon Orbach, writing for her brother's wedding).

Procession and Escort

The procession can also signal the Jewish nature of the ceremony. In most Christian weddings, the man does not walk down the aisle, but waits at the front. After the bridesmaids enter, the woman is brought to her new husband by her father, signifying the handing over of possession of the woman from one man to another. The traditional Jewish wedding procession, on the other hand, generally includes first the *chuppah* bearers, and then both members of the couple, accompanied by both sets of parents, who stand around the *chuppah* throughout the ceremony. You can each ask your parents to accompany you down the aisle, or the woman can be accompanied by both mothers and the man by both fathers. You can have no escort at all or you can walk down the aisle together. You don't have to have a procession at all, if you don't want to.

If you are the children of parents who are no longer married, and especially if your parents have remarried, these arrangements can become sticky and fraught with politics and emotion. Try to remember that the ceremony is only half an hour of your life. You can afford to be generous.

Circling

In the traditional Jewish ceremony, the woman binds the man to her by walking around him seven (or three) times. In modern ceremonies, each participant can circle the other seven times, or each can circle the other three times and they can circle each other once. You can use any combination you like, or not bother at all.

Saul Tchernikovsky's poem "With This Ring I Thee Charm," in its entirety, has the word *ring* seven times, and is appropriate either at this point or at the giving of the wedding rings.

Sharing Wine

It is a Jewish tradition for the couple to drink out of one glass of wine. In some ceremonies, there are two occasions on which they drink. Some couples prefer to use two cups, pouring each other's cup, but drinking out of their own.

Here are some things that can be said at that time:

> We rejoice in our heritage, which has given us the cup of wine as the symbol of our happiness. May your lives be as sweet and full as this goblet of wine and may you always drink from a full cup.

Wine is a symbol of joy, of the richness of life, and the sweetness of love. We rejoice in life, health, and love, which enable us to celebrate the happiness of this beautiful day. As you have shared the wine in this cup, so may you in enduring union and devotion to each other, draw contentment, comfort, and happiness from the cup of life. May you find life's joy doubly gladdening, its bitterness sweetened, and all things shared in true companionship. (Dan Friedman.)

Ketubah (Marriage Contract)

The *ketubah* is the ancient wedding contract, a premarital contract, which protects the wife if the husband should divorce her. It also provides that the couple will honor and care for each other. In traditionally religious weddings, the husband and two witnesses sign it; then it is read at the ceremony and the wife accepts it.

You can have a *ketubah* made by a calligrapher, use a preprinted one, or produce your own. You can write your own contract, or make up a certificate, instead, with your vows and a short poem or phrase on it, or not use one at all. If you use a *ketubah,* you can have it read at the ceremony or not. You can sign it before or during the ceremony. If you make a large one, you can ask all your guests to sign as witnesses. A beautiful *ketubah* is often framed and hung in the home.

Seven Benedictions

In the traditional Jewish wedding, the rabbi recites seven blessings. Sometimes friends and relatives are honored by being asked to recite one of the blessings. You can ask people to make statements or wishes for your future, or to read a piece of poetry. A friend or relative might sing. Or you can ignore this.

If you'd like to use the seven blessings format, you might want to use reworkings somewhat like these that I adapted from the religious blessings. The Hebrew is by Benjamin M. Ben-Baruch.

Melissa and Daniel's Ketubah

אני לדודי ודודי לי

I give you my hand!
I give you my love more precious than money.
I give you myself before preaching or law.
Will you give me yourself?
Will you come travel with me?
Shall we stick by each other as long as we live?

This I promise:
To be the companion of your heart
To live with you and laugh with you
To stand by your side and sleep in your arms
To have you and to hold you,
For better or for worse
To love you and to cherish you
To play with you as much as I can until we grow old
And still loving each other
Sweetly and gladly, our lives shall come to an end.

I love you without knowing how, or when, or from where,
I love you simply, without problems or pride:
I love you in this way because I don't know any other way of loving
but this, in which there is no I or you,
so intimate that your hand upon my chest is my hand,
so intimate that when I fall asleep it is your eyes that close.

Signature of Melissa

Signature of Daniel

Signature of witness

Signature of witness

Signature of officiant

Ruth and John's Ketubah

אני לדודי ודודי לי

I am my beloved's

and my beloved is mine

*On the eighteenth day of June in the year of 1995,
corresponding to the twentieth day of Sivan in the year
5755, in Kalamazoo, Michigan
שיינדל רבקה / S-R-P-, daughter of
רחל לאה / Rena and שלמה לייב /Lester
and J-L-V-, son of Mark and Laura
married and dedicated themselves to each other in the
presence of:*

_____   _____

_____

*"As I dig for wild orchids in the autumn fields,
it is the deeply bedded root that I desire,
not the flower"*

_____   _____

1. We rejoice in our heritage, which has given us the cup of wine as the symbol of our happiness.

2a. We rejoice in our heritage, which teaches us to love our beautiful earth.

or

2b. We rejoice in the beauty of the earth, home to all creation.

אַשְׁרֵינוּ בְּיוֹפִי טֶבַע הַתֵּבֵל בֵּית-הַבְּרִיאָה
וִיצִירָה
הַבַּיִת לְכָל אֲשֶׁר נִבְרָא.

*Ashreynu b'yofee teva, ha'teyvel beyt ha'briyah
v'tsirah, ha'bayit l'khol asher nivrah.*

3. We rejoice in humanity and in being part of the vast sister- and brotherhood that embraces us all.

אַשְׁרֵינוּ בִּבְנוֹת-חַוָּה וּבְנֵי-אָדָם
וּבְחֶלְקֵנוּ בַּחֲבֵרוֹת הַמְחַבֵּק כֻּלָּנוּ.

*Ashreynu b'vnot Chavah u'vney Adam u'v'chelkeynu
b'chaverut ha'mechabek kulanu.*

4. We rejoice in (or we are thankful for) the capacity of people to join together in intimacy.

אַשְׁרֵינוּ בְּכִשְׁרוֹנוֹת בִּבְנֵי-אָדָם
וּבְנוֹת-חַוָּה
לְהִתְיַחֵד וּלְהִתְיַחֵס וּלְהִתְקָרֵב
בְּרֵעוּת וּבְאַהֲבָה.

*Ashreynu b'kishronut b'vney Adam u'b'not Chavah
l'hityached u'l'hityacheys u'l'hitkareyv b'reyut
u'v'ahavah.*

5. We invite all of our family and friends (and all of the People of Israel) to rejoice with us at our union.

אַשְׁרֵינוּ בְּשִׂמְחָתֵינוּ חֲפָתֵינוּ וְאִיחוּדֵנוּ
וּבְכֵן אָנוּ שְׂמֵחִים לְהַזְמִינְכֶם

מִשְׁפַּחְתֵנוּ וְחֶבְרֵנוּ וְכָל עַם יִשְׂרָאֵל
וְכָל הַנּוֹכְחִים כַּאן לְהִצְטָרֵף
בְּשִׂמְחָתֵינוּ.

*Ashreynu b'simchateynu chupateynu v'ichudeynu u'v'ken
anu smeychim l'hazminchem mishpachateynu
v'chevreynu v'khol am yisrael v'chol ha'nochechim
kahn l'hitztaref b'simchateynu.*

6. We rejoice in our heritage and honor our ancestors, our parents, and grandparents at this joyous occasion. We thank them for their example and their love.

אַשְׁרֵינוּ בִּירֻשָׁתֵנוּ
וְכִבְּדֵינוּ בְּשָׁעַת חֻפָּתֵינוּ אֲבוֹתֵינוּ
וְאִמוֹתֵינוּ
הוֹרֵינוּ וְהוֹרֵיהֶם
וּמוֹדִים אֲנַחְנוּ לְכָל הַדְרָכַתָם
וְאַהֲבָתָם.

*Ashreynu b'yerushateynu v'chabdeynu b'sha'at chupateynu
avoteynu v'imoteynu, horeynu v'horeyhem u'modim
anachnu l'khol hadrachatam v'ahavatam.*

7a. We are thankful for (or we rejoice in) the joy and gladness in our lives, for mirth and exultation, pleasure and delight, love, friendship, peace, and fellowship.
or
7b. We are thankful for the joy and gladness in our lives, for mirth and exultation, pleasure and delight, love, friendship, peace, and fellowship. May we all witness the day when the sounds throughout the world will be these sounds of happiness:
The voices of lovers,
the sounds of feasting and singing
and the songs of peace.
May these beloved companions rejoice together.

אַשְׁרֵינוּ לְהוֹדוֹת תּוֹדוֹת
וּלְשָׂשׂוֹן וְשִׂמְחָה גִּילָה רִנָּה דִּיצָה

וְחֶדְוָה
אַהֲבָה וְאַחֲוָה וְשָׁלוֹם וְרֵעוּת
עוֹד יִשָּׁמַע בְּאַרְבַּע כַּנְפוֹת הָעוֹלָם
כָּל הַקּוֹלוֹת קוֹלוֹת שָׂשׂוֹן וְקוֹלוֹת
שִׂמְחָה.

*Ashreynu l'hodot todot u'l'sasson v'simchah, gilah,
rinah, ditzah, v'chedvah, ahavah ve'achavah,
v'shalom v'reyut. Od yishama b'arba kanfot ha'olam
kol hakolot kolot sasson v'kolot simchah.*

8. We rejoice in our heritage, which teaches us to find inner happiness and to seek out and bring forth joy and happiness despite
the troubles and difficulties that exist in the world.

אַשְׁרֵינוּ בִּירֻשָּׁתֵנוּ הַמּוֹרָה לָנוּ
לְהִתְרַנֵּן וּלְהַמְצִיא
רִינָה וְגִילָה
דַּוְקָא בִּפְנֵי הַצָּרוֹת וְהַקָּשׁוֹת שֶׁבְּעַלְם.

*Ashreynu b'yerushateynu hamorah lanu l'hitraneyn u'l'hamtsee
reenah v'gheelah dafka bifney ha'tsorot v'ha'kashot
she'b'olam.*

Shehechianu: We rejoice in our heritage, which has given us the
indomitable spirit that has preserved our people and sustained
us and brought us forward to this moment.

אַשְׁרֵינוּ בִּירֻשָּׁתֵנוּ הַכֹּחַ שֶׁהֶחֱיָנוּ
וְקִימָנוּ וְהִגִּיעָנוּ לִזְמַן הַזֶּה.

*Ashreinu b'yerushateynu, ha'ko-ach shehechiyanu v'kimanu
v'highi'anu lazman hazeh.*

Breaking the Glass

In a traditionally religious Jewish ceremony the man breaks a
wine glass by stepping on it. If you are having a Jewish wedding,
you probably have to break a glass. You can forgo almost every

other element, but if you don't break a glass, folks will not believe you are really married. You can have one person break the glass, you can each break a glass, or you can break one glass together.

You can explain the symbolism in any way that makes sense to you. Since the origin was probably an ancient ritual to scare away evil spirits, all the other explanations were made up to explain something that people were already doing. Your own explanation is just as valid as any other. You or the officiator can say something like one of these statements:

*

May your years together be as many as the fragments of this glass.

*

May you be happy together until all the fragments of this glass are rejoined.

*

May all your happiness be as great as the number of shattered pieces of this glass, and may all your troubles be as easily shattered.

*

We break the glass to symbolize that this cup of life that we drink from together shall be an exclusive commitment we shall always share. Just as the now-shattered glass can never again be used for a lesser purpose, never will we serve a lesser purpose than this everlasting commitment.

*

The tradition tells us that the breaking of the glass reminds us of the destruction of the second Temple in Jerusalem in the year 70 CE and of the subsequent exile of the people of Israel. It reminds us that we have only today to rejoice and love each other, for our happiness may be destroyed by forces beyond our control at any time. In the words of Robert Ingersoll, "The place to be happy is here. The time to be happy is now."

How to Have an Intermarriage

Sherwin Wine, teaching at the International Institute for Secular Humanistic Judaism, reformulated the term *intermarriage* into two separate phenomena. An intercultural marriage is one in which the two partners have come from different backgrounds, but share a basic worldview. Both may be atheists, or they may believe in a god that they define in the same way. They believe the same thing about human nature, about values, about their understanding of the nature of the universe.

An interfaith marriage, on the other hand, involves two people who may be of the same or different cultural backgrounds but who don't have the same worldview or religious ideas. A marriage between a Jewish atheist and a religious Jew is just as much an interfaith marriage as is one between a devout Catholic and a religious Jew. These partners truly do not believe the same things about humanity, God, or the universe, and they have a lot more difficulties to work out than do partners in intercultural marriages. There are several good books on interfaith marriages and how to work out the difficulties. The best of these, I think, is *The Intermarriage Handbook* by Judy Petsonk and Jim Remsen. It doesn't come to you with a preconceived notion of the right way to solve the problems you may have.

If yours is an intercultural marriage, you will be able to work elements of both cultures into your wedding ceremony and into your lives together. It will be easy to follow the One Rule For Weddings—that everything said will be something both of you believe. If yours is an interfaith wedding, both of you and the officiator(s) will have to take great care over the words you say at the wedding. If you have a coofficiated ceremony (that is, with an officiator from each tradition), the officiators will need to agree to your requirements for the ceremony. You may have to look hard, but it is worth it to find the right people, those who will agree not to say anything that you have not already okayed. No matter how much you trust the clergy, it's best not to allow improvisation. It's too easy for one to say something *with the best will in the world and not meaning to offend* that will, only through ignorance, make half the people at the wedding feel upset or excluded.

Here are some elements you might like to consider, and notes about whether they are acceptable to both Jews and Christians (the most common intermarriages).

Typical Christian Elements and Jewish Responses

Christian clergy typically use words like "Jesus," "Christ," "Savior," or "Redeemer." These terms make Jews shudder. It's better not to use them in an intercultural wedding ceremony.

Christian ministers often announce "Let us pray" or ask people to bow their heads. These customs are alien to Jews. If someone is going to offer a prayer at your wedding, let him or her just start praying, rather than prefacing the prayer with a request that all pray or bow their heads.

Communion is an important part of many Christian services, but it is exclusive; not even all Christians can participate in communion offered by other Christian clergy. It can only create feelings of alienation and is better left out of the wedding service.

The pronouncement, while not included in the Jewish ceremony, is not offensive in any way to Jews. You'll want to be sure you are introduced in a way that you like. If you are both taking the same name, you can be introduced as Mr. and Mrs. It can be announced that you are now husband and wife. Or you can ask the officiators to say that, in the presence of this company, you have married yourselves to each other.

The assent of the congregation, not traditionally Jewish, is perfectly acceptable to Jews.

Many Christian ceremonies we've seen in the movies ask for any objections. Does anyone still do this? In some Christian ceremonies, and even some Jewish ceremonies that borrow from Christian traditions, the bride is given away. This has an unpleasant connotation of ownership, but should be no more offensive to Jews than to non-Jews.

The Catholic unity candle is attractive to Jews because, although this specific tradition is not Jewish, lighting candles always seems Jewish.

Many Christian services include kneeling. Jews don't kneel. Don't ask them to. And it would be exclusive and not pertaining to both members of the couple if the officiator invited anyone to do so.

Vows are not traditionally Jewish, but there is no reason not to add this element to a wedding that includes a Jew as a partner.

Typical Jewish Elements and Christian Responses

In the traditional Jewish wedding, the *ketubah,* or wedding contract, is read out loud (in Aramaic). The contract is all about what happens if the couple divorces. Do you really want to talk about that during your wedding ceremony?

The Jewish wedding includes the sharing of wine. Some Christian traditions do not allow the consumption of alcohol. If this is the case for you (or if you don't drink), you can use grape juice and refer to *the fruit of the vine* rather than to *the wine*.

The hallmark sign of the Jewish wedding, the breaking of the glass, has no parallel in Christian tradition, but shouldn't offend or alienate anyone.

The Jewish tradition of the bride circling the groom seven times is not used often even among Jews. Although it is not intrinsically offensive to Christians, it will seem rather alien.

The use of Hebrew, which is typical of a Jewish wedding, is exclusive and can be alienating to the Christian family members and guests.

The Jewish marriage statement, in which the man marries the woman "according to the laws of Moses and Israel" doesn't make any sense in an intermarriage, because those laws don't allow intermarriage. It is also confrontational and exclusive.

Different Traditions for the Same Element

When entering, the Christian tradition is that the bride enters with her father. In the Jewish tradition, both enter with their parents (or the woman with both mothers and the man with both fathers). This is a more inclusive alternative and avoids the implication that the woman is a piece of property to be transferred from one man to another.

In the Jewish ceremony, only the man makes the statement of marriage. Christian weddings include vows by both, which is more inclusive.

A Christian wedding is typically held in a church, at the altar. A Jewish wedding is held beneath a *chuppah,* which is less exclusive.

Christian weddings often include intercessions or prayers, while Jewish weddings include the seven blessings. Benedictions are more inclusive than either the Christian or Jewish alternative.

In older Jewish traditions, the man gives a gift to the woman. In older Christian traditions, the man gives a ring to the woman. In both modern traditions, there is an exchange of rings, which seems to suit everyone better.

13

Funerals

Some things happen to us only once. The death of a mother is like that, and we have no precedent to follow. At such times, we don't have the emotional capacity to search out the way we want to deal with a funeral and mourning, so we fall into the easiest way to do it. Most of us just call the local Jewish funeral home and let the funeral director arrange for a religious Jewish funeral. But you don't have to do that. If you've thought beforehand about the decisions you'll want to make, and discussed them with the rest of your family members, you'll be able to create a meaningful way to respond to the death, a way that will not leave you feeling alienated from your own emotions and from the Jewish community.

Traditional Jewish funerals and mourning practices uphold three values: dignity, equality, and faith. The entire funeral service deals mostly with the glory of God, and the traditional religious response to hearing about a death is "Blessed is the true judge." Although the kind of faith expressed here may not appeal to you, the elements of dignity and equality and some of the cultural norms may resonate with your own Jewishness.

Jewish funerals are held as soon after the death as possible, usually within a day. Funerals are not held on Saturdays. The body is washed and then watched and prayed over all night. In Orthodox communities this is done by the *chevrah kaddishah*, a group of vol-

unteers. Jewish corpses are not embalmed and are buried in un-
seamed shrouds and plain wooden coffins. Although some Jewish
cemeteries allow elaborate gravestones, many require all stones to
be the same, symbolizing, as does the plain coffin, that all are equal
in death. Pregnant women and *Cohanim* (those eligible for the
hereditary High Priesthood) do not go into cemeteries. The mourners remain in the cemetery until the grave is covered, and many
help to throw dirt on top of the coffin. After leaving the cemetery
or before entering the house of mourning, anyone who has been in
the cemetery ritually washes his or her hands.

After the burial, everyone usually goes to the house of the deceased, bringing food for the family. In recent times, the family of
the deceased has been expected to provide the meal, but this seems
hideously offensive to some of us. The friends of the bereaved can
surely manage to buy bread, boil eggs, and pick up some cakes,
rather than expecting the bereaved to accomplish this in the short
time available. The mourners' meal includes boiled eggs, which
symbolize the renewal of life, and the egg is the first thing the
mourners eat after the funeral. Mourners are brought plates of
food by their friends without having to ask for it.

The first (up to) seven days after the funeral is the period known
as "shivah," which means "seven." (Shivah pauses and sometimes
ends altogether at the beginning of the Sabbath.) The family is said
to be "sitting shivah." Friends and relatives come to visit and may
bring food for the family. Mirrors are covered and Orthodox Jews
do not sit on chairs or wear leather. The afternoon and evening services (Mincha and Maariv) are conducted at the shivah house. Be
careful whom you invite to conduct services—if you choose an
Orthodox rabbi out of respect to the deceased, as did Hildy
Goldfeld, you may be in for a nasty surprise. "The rabbi made me
and my mother go into the kitchen during the services when my father died," she explains, "because he didn't conduct services with
men and women together. I wasn't allowed to say Kaddish for my
own father, and my mother, his wife, couldn't even be in the
room."

After shivah, there is a thirty-day period of partial mourning
followed by a year of remembrance. Some people recite Kaddish
every day for this year. (Others say Kaddish for only eleven
months, believing that Kaddish is said only for souls that have not

yet ascended to heaven. All souls are said to ascend within a year, and nobody wants to imply that the deceased was so evil that he did not deserve to ascend for the whole year.) Following that, we observe the *yortseit* (literally *year time*) or death anniversary each year.

It should be noted that funerals and mourning are not held if the person who died was under thirty days old. This seems cruel to us in modern times, but, since throughout most of history so many babies didn't live beyond the first few days, it was simply a practical matter. Some religious Jews still uphold this tradition, but most Jewish leaders will now conduct mourning observances for newborns.

What to Do With the Body

The first question that must be answered is the disposition of the body. Each state has its own rules about who may handle a dead body. In some states, only a licensed funeral director can touch or transport a body from the place of death until the final disposition. In other places, a body may be brought or left home, tended by the family or community, and transported to a burial site privately. You must find out the law in your own state before making any plans for disposition.

If the deceased donated his or her entire body for medical use, that particular question is settled. If the person was an organ donor, however, the remains are typically returned to the family. You can ask the medical center to dispose of these remains; most of them do incinerate amputated limbs and organs that have been removed. It may not be aesthetically pleasing, but if you are not sentimental about the body, it might be the right choice, since it involves no expense and no immediate ceremony to prepare for.

If you are going to be responsible for disposition of the body, you can choose burial or cremation. You will generally want to honor the wishes of the deceased, but many people don't make their wishes known. In addition, Orthodoxy does not allow cremation, so if you are burying your relative in a Jewish cemetery, it's important to find out if they will accept cremated remains. If your parent has already bought a plot, you still have to find out; many people do not ascertain the regulations before actually buying a plot in their congregation's cemetery. In addition, you should know that many Jewish cemeteries do not allow burial of a person not born Jewish and not converted according to the Orthodox understanding of Jewish law. If there is a such a person in the family and that person wants to be buried together with the person you are burying, you may have difficulty finding a Jewish cemetery. Be sure to ask!

The Conservative movement tends to follow Orthodox law unless there's a good reason not to. Rabbi Rob Dobrusin of Beth Israel Congregation in Ann Arbor, Michigan, says, "We do not allow cremation at the Beth Israel cemetery except in extreme circumstances" (for example, if someone were to die overseas and the return of a body were held up in customs/legalities). The movement strongly discourages cremation but rabbis are permitted to officiate at services before or after and to bury people in cemeteries that allow it. Some rabbis might officiate at ceremonies in which cremated remains are buried, but the vast majority do not. In general, Conservative cemeteries do not allow burial of non-Jews, but rabbis vary in the degree of leniency on this issue and the degree to which they will accept converts from other movements.

Reform congregations that maintain cemeteries vary in their regulations. The CCAR, the professional organization for Reform rabbis, holds that Reform rabbis may discourage cremation but must not refuse to officiate at a funeral for someone who has chosen cremation. Reform cemeteries generally allow burial of cremated remains and will allow the burial of a non-Jew who was closely related to a Jew buried in the cemetery. They generally accept converts from other movements as Jews.

Rabbi Richard Hirsh, the executive director of the Reconstructionist Rabbinical Association, says that Reconstructionist rabbis make their decisions based on both tradition and circumstance, but in general would "discourage, but not prohibit" cremation. Likewise, the individual rabbis must decide if they will officiate at funerals of non-halachically converted Jews. Since the movement is a new one, most Reconstructionist congregations and *chavurot* don't have their own burial sites, so decisions about burial are made by the cemetery. He adds, however, that cemeteries are now mostly owned by private corporations, not congregations, and that if a rabbi says she or he will officiate at a funeral, the cemetery administrators tend not to question who or what is being buried.

The Secular Humanistic Jewish movement allows cremation, and the Secular and Humanistic Jewish organizations that have their own memorial gardens allow cremated remains to be buried there. They are also open to people of all backgrounds and religions.

Cremated remains can, almost everywhere, be kept or disposed of without any regulations or licenses, so if you want to scatter the remains in a place that was meaningful for your relative or is meaningful for you, you can do that. You can keep the remains (they'll be given to you in a heavy cardboard box, but you can buy an urn from most crematoriums) until you decide where to scatter or bury them, or until the entire family can gather at the chosen place. It is also possible to divide the remains among family members and allow each to do whatever is meaningful for him or her.

If you choose burial, you will have to abide by the laws of your jurisdiction regarding caskets and coffins. Traditionally, Jews do not embalm; if you want to have the body embalmed, you will probably not be able to use a Jewish funeral home and may not be able to bury the body in a Jewish cemetery.

Jewish funeral homes often operate according to Jewish law. They will require you to hire a person to sit with the body all night. They will provide a kosher coffin and will generally not allow an open-coffin funeral, although the family may be allowed to view the body privately before the ceremony. They also typically require the pallbearers to be Jews. Most Jewish funeral homes require a rabbi to officiate at the funeral, although those in cities with Secular Humanistic clergy can be persuaded to allow them to officiate. Most Secular Humanistic Jewish ordained clergy are *leaders* or *senior leaders* rather than rabbis, but you can refer to one as a *rabbi* if you need to convince the funeral home to allow one to officiate.

If you don't want to follow the rules of the Jewish funeral home, or if there isn't one near you, you can use a nonsectarian mortuary. You will probably need to be very clear about your decision not to embalm. The funeral director may try to tell you it is required. You will need to stand firm and say that it is against your religion. If the funeral director says it is required, inform him that according to the National Funeral Directors Association there is no state that requires embalming. It is done only for the sake of those viewing the body. You may also have a hard time finding a kosher coffin, one that is made only of wood and has no metal screws or nails. You may decide to have a plain wood coffin, as is traditional, but allow metal in the construction. Either way, you may have to resist attempts to sell you more elaborate coffins. Again, just say that it is against your religion. The invocation of religion has great power and generally puts an end to sales arguments.

The Funeral or Memorial

Once you have decided on the disposition of the body, you have to decide whether to conduct a funeral or memorial ceremony. Despite pop psychology's demand for closure, you should know that you do not have to have any ceremony at all. Each family is different and each family has different needs. When my own father died in 1990, neither my mother nor my sisters and I saw any need for a ceremony of any kind. My father's ashes were scattered over the ocean, where he had liked to sail, and none of us was there. That suited our way best, but it isn't best for everyone.

If you decide on a ceremony, you can have a funeral or a memorial ceremony. A funeral means that the body is present. In earlier times, when Jewish families lived in the same town for generations, and in hot climates, the funeral was held within twenty-four hours. Now, a non-Orthodox Jewish funeral is usually held at the soonest time that the family can gather. If you feel you need a few days to put together a funeral, take the time you need. At a memorial ceremony, there is no body; it has already been buried or cremated, so the ceremony can be held at a later time. If you have a memorial service, you might want to create some sort of visual focus, since there is no coffin or urn. A picture or picture collage or a collection of the deceased's favorite items are all appropriate.

Of course, you can just allow the Jewish funeral home to arrange the funeral. If you are lucky, the rent-a-rabbi who works for the funeral home will listen to your stories and incorporate them into a reasonable eulogy, and you'll be encouraged to help fill the grave. If you're not lucky, you'll hear a few traditional prayers, allow the black ribbon the funeral director has pinned to your shirt to be cut, and follow along the transliteration with the rabbi's recitation of Kaddish. The religious Jewish funeral is quite short. It includes an introductory reading including the phrase "teach us to number our days," followed, often, by the twenty-third Psalm, "The Lord is my shepherd." The heart of the ceremony is the two prayers, El Moley Rachamim and Kaddish. El Moley Rachamim refers to God as compassionate and asks him to take the soul of the deceased. Kaddish does not mention the deceased at all; it is an Aramaic prayer about the glory of God. The funeral can end with another Psalm, typically Psalm 121, and then the final prayer asking that the soul of the deceased be bound together with the souls of all the matriarchs and patriarchs and righteous men and women in heaven. The entire service can easily be over in five minutes, even if everything is said both in English and Hebrew/Aramaic. If the El Moley Rachamim is sung instead of recited, it could take a few more minutes. And you may be left bewildered and uncomforted.

For those of us from secular homes, especially the children of leftists, this is an especially unappealing picture. If, in life, our family member had no patience with religion, it seems disrespectful to memorialize such a person with a ceremony that would have had no meaning for him or her, or one alien to his or her true beliefs.

On the other hand, if our parents were religious, it might seem disrespectful to have anything other than a religious funeral. And, of course, there are the feelings of other family members to consider. How can all the conflicting needs be satisfied? While it may not be possible to craft a single ceremony that will fill everybody's needs, you can create several ceremonies. You may decide to have a funeral that reflects the beliefs of the deceased. Your graveside service might be one that the most traditionally religious members of the family need. You could also have a ceremony at home that evening or soon after, one that is Secular and Humanistic in nature. Or you can agree that everyone involved can say what he or she believes, without any expectation that anyone else will join in that belief. Secular Humanistic poetry, readings, and songs can be interspersed with religious prayers, as long as participation in group readings or amens is not assumed. For example, a prayer leader can say, "Please join me, if you wish to, in the recitation of . . ." rather than "We pray . . ."

A funeral can have two separate parts: a ceremony in the funeral home or synagogue and a ceremony at the graveside. You can choose to do both or either, depending on the length of the ceremony, the weather, and your personal preferences. A longer ceremony with many participants is better held inside, where the acoustics are better and the seating is typically more comfortable. In addition, buildings usually provide the bereaved family with more privacy than can be had at a graveside. Graveside ceremonies are better suited to good weather, shorter readings, and smaller groups.

Who conducts a funeral or memorial service? This depends on the family preferences and the resources available. You can have a rabbi of a religious Jewish movement conduct the service. Depending on his or her own feelings, many beautiful Humanistic readings could be included. Religious prayers, however, will also probably be included. If there is an ordained Secular Humanistic Jewish leader in your city, he or she will be able to conduct the funeral or help you put one together on your own. Most leaders will not participate in religious prayers, though, so if members of your family need to hear or recite Kaddish, you may need to ask a religious friend to lead that prayer. You don't need a professional officiator to have a funeral (unless the funeral home or cemetery demands it); a family member or friend can conduct the ceremony.

What happens at a funeral or memorial service? A good funeral helps the mourners understand the significance of the life of the deceased. It can be comforting or challenging, and should acknowledge the grief of the mourners as well as their gratitude for having known the deceased. John Lovejoy Elliott once said at a memorial service that those who did not know the person he was eulogizing should miss him more than those who did know him, because they missed his entire life.

A funeral can include poetry and other readings, responsive or group readings, music, and eulogies, both planned and spontaneous. If you choose to have responsive or group readings, someone will have to put together some sort of handout for the ceremony. If you have time and resources or an officiator who will do this, it is a good way to show the people who attend that you recognize their loss as well as your own and to allow them to participate in honoring the deceased.

Typically, whoever is officiating will open the ceremony with one or two poems or readings. He or she may speak about the deceased or may ask someone else to deliver a eulogy. Family members with very sick or aged relatives should probably start writing eulogies while the relative is still alive; it's a lot easier to come up with the funny or telling stories when you're not overcome with the grief that even an expected death brings. Any number of people can be asked to speak either briefly or at length about the deceased. It's particularly effective to ask people who knew him or her in different capacities to tell one story each about the person's interactions with the speaker. You can also open the floor after the prepared eulogy and ask anyone who wants to speak to come forward.

If your congregation, *chavurah,* or organization has a chorus, it can sing, or you can ask a friend or family member to sing, lead a song, or play an instrument. You can play recorded music, too, if you'd like. Appropriate music includes anything the deceased really liked, or memorial songs.

You can light a candle, or ask each person who speaks to light a candle. Younger children might help light a candle or bring up a flower to place in a vase. You may choose to give each person a flower to place in a vase. Or, if you are going to the cemetery, you might give each person a flower to throw into the grave. The symbolism can be implicit, or you can explain that each candle symbolizes a light in the heart of the mourner, and that the vase full of flowers shows the beauty that the deceased brought into the lives of others.

A group or responsive reading and a closing poem or ritual statement end the funeral or memorial service.

What happens at the cemetery? Whether there's an earlier ceremony or not, at least some people will probably want to go to the cemetery for the burial, or to another place if you are depositing ashes elsewhere. A short poem or reading, a group reading, and a dedication are appropriate. Traditional Jewish burials often include the covering of the coffin with dirt, or even the filling of the whole grave. You can choose to carry out this tradition or not. If you choose to do so, be sure the cemetery personnel know your intentions, and they will have several shovels ready for your use. First the family and then any others put a shovelful or two of dirt on the coffin. People can take as many turns as they want to. If there are members of the family who want to say Kaddish, and it has been decided not to include this prayer in the ceremony, they may wish to stay behind after others have left the cemetery to recite the prayer then.

Resources

How do you find the right readings? Resources are available through the CSJO or SHJ or individual leaders, whether local or far away. Not long ago I received a phone call from a state about one thousand miles away. An old Jewish socialist had died and nobody wanted to dishonor him with a religious ceremony. I was able to fax over several pages of appropriate readings for the family to choose. Don't be afraid to call. Most leaders have a considerable file full of beautiful secular readings and are honored to be asked to help out. You can also find readings in Sherwin Wine's *Celebration,* available from the SHJ and in works by Algernon Black and John Lovejoy Elliott, non-Jewish Humanists. Several appropriate songs can be found in Kopinvant Press's *Kumzits! A Festivity of Instant Jewish Songs.*

IV

NOW WHAT?

14

How to Find a Community or Start Your Own

Finding a Group

Before you decide to put the time and energy into starting a group of your own, you might want to put a little effort into finding a local group that will suit you. This might be a Secular Humanistic affiliate, a comfortable religious congregation, or an independent *chavurah* or Sunday school.

Finding a Secular Humanistic affiliate is the easiest of the possibilities. Secular Humanistic Jewish groups and schools are affiliated with one of three organizations. Contact the headquarters for information on the group nearest you.

Congress of Secular Jewish Organizations
19657 Villa Drive North
Southfield, MI 48076
http://www.csjo.org

Society for Humanistic Judaism
28611 W. Twelve Mile Rd.
Farmington Hills, MI 48334
http://www.shj.org/

Workmens Circle/Arbeter Ring
45 East 33rd Street
New York, NY 10016
http://www.circle.org

If there's an affiliate near you, one of these organizations can put you in touch. But even if there is a nearby affiliate, it may be primarily organized around an age or interest group that isn't your preference. All the umbrella organizations will be happy to help you expand the group to include your particular interests. If you find a group that is mainly interested in adult discussion, but you need a Sunday school for your kids, you can probably make it happen within the already-organized group. Just ask for help.

What if there's no affiliate near you, but you really need an already-organized group? Check out one of the religious congregations that has active programs you're interested in. You can join the congregation's social-action committee or sisterhood/brotherhood group and never participate in any religious activity that doesn't suit you. You may be happiest in a Reconstructionist congregation, but there are many Reform and Conservative congregations that are welcoming to nontheists or people whose religious beliefs don't include the ruler-of-the-universe god that Jews address in prayer.

How to find the right congregation? Call up a local organization that works on issues you find meaningful—the ACLU, an ecology organization, or your local food bank, for example—and ask if there are representatives from liberal Jewish congregations who participate. Ask the parents of your children's friends if they belong to a congregation. Look in your local newspaper for congregational news and attend a lecture or activity sponsored by a congregation. Or, if you're in a small enough city, open the Yellow Pages and start calling around.

It's not easy to find the independent Sunday schools and *chavurot* that exist in a number of cities. The Congress of Secular Jewish Organizations has contact with some of them and will direct you to them if there's no CSJO affiliate in the area. Others can be found through listings from Jewish federations or in small community directories. The rabbi or administrator of a synagogue may know of the independent groups in the area. Or you can just start asking around. Check with people in progressive organizations, the local folk-music society, progressive private schools, the health-food store. You might even put up a few flyers reading,

Wanted: An Alternative Jewish Experience.

Founding a Group

If you've determined there's really no Jewish home for you in your area, it's time to start thinking about how to make one happen. Any of the three organizations will help you start an affiliate.

The most important thing to remember when starting a group is that you are not alone. Many Jews in the U.S. and Canada, according to rabbis and national surveys, do not believe in the god of Jewish prayer, even if they do believe in some sort of supernatural force. And many, if not most, are interested in a congenial community of like-minded people. There are people just like you everywhere; all you have to do is let them know you're there.

How do you get the word out? Here's an excerpt from the CSJO New Community Organizing Manual:

> There are two kinds of publicity—free and paid. Free is better. Your best free publicity, as you grow, will be word of mouth. People who find you will tell their friends. People who come to your ceremonies and programs and who find them meaningful and enjoyable will join and bring their friends and families. But how do you get them to come in the first place?
>
> Your second best free publicity is articles in local papers and magazines. Here are the places you can contact:
>
> - Local Jewish newspapers. When you contact your Jewish newspaper, position yourself as performing outreach to the unaffiliated, as this is a hot topic in the mainstream Jewish press.
> - Local community newspapers in your neighborhood and in the heavily Jewish neighborhoods of your city. The focus of these papers will be on community personalities. Pitch a person in the community who will be involved. You're

looking for a headline that might read *Longtime community activist returns to Jewish roots,* or *Local businesswoman involved in Jewish pluralism.*

- Alternative weeklies, gay/lesbian newspapers and magazines. Stress the alternative and inclusive nature of your new community. These are the publications that appeal to those who have abandoned religious Judaism but may be searching for a Jewish community.
- Local family centered magazines. If you are interested in setting up a Sunday school or Bar/Bat Mitzvah program, call the magazine and describe how hard it is for parents to get kids to go to Sunday school. Then tell them that your Sunday school is different—kids like it.
- Major newpapers. Make an appointment with the religion editor. That's the only place you'll be covered, and people who are looking for Jewish affiliation will be looking on the religion page because they won't know there's any alternative.
- Local television, public television and radio stations.

Be persistent. Keep calling, and sending articles and faxing press releases. The more the news media see your name, the more likely they are to believe you really are there and are newsworthy.

The manual also gives ideas for advertisements, brochures, and business cards, as well as examples of flyers. Flyers can be produced on bright paper and posted places where people like you are found:

- Book and music stores
- Coffee shops
- Nursery schools
- Libraries
- Stores that sell clothes or educational toys for kids
- Health-food stores or co-ops
- Jewish Community Centers, senior centers, and Yiddish groups
- Community pools
- Spas or gyms
- Bagel shops and delis

Try to think of places that attract different populations: people with young kids, empty-nesters, the gay/lesbian community, older people. A mixed-age, diverse group will give you your best chance of creating a real, lasting community of people who can offer each other support and broaden each other's experiences. It will also give you a greater population from which to find like-minded people.

Flyers should have very little information—they need to be easy to read at a glance. Be sure to include a phone number.

What should be on your flyers or in your ads? Information about upcoming programs is better than general information. Any of the umbrella organizations will send in a speaker, if you'd like to start with a large public event. Or you can start by inviting a few people you know to share Shabbes or a holiday with you and then open the occasion to others. Alternatively, you might want to start with a discussion or series of discussions of a current hot topic such as intermarriage. For example, in December, you could have an open forum on the problems of intermarried couples at Hanukkah/Christmas. In May or June, the topic could be how to negotiate an intercultural wedding. Early fall is a great time to sponsor a panel discussion for Jewish grandparents with non-Jewish grandchildren.

The key to creating a group for yourself is to commit to doing it. Don't spend a lot of time planning. Don't spend a lot of time finding every possible person who might be interested. Just plunge in. Schedule some activities and publicize them. People will find you when you have something to offer them.

What *do* you have to offer? Community, acceptance, an authentic way to express their Jewish identity. How do you do it? Through programming that meets your own needs.

Holiday programs: The umbrella organizations have holiday programs available, so you don't have to write your own. Just arrange to make enough copies. Be sure that you have coffee and dessert, at least (unless it's Yom Kippur, of course!) so that people feel like it's a real Jewish event and so they have a time for informal discussion.

Shabbes gathering: You can have a Friday night dinner—make it a potluck, but be sure that you cook extra—or an after-dinner event (with coffee and dessert, of course). You'll want to do a short ritual and have a presentation or discussion topic. Rituals, songs, readings, and discussion ideas are available from the CSJO and SHJ.

Lectures and discussions: Sunday mornings and Sunday evenings are the typical times for such events. If you or someone in your new group is knowledgeable on a subject of interest, you can present a talk. Representatives of the movement are happy to travel to give talks and lead discussions. Rabbis, cantors, professors, and graduate students are often pleased to be asked as well. Or invite a speaker on a current issue and discuss how being Jewish affects your response to the issue. You can have a lecture/discussion series on intermarriage, current events, Jewish history, etc., or you can discuss unrelated topics at each meeting. You'll want to create a safe space in which everyone feels welcome to express an opinion and to ask questions.

Community service: Your group can give people an organized way to serve the community. You don't need to invent your own programs—there are lots of worthwhile activities that could use an active group on a regular basis. You can adopt a highway or take responsibility for serving at your local meal program once a month. You can have a book drive for your local battered women's shelter. You can work with Habitat for Humanity once a month. These community service opportunities are fulfilling for the participants and also help to build your community. These activities can also help to integrate high school students—too old for Sunday school but too young for adult programming—into the community.

Education for kids: You don't have to start out with a full-fledged Sunday school. You don't even have to end up with one. There are lots of models that will work, and you can change your model as your group changes and grows.

One possibility is to start out with a parent-preschool and/or parent-kindergarten workshop series. You set up an hour-and-a-half or two-hour session about a week before each of four to six holidays, say, Rosh Hashanah/Yom Kippur/Sukkot (all in one because they really happen all at once), Hanukkah, Tu b'Shvat, Purim, Pesach, and Shavuot. Add Israel Independence Day if you like. If there's a long break you'd like to fill, like the time between

Sukkot and Chanukah, add a session on Shabbes. You'll teach a song or two and a dance (simplified for little kids to just running, jumping, and clapping). A cooking project or food tasting is always good. A craft project and a story round out the workshop. While the kids are eating their cooking project, you can even give the parents a short outline of the holiday.

If people are happy the first year, they'll want to continue. By kindergarten or first grade, you can establish a weekly, biweekly, or monthly school with a classroom teacher. Each year, as the kids get older, you add a year to your school, continuing to replace kids in the younger grades with new members.

Alternatively, you can start with the older kids. Every city has ten, eleven, and twelve-year-olds who haven't had a Jewish education but would like a Bar or Bat Mitzvah ceremony. Many religious congregations require three or four years of Sunday school attendance, and most also require attendance at religious services. Secular Humanistic Jewish schools can choose different requirements, as described in the Bar/Bat Mitzvah chapter. If you advertise a two-year program leading to a Secular Humanistic Bar or Bat Mitzvah ceremony, you will probably find several takers. You can establish weekly, biweekly, or monthly meetings of kids and parents to study together, or you can arrange for a single teacher. At the end of the two-year period, the students can celebrate becoming Bar or Bat Mitzvah together or in individual ceremonies. Each year you can add a new class of kids, and, when you're ready, you can add an earlier year to the program, working with younger and younger children until you have a full age program.

A third possibility is occasional or monthly educational programming for the entire family, based on a theme like Israel, Jewish literature, holidays, Bible times, or shtetl life. Children would be divided up into two or three age groups with appropriate activities and adults would also have activities or a lecture to attend. At the end of the session, everyone can gather to sing a few favorite songs and dance together. Don't forget food!

Whether you choose to have a few programs for a few ages, or a full Sunday school, the umbrella organizations can help with detailed curriculum materials and even lesson plans, song books, games, and craft instructions. CSJO will even send an experienced teacher to your area to conduct teacher training

SUNDAY SCHOOLS

Here are some ideas from CSJO for a Secular Humanistic
Jewish Sunday (or Saturday) school curriculum.

Kindergarten: Family, family stories, holidays, and Hebrew relating to family and the home. Songs about family
and holidays.

First Grade: Life in biblical times. What did people eat,
wear, do for jobs? Who were the kings, judges, and prophets,
and what were their ideas about values, justice, and fairness?
Hebrew relating to these concepts and songs about these
concepts.

Second Grade: The Jewish life cycle and Hebrew relating
to these events. Songs for life-cycle events.

Third Grade: Jews around the world, including Israel,
India, Ethiopia, Turkey, South America, northern Africa, and
China. What do these Jews wear, eat, do for jobs? Songs
from Jews all over the world.

Fourth Grade: Jews during the Middle Ages, including
Jewish self-rule in Persia and Europe; the Crusades; the
Golden Age in Spain; and the Inquisition. Try out the arts-
and-crafts forms of these Jews, such as poetry, metalwork-
ing, and weaving.

Fifth Grade: Jews in America, including the Sephardic immigration, the Westward movement, Eastern European Yiddish culture, the Jewish labor movement. Yiddish songs and
labor songs.

Sixth Grade: Eastern European Jewry: Yiddish language
and culture; Enlightenment and its movements—Reform
Judaism, Zionism, and Secularism; the Holocaust and resistance. Songs and dances of Europe and early Israel.

Seventh Grade: Jewish religion and religious practices, including services, kashrut, and Shabbes. Comparative Judaism, examining the responses of the different movements
in Jewish life to questions that the students develop.

Secular Humanistic Jewish Sunday schools are usually activity-based rather than text-based, and the best teachers are camp counselors, not Judaic Studies majors. Each class should include a combination of learning techniques and should emphasize hands-on activities. The goal is to produce Jews who not only know about the Jewish past but are competent to participate in the Jewish future. We don't just teach kids about Jewish music, we sing every week. We don't just teach them that the pioneers in Israel danced, we teach them Israeli folk dances. We don't only learn about traditional religious Jewish literature, we read Yiddish stories in translation, and poetry, and plays, and then we perform the plays and write our own poems. We cook, we weave, and we do metalwork when we learn about Jews in history who worked in those professions. We talk about modern events that relate to Jewish history. Our goal is not to fill our children's heads with lots of facts. Rather, we want them to leave Sunday school with an appreciation for the enormous diversity and beauty of Jewish life and with the idea that there is something in Jewish life that is meaningful and interesting to them.

Starting a new Secular Humanistic Jewish organization is a lot of work, but the rewards are great and many. It's true you'll spend hours on the phone and in front of the computer. It's true you'll always be scrambling to meet a publicity deadline. It's true that you'll always be finding something new that you have to learn about. But you'll also meet people you can talk to without constantly explaining the kind of Jew you are. You'll have a place to educate your children that won't teach them things you don't believe. You'll have a forum to take social action in a Jewish context. You'll have a place to come together as Jews on happy and sad occasions and on holidays. You'll have a place where you can feel validated as a Jew, as a Humanist, and as a part of the greater Jewish world. And you won't be alone.

15

How to Answer Questions about Secular Judaism

Once you begin to identify yourself as a Cultural, Secular Humanistic, or God-Optional Jew, you'll need to be able to answer the questions that your friends will ask. Here are some of the questions we often hear along with some short (and not-so-short) answers. You'll formulate your own answers over time.

What do you mean by Secular? Does that mean you don't believe in God?

The word *secular* tells both what we believe and what we don't believe. In one sense, it means *not religious*. It means we believe that this natural world is the only one we can know about. It means that we don't believe that any nonnatural or supernatural powers have influence on this world. It means we believe that religious authorities should have no control over government or public functions, and that the government should not dictate religious beliefs or practices.

But *secular* is also the translation of the Yiddish name for the movement, *veltlich,* which means *worldly.*

In this sense, the word has a positive meaning, the meaning of being involved, passionately involved, in the world and integrally connected to it.

It means that we believe that this is the only world we have, and if we want it to be better, we have the responsibility to make it better, and if we want it to survive, we have the responsibility to take care of it.

It means that all the things the world has to offer are ours, if we want them—art, music, literature, science, nature, the immense variety of intellectual and cultural expressions. What the world has to offer is good and interesting and worthwhile. We can be a part of those expressions, enjoy them, add to them, and share them with others.

It means that what happens in the world has meaning to us, that what happens to any of the world's people happens to us, that human relationships are powerful, and that our lives can affect the lives of others.

But what's Humanistic? Is it different from Secular?

Secularism tells us about human power. Humanism tells us how to use that power. It gives us a framework to decide what's right and what's wrong. Israel Kugler writes that humanism is "compassion, justice, and equality." Humanism teaches us that each person is worthy of respect, dignity, and self-determination. It teaches that neither God nor the state is an ultimate authority on right and wrong. It teaches us to judge acts according to their consequences, not according to the authority that dictates these acts. It teaches us that human beings are their own end and not a means to someone else's end.

I always thought of Judaism as a religion. How can you be Jewish if you don't believe in God?

The idea that Judaism is a religion dates back only to the 1700s. Before that, the Jews were considered to be a national entity, like the French or the Mexicans or the Native Americans. Submerging our national identity was the price we paid for becoming first-class citizens of the countries we lived in. The Reform movement, one outgrowth of the Enlightenment, made this shift one of its central principles and stated that Judaism is only a religion. But if we consider ourselves less like Protestants or Catholics and more like Mexicans or Native American tribes, we come to a better understanding of what being Jewish is all about. Nobody would say to a

Mexican "How can you be a Mexican if you're not a Catholic?" And certainly nobody would say to a Native American "How can you be Piute if you're Christian?" That's because, although there are typical, majority religious forms for each national culture, and the culture is enriched by those religious forms, the religion does not define the civilization.

But just as much as calling Judaism a religion rather than a national civilization flies in the face of history and tradition, calling Judaism *a* religion is historically inaccurate. Judaism is not one religion and has never been only one religion. The diversity of beliefs that has always existed in Judaism is testimony to that. And modern mainstream Judaism is just as diverse. Reform and Orthodox Jews believe very little, if anything, in common. They differ on the nature of God, the nature of humanity, the existence of an afterlife, the authority of the halacha, and just about everything else. There is no creed that defines Jewish religion, and there is no one set of Jewish beliefs that can be defined as *the* Jewish religion.

Religion is what divides the Jewish People. What holds us together is our sense of heritage, culture, and commitment to our people.

The center of Secular Humanistic Judaism is *not* the denial of a god. It is Jewish Peoplehood. We're not obsessed with the nonexistence of gods; they are irrelevant to us. The most important thing we can say about God is that whether or not there are any gods, whether or not there is a god named YHVH who told the Jews to do certain things, *we would live our lives exactly the same way we do now.* Our important statement is *not* that there is no god, but that God is not our authority.

Then how can a person convert to Judaism?

A conversion means a change. People change from not identifying themselves as Jews to identifying themselves as Jews. This is not a revelatory conversion, in an instant, as a result of a ritual immersion. Rather, it is a process that may or may not be marked with ceremony.

David Max Einhorn, in *Conversion to Judaism: A History and Analysis,* puts it this way: "Such a person does not change his religious way of life; he enriches the way of life he already has. He enriches it by becoming part of the Jewish people. . . . The Hebrew word *ger* . . . means 'someone who has come to live with us' . . .

The Hebrew verb root *gayer* does not mean *to convert*. It means *to invite a non-Jew to become a member of the Jewish people.*"

People become Jews by learning about Jewish life and by becoming part of the Jewish community. The Secular Humanistic movement defines a Jew as "a person of Jewish descent or any person who declares himself or herself to be a Jew and who identifies with the history, ethical values, culture, civilization, community, and fate of the Jewish People." Anyone who declares this identification, then, is a Jew and is accepted as one in our communities.

If someone becoming a Jew wants a formal course of study, the community's leader(s) will help him or her. If someone who has become a Jew would like to have a ceremony, that's fine. Among some congregations, this ceremony is called an *adoption*. Others call it a *Kabbalat nilvah* (welcoming the newcomer) or just a *welcoming ceremony*. Some use the adult Bar or Bat Mitzvah ceremony to welcome an adult into Jewish life.

What's the place of Torah and Jewish law?

We believe that the Torah, by which we mean all of Jewish religious teaching, is a creation of the Jewish People and that it evolved over the generations. We know that the existence of the law and the legal codes, the stories in the Torah and Midrash, discussions in the Talmud and syntheses of all of these in the responsa literature have been and continue to be important to the development of Jewish civilization. We think that culturally literate Jews should have a working knowledge of these laws and stories and discussions and be able to appreciate allusions to them in Jewish literature and music and to understand the way they have influenced Jewish culture and history.

Because we believe that Torah is a creation of the Jewish People, we do not accept it as authority for our actions or beliefs.

Is this like Jews for Jesus?

Well, no. And yes. And no. The first no is the quick answer. We're not like Jews for Jesus because they want more gods and we want fewer.

And yes, we are like Jews for Jesus because our religious beliefs are not what the Official Story teaches us are the correct or dominant or only possible Jewish religious beliefs. We are like Jews for

Jesus because, like many modern Jews, we believe that Judaism can encompass more than one set of beliefs.

But no, ultimately, we aren't like Jews for Jesus. Like religious Jews, Jews for Jesus or Messianic Jews use the Bible as authority and attempt to show that their beliefs are rooted in the Jewish religious tradition. Secular Humanistic Jews use the Bible as a source of history and literature but not as an authority that justifies our beliefs and actions.

Jews for Jesus are different from Secular Humanistic Jews in another way, as well. The International Federation of Secular Humanistic Jews' official answer to the question of who is a Jew—"a person of Jewish descent or any person who declares himself or herself to be a Jew and who identifies with the history, ethical values, culture, civilization, community, and fate of the Jewish people"—is clear that the fate of the Jews is a communal, not an individual fate. Therefore, anyone who would chose for him/herself an individual salvation has cut him/herself off from the communal fate of the Jewish People.

Jews for Jesus, a small group, has beliefs not appreciably different from Jews throughout the ages who followed messiahs. Messianism isn't our path. It isn't a majority path. But it is an expression of one path in Judaism and it's nothing for the Jewish community to be afraid of.

Aren't you speeding up the process of assimilation and the death of the Jewish People by encouraging intermarriage? Aren't children of intermarrieds less likely to be Jewish?

No. By accepting and performing intermarriages, we are acknowledging the truth of living in a modern Western democracy in which Jews are a tiny minority. Jews are going to meet and fall in love with and marry non-Jews. Our choice is whether to give an inclusive or an exclusive message to those who do. We choose to celebrate love and commitment and to welcome intermarrieds into our communities. Judaism's historic semipermeable membrane has always accepted outside influences that enrich our community, as well as sharing our cultural riches with others.

Many religious congregations welcome intermarried couples, even if the rabbi refuses to perform the ceremony. Unfortunately, there can be strings attached. The non-Jewish spouse is usually not a full member and is not allowed to participate fully, and the children are held to different standards than children of two Jewish parents. If we want to retain the children of intermarriage, we have to make them welcome in the Jewish family and we cannot make that welcome a grudging one.

The Reform movement recently decided that congregations should deny a Jewish education to children who are also receiving a Christian education. This decision, which was approved of by many both inside and outside the Reform movement, indicates a deep misunderstanding of the nature of Judaism and Jewish education. It is counterproductive to our shared goal of strengthening the Jewish community, and it betrays an insecurity about the value of being Jewish.

We professional Jews are always complaining about the state of Jewish education. We bewail the fact that not enough people are spending enough time learning about Jewish history, culture, and religion. We devise all sorts of ways to get adults interested in learning; we invest lots of time trying to make Jewish school interesting and appealing to our children. Why on earth would we want to turn away someone who actually wants a Jewish education?

Refusing to allow a child both Jewish and Christian education makes sense only if we conceive of Jewish education as solely religious. But it is not. The true aim of Jewish education is not religious indoctrination but the development of an appreciation of the diversity of Jewish culture and the development of a Jewish identity and a sense of connection.

This sense of Jewishness is crucial as children approach the ages when identity decisions are made. The fact is that, in modern America, Jewishness is a choice. All of us have chosen to be Jewish; we could have chosen otherwise. Many of us, however, did not choose exactly the form of Jewishness that our parents did, if, indeed, our parents were Jewish. We all decided for ourselves, and we all chose our own paths. Why do we think our children will be exactly what we tell them they are? They, too, will decide for themselves as they grow up. Should we deny them the opportunity to make an informed decision? Should we arrange for them to decide for or against Judaism knowing nothing about the delights and responsibilities of being Jewish? Should we deny potential Jews the chance to learn about being Jewish, the chance to feel part of the

Jewish world? Why should we try to choose an identity for them; and if we are to choose for them, why are we choosing that they should not be Jews?

Should we deny them a Jewish education just because they may not choose Judaism for themselves? If we did that, we might deny any of our children a Jewish education, because any of them could choose not to be Jewish, or to be a kind of Jew different from their parents.

The decision of the Reform movement (which is not, thankfully, followed by all Reform congregations, some of which are very welcoming to intercultural families) is unnerving in one other respect. It implies a belief that Christianity is more appealing than Judaism. The assumption is clear: If children are given both a Jewish and a Christian education, they will choose Christianity. According to this viewpoint, allowing them to attend Jewish schools is a waste of the Jewish community's resources.

The reality is that while Christianity has some very attractive elements, both religiously and culturally, Judaism is also an attractive choice. It gives us a community anywhere in the world. It is rich in music, dance, literature, and art. Its history teaches us ethical lessons. Judaism is strong and meaningful enough to compete with Christianity for adherents. We do not have anything to fear from the dual religious education of children with one Jewish and one Christian parent. We should not reject the opportunity to welcome a committed Jew who understands what he or she is choosing. And if a bicultural child does, indeed, choose Christianity, he or she will be a Christian appreciative of Jewish culture, with strong family connections to Jews and memories of interesting, meaningful, and accepting Jewish experiences rather than one whose only experience with Jewish organizations was rejection.

How do you give kids a Jewish identity that will last?

There's no one sure answer to this one. Children from committed Jewish homes sometimes leave Jewish life because it just doesn't suit them. The best we can do is to make sure that our children find something in Jewish life that is interesting and meaningful to them. If the child is interested in nature, we have to be able to provide a Jewish perspective on ecology and the outdoors and a Jewish role model for someone who can live in harmony with the natural world. If the child is interested in social justice, we should be able to provide historical examples and role models of Jews involved in these issues. If the child is of a mystic turn of mind, we need to acquaint him or her with Jewish mystic traditions. If the child is family oriented, we should make Jewish activities a normal part of family life. In the last century, the Jewish historian Simon Dubnow, a Diaspora Nationalist Secularist, wrote, "Judaism is comprised of religious, moral, social, messianic, philosophical, political ideas . . . so broad and multifaceted that each Jew can choose whatever is in keeping with his convictions . . ."

What about Israel?

Secularists are all over the map on this one. Both the most politically conservative and politically liberal Zionist positions have been promulgated by Secularists. Secularism has promoted political Zionism, cultural Zionism, anti-Zionism, and non-Zionism. Today, many Israelis on both the left and right are Secularists. Many anti-Zionists are Secularist. Many non-Zionists are Secularists. The official position of the Secular Humanistic Jewish movement is of the non-Zionist variety, which accepts Israel as an important Jewish community because of its population, the diversity and extent of Jewish life there, and because of its historical and cultural significance. We are concerned for Israel's Jews just as we are concerned for Jews in the former Soviet Union, in South America, Africa, and Asia. We accept the Israeli Jewish community as important in Jewish life, but not as the center of Jewish life.

We support Israel as a democratic country that will always be a safe place for Jews. The Congress of Secular Jewish Organizations has for many years supported a two-state solution in the Middle East.

Where do you get strength? Even if God can't or won't do anything to change the world, don't you need a strong arm to lean on and a loving ear to talk to? Doesn't Harold Kushner's idea of a weak but good god appeal to you?

Some Secular Humanistic Jews may connect to a god like Kushner's who can't keep bad things from happening but nevertheless helps them to find their own strength, or "gives us strength and patience and hope, renewing our spiritual resources . . ." as Kushner writes in *When Bad Things Happen to Good People.* But even Kushner says that the reason people pray is not to influence

God but to connect with their communities and the people who care about them. If it is meaningful for you to call your connection with others *God,* nobody will stop you. But, in general, Secular Humanistic Jews don't use the word *God* to describe things that already have other names. We don't say "God is love." We say, "Love is love." Likewise, we don't call on God when we need our community's strength. We call on our community. And we don't call on God when we need inner strength. We call on our own inner strength.

But, then, what's the meaning of life?

This is something we all need to decide for ourselves. Ask yourself, "What would make my own particular life one that was meaningful?" Then live that meaning. Ahad Ha-am, the theoretician of cultural Zionism, recognized the importance of the question and answered this way: "When the individual values the community as his own life and strives after its happiness as though it were his individual well-being, he finds satisfaction and no longer feels so keenly the bitterness of his individual existence because he sees the end for which he lives and suffers."

What is the purpose of my life? My own one-sentence answer is "to make the world better for the next generation." Others might say "to repay the great gift of life by using it and enjoying it to its fullest," or "to use up every bit of my potential and not to waste an iota of my precious time and energy," or "to be a blessing to those who know me." Leo Rosten put it this way, "The purpose of life is to matter—to count, to stand for something, to have it make some difference that we lived at all."

The shorthand answer is that you should write the obituary you'd want read at your funeral. Then live a life that will make it true.

How do you know you're right?

We don't. But we're willing to live with uncertainty because we are not willing to accept something as truth just because it is comforting to think we know the truth. The Reverend Mr. William Sloane Coffin said, "Almost all of us tend to hold certainty dearer than truth." It's grounding, anchoring, to believe unwaveringly in something. But as Nietzsche wrote, "Believing something passionately does not make it true."

All of our knowledge is tentative. Anything we know can be disproved with only one example. But this is the difference between science and religion. Science is responsible to the facts and religion is not. With religion, the truth is known; if the facts don't fit, there's something wrong with the facts or there's something wrong with our understanding of the facts. With science, if the facts don't fit, we are forced to change our minds about what's true.

Can we ever know the real truth about anything? Maybe we can about some things, and maybe we can't about others. But a lot of times we can come close and we can keep trying. Still, lest hubris trip us up, we should probably remember what Gene Bocknek, a participant on the Humanistic Judaism on-line discussion group wrote: "Seeking reason and truth is no guarantee that one will recognize it."

What if you're wrong and there is a god who rewards and punishes?

Okay, let's say there is only one god and it's a god like the one you believe in and it rewards and punishes. How are we to know what that god is going to reward and punish, when every religion has a different answer? Is it sinful to eat meat? To eat certain kinds of meat? To eat meat prepared improperly? Is it sinful to accept a blood transfusion? Is it sinful to refuse to lay your life on the line to save an embryo? Is it sinful to enjoy sex? To have more than one wife? To be celibate?

How do we decide on our religion? We can receive it through the authority of our parents or community, through revelation, or through decision, but in every case we accept a religion with which we agree. When we don't agree with a religion's major ideas, we tend to leave that religion and seek another that suits us better.

Secular Humanistic Jews don't usually believe a god who rewards and punishes, but we live in such a way that if there were a just and good god, we would have no worry over our reward. We try to live good lives that are fulfilling and help others, and if this isn't what a god wants, then such a god is not worthy of worship.

But if there's no reward or punishment in the afterlife, why should people be good?

First of all, lots of terrible things have been done throughout the ages by people who believed that there *is* an afterlife of reward and punishment. But even if this fear does deter some people from a life a crime, it's a very low level of morality. A higher morality is actually caring about other people and about the world we live in. Good is good and evil is evil, whether or not there's a god watching.

If there's no reward and punishment in the afterlife, what happens after you die?

Most, but not all, Secular Humanistic Jews tend to believe that there is no eternal self-conscious soul. We live so that our lives will have an impact on this world throughout the generations, whether that means being good parents or friends to the next generation, working for social justice, or creating works of art and truth that will influence lives yet to come. Our immortality is in this world, and even if our individual name and accomplishments aren't remembered past the lifetimes of those who knew us, our lives have mattered.

Do you think it's fair that you get all the fun of being Jewish with none of the responsibilities?

None of the responsibilities? On the contrary, we have many responsibilities and we take their fulfillment seriously. We are responsible to be truthful about the past, to be contributors in the present, and to be believers in the future. We have the responsibility of carrying on a wealth of Jewish music, literature, history, and folk culture from three thousand five hundred years and on six continents. We have the responsibility of bringing the lessons of Jewish history into our daily lives. We have the responsibility of helping to create a world that truly appreciates the dignity of the individual and the power of the community. We have the responsibility to respond to one another's needs in real, concrete ways. We have the responsibility to continue the Jewish People as a relevant identity for generations to come.

But thank you for noticing that being Jewish is fun. With all the tsuris (troubles) and the weight of history, we have all chosen this path because it is meaningful and rewarding for us. We choose to be Jewish and to accept the responsibilities that come with it, and we fully enjoy the pleasures and satisfactions that being Jewish brings us.

APPENDIX A:
HOLIDAY RESOURCES

Ritual

We Rejoice in Our Heritage: Home Rituals for Secular and Humanistic Jews by Judith Seid. Kopinvant Press, distributed through CSJO, 19657 Villa Drive North, Southfield, MI 48076. Ashreis, or short ritual statements for all Jewish occasions: candlelighting, wine, challah, holiday celebrations, etc. In English, Hebrew, and Yiddish with transliteration. $10.20 postpaid. Bulk discounts available.

Marcia Falk's *The Book of Blessings* (HarperCollins, San Francisco, 1996, available in bookstores) contains many blessings for special occasions. Falk's blessings are religious, but refer to *The Source of Life*.

Songs

Kumzits! A Festivity of Instant Jewish Songs, Kopinvant Press, distributed through CSJO, 19657 Villa Drive North, Southfield, MI 48076. Easy to sing, easy to learn songs in English, Hebrew, and Yiddish. Songs in Hebrew and Yiddish have very few words. Melody line and chords. $17.95 + shipping. Bulk discounts available.

Stories

Pushcarts and Dreamers: Stories of Jewish Life in America is a wonderful collection of Yiddish stories translated (and with a fine introduction) by Max Rosenfeld. The translations are as colorful and colloquial as the original stories and are just made to read out loud. $9.95 + $2.00 s/h. Sholem Aleichem Club Press, 443 E. Wadsworth Ave., Philadelphia, PA 19119.

Any kids' books by Patricia Polacco, who writes from her own experiences, and Barbara Cohen, who retells folk tales. Also look for collections of stories edited by Howard Schwartz and Penina Schram.

Fall Holidays

Apples and Honey: Music and Readings for a Secular Observance of the Jewish New Year edited by Julie Gales and Pat Martz, published by the Congress of Secular Jewish Organizations (CSJO) 19657 Villa Drive North, Southfield, MI 48076. A collection of songs, poetry, and readings used by Secularist groups all over the U.S. and Canada. $19.95 + s/h.

You can also go to the CSJO Web page (http://csjo.org) for links to groups all over the U.S. and Canada. Many will share their holiday programs with you.

Haggadahs

Haggadah for a Secular Celebration of Pesach, Sholem Aleichem Club Press, 443 E. Wadsworth Ave., Philadelphia, PA 19119 (original illustrations and calligraphy, description of the foods and symbols, songs with music, in English with excerpts in Yiddish and Hebrew with transliteration, egalitarian language, 64 pages) $8.95 + $1.50 s/h. Bulk discount available.

Songs for a Secular Celebration of Pesach is a sing-along tape with all the songs from the *Haggadah for a Secular Celebration of Pesach*. It includes the Four Questions in English, Hebrew, and Yiddish. $7.95 + $1.50 s/h. (Combination discount if ordered with *Haggadah.)*

Sholem Family Hagada published by the Sholem Community Organization of Los Angeles and distributed through CSJO, 19657 Villa Drive North, Southfield, MI 48076. A particularly universalist, socially aware Haggadah suitable for adults and children. $5.00 + s/h.

The Shalom Seder: Three Haggadahs Compiled by New Jewish Agenda, published by Adama Books (NY) in 1984, is a collection of Haggadahs with themes of environmentalism, feminism, and universal freedom. I found a copy at my local chain bookstore for $12.95.

You can also find good stuff in traditional Haggadahs translated and edited by Phillip Birnbaum and Nahum Glazer and in Haggadahs prepared by Kadima and the Liturgy Committee of the Task Force on Equality of Women in Judaism, New York Federation of Reform Synagogues. Also check out "An Egalitarian Haggadah" by Aviva Cantor in *Lilith* magazine, 1982.

Tu b'Shvat

The Lorax by Dr. Seuss is a great book for Tu b'Shvat. It's in every library I've ever been in.

Seder Tu Bishevat: The Festival of Trees by Adam Fisher, from the Central Conference of American Rabbis, is a Reform Tu b'Shvat seder. Kar-Ben Publishers also puts out a Tu b'Shvat seder for kids.

Other

Do a Web search for "Jewish holidays" or "Jewish family" and you'll come up with a lot of good stuff.

http://www.jewishfamily.com is a Web site with articles, ideas, and discussions about how to conduct a Jewish life, celebrate holidays, teach your kids.

S&S Crafts has a Judaic catalog. You can reach them at 800/243–9232. Another Jewish crafts catalog, "Just for the Mitzvah," can be accessed on-line at mitzvahcrafts@jewishyouth.com

The Jewish Kids Catalog by Chaya Burstein, Jewish Publication Society of America, Philadelphia, 1983, is full of information on the holidays (as well as other stuff) and has lots of holiday stories and ideas for crafts.

APPENDIX B:
OUT-OF-THE MAINSTREAM RESOURCES

For Mixed-Race Households

Non-European Jews are generally ignored both in books about Jews and in Jewish communities in America. Claire Kinberg, editor of *Bridges*, a progressive feminist Jewish magazine, and herself a member of a mixed-race household, recommends these two books:

Azoulay, Katya Gibel. *Black, Jewish and Interracial*. Durham: Duke University Press, 1997.

Funderberg, Lise. *Black, White, Other*. New York: W. Morrow and Co., 1994.

For Intermarried Couples

There's a great deal of interest in the mainstream Jewish community in getting intermarrieds to join temples and synagogues and feel welcome in Jewish life. Most books on the topic are written by Jews and tend to be biased toward a completely Jewish home life. A more balanced viewpoint is presented in:

Petsonk, Judy, and Jim Remsen. *The Intermarriage Handbook*. New York: Arbor House, 1988.

Reuben, Steven Carr. *Making Interfaith Marriage Work.* Rocklin, California: Prima Publishing, 1994.

Books on Secular Judaism

If you're interested in books specifically about the philosophy of Secular Humanistic Judaism, take a look at:

Goldfinger, Eva. *Basic Ideas of Secular Humanistic Judaism.* Farmington Hills, M.I.: International Institute for Secular Humanistic Judaism, 1996.

Goodman, Saul L., ed. *The Faith of Secular Jews.* New York: KTAV Publishing House, Inc., 1976.

Kogel, Renée, and Zev Katz, eds. *Judaism in a Secular Age.* New York: KTAV Publishing House, Inc., 1995.

Rosenfeld, Max. *Festivals, Folklore and Philosophy: A Secularist Revisits Jewish Traditions.* Philadelphia: Sholem Aleichem Club, 1997.

Wine, Sherwin T. *Judaism Beyond God: A Radical New Way to Be Jewish.* Farmington Hills, M.I.: Society for Humanistic Judaism, 1985.

Periodicals on Secular Judaism

There are a number of Jewish periodicals that are specifically Secular and Humanistic or are friendly to Secular Humanistic Judaism. Among them are:

Humanistic Judaism. Published three times a year by the SHJ. 28611 W. 12 Mile Rd., Dept. HJ, Farmington Hils, MI 48018. ($15.)

Jewish Currents. A fifty-year-old monthly published by the Association for Promotion of Jewish Secularism. 22 E. 17th St., Suite 601, New York, NY 10003–1010. 212/924–5740. ($30.)

Bridges: A Journal for Jewish Feminists and Our Friends. Published semi-annually. Box 24839, Eugene, OR 97402. ($15.)

BIBLIOGRAPHY

Adelman, Howard. *Medieval Jewish History*. Jewish University in Cyberspace, juice@wzo.org.il, 1998.

Adelman, Howard. *Modern Jewish History*. Jewish University in Cyberspace, juice@wzo.org.il, 1998.

Anderson, G.W. *The History and Religion of Israel*. London: Oxford University Press, 1966.

Azoulay, Katya Gibel. *Black, Jewish and Interracial*. Durham: Duke University Press, 1997.

Balka, Christie, and Andy Rose, eds. *Twice Blessed*. Boston: Beacon Press, 1994.

Baron, Salo W., and Joseph L. Blau. *Judaism: Postbiblical and Talmudic Period*. New York: Bobbs-Merrill Company, 1954.

Beck, Evelyn Torton, ed. *Nice Jewish Girls*. Watertown, Mass: Persephone Press, 1982.

Bickerman, Elias J. *The Jews in the Greek Age*. Cambridge, Mass: Harvard University Press, 1988.

Black, Algernon. *Without Burnt Offerings*. New York: Viking Press, 1974.

Bridger, David, ed. *The New Jewish Encyclopedia*. West Orange, N.J.: Behrman House, Inc., 1962.

Cantor, Norman. *The Sacred Chain: The History of the Jews*. New York: HarperCollins Publishers, 1994.

CCAR, *American Reform Responsa* No.100, http://ccarnet.org/cgi/respdisp.pl5?file=100&year=arr

Chill, Abraham. *The Minhagim.* New York: Sepher-Hermon Press, 1989.

Coogan, Michael D., ed. *The Oxford History of the Biblical World.* London: Oxford University Press, 1998.

Daffodils; A Monthly Newsletter of Holiday Stuff, History, Stories. http://bc.emanon.net/cgi-bin/daffodils/newsletter.

Diamant, Anita. *The Jewish Baby Book.* New York: Summit Books, 1988.

Dobrinsky, Herbert C. *A Treasury of Sephardic Laws and Customs.* New York: Yeshiva University Press, 1986.

Dorfman, Toby, and Rosalie Gottfried. *Answers in a Nutshell to Questions on Humanistic Judaism.* San Diego: Humanistic Jewish Congregation of San Diego, undated pamphlet.

Dubnow-Erlich, Sophie (tr. by Judith Vowles). *The Life and Work of S.M. Dubnow: Diaspora Nationalism and Jewish History.* Bloomington: Indiana University Press, 1950/1991.

Eichorn, David Max, ed. *Conversion to Judaism: A History and Analysis.* New York: KTAV Publishing House, Inc., 1965.

Friedman, Richard Elliott. *Who Wrote the Bible?* New York: Summit Books, 1987.

Funderberg, Lise. *Black, White, Other.* New York: William Morrow, 1994.

Gaster, Theodore H. *Festivals of the Jewish Year.* New York: Commentary/William Morrow, 1952.

Ginzberg, Louis. *On Jewish Law and Lore.* New York: Atheneum,1970.

Goldfinger, Eva. *Basic Ideas of Secular Humanistic Judaism.* Farmington Hills, Mich.: International Institute for Secular Humanistic Judaism, 1996.

Goodman, Saul L., ed. *The Faith of Secular Jews.* New York: KTAV Publishing House, 1976.

Gruen, Erich S. *Heritage and Hellenism: The Reinvention of Jewish Tradition.* Berkeley: University of California Press, 1998.

Hartman, Hershl. *The Hanuka Festival: A Guide for The Rest of Us,* Los Angeles: Sholem Community Organization, 1992.

Hartman, Hershl. *The Jewish New Year Festival: A Guide for the Rest of Us.* Los Angeles: Sholem Community Organization, 1992.

Hoenig, Samuel N. *The Essence of Talmudic Law and Thought.* Northvale, N.J.: Jason Aronson, 1993.

Howe, Irving, and Eliezer Greenberg, ed. *Voices from the Yiddish: Essays, Memoirs, Diaries.* Ann Arbor, Mich.: University of Michigan Press, 1972.

Husik, Isaac. *A History of Mediaeval Jewish Philosophy.* New York: Atheneum, 1976.

Idel, Moshe. *Devekut.* Class lectures, 1995.

Kaganoff, Benzion C. *A Dictionary of Jewish Names and Their History.* Northvale, N.J.: Jason Aronson, 1996.

Kamenetz, Rodger. *The Jew in the Lotus: A Poet's Rediscovery of Jewish Identity in Buddhist India.* New York: HarperCollins, 1994.

Kaplan, Mordecai. *Judaism as a Civilization.* New York: Reconstructionist Press, 1934.

Kaplan, Mordecai. *Questions Jews Ask: Reconstructionist Answers.* New York: Reconstructionist Press, 1956.

Katz, Jacob. *Tradition and Crisis: Jewish Society at the End of the Middle Ages.* New York: Schocken, 1993.

Kogel, Renée, and Zev Katz, eds. *Judaism in a Secular Age.* New York: KTAV Publishing House, 1995.

Kushner, Harold S. *When Bad Things Happen to Good People.* New York: Avon Books, 1981.

Leftwich, Joseph, ed. *Great Yiddish Writers of the Twentieth Century.* Northvale, N.J.: Jason Aronson, 1969/1987.

Levy, Karen, ed. *The Early Modern European Roots of Secular Humanistic Judaism.* Farmington Hills, Mich.: International Institute for Secular Humanistic Judaism, 1998.

Lewy, Hans, Alexander Altmann, and Isaak Heinemann, eds. *Three Jewish Philosophers.* New York: Atheneum, 1969.

Lutske, Harvey, *The Book of Jewish Customs.* Northvale, N.J.: Jason Aronson, 1986.

Luzzatto, Moshe Chaim (tr. by Yaakov Feldman). *The Path of the Just.* Northvale, N.J.: Jason Aronson, 1996.

Mendes-Flohr, Paul, and Jehuda Reinharz. *The Jew in the Modern World: A Documentary History.* 2nd ed. London: Oxford University Press, 1980/1995.

Meltzer, Milton. *A History of Jewish Life from Eastern Europe to America.* Northvale, N.J.: Jason Aronson, 1996.

Milgram, Abraham. *Jewish Worship.* Philadelphia: Jewish Publication Society of America, 1971.

Mor, Menachem, ed. *Jewish Sects, Religious Movements, and Political Parties.* Omaha, Neb.: Creighton University Press, 1992.

ibn Pakuda, Bachya (tr. by Yaakov Feldman). *The Duties of the Heart.* Northvale, N.J.: Jason Aronson, 1996.

Passow, Isidore David. "Shmuel Niger's Ideas on Building a Jewish Comunity in the United States, 1920–1933," *YIVO Annual of Jewish*

Social Science XV, p. 188, New York: YIVO Institute for Jewish Research, 1974.

Petsonk, Judy, and Jim Remsen. *The Intermarriage Handbook.* New York: Arbor House, 1988.

Phillips, Rebecca, et al., "What Jewish Students Believe . . . and What They Don't," *New Voices* vol. 7, Number 3, November 1998, p. 20.

Posy, Arnold. *Mystic Trends in Judaism.* New York: Jonathan David Publishers, 1966.

Redford, Donald B., *Egypt, Canaan, and Israel in Ancient Times.* Princeton, N.J.: Princeton University Press, 1992.

Reuben, Steven Carr. *Making Interfaith Marriage Work.* Rocklin, Cal.: Prima Publishing, 1994.

Rivkin, Ellis. *The Shaping of Jewish History: A Radical New Interpretation.* New York: Charles Scribner's Sons, 1971.

Rosenbloom, Joseph R. *Conversion to Judaism: From the Biblical Period to the Present.* Cincinnati: Hebrew Union College Press, 1978.

Rosenfeld, Max. *Festivals, Folklore and Philosophy: A Secularist Revisits Jewish Traditions.* Philadelphia: Sholem Aleichem Club, 1997.

Sachar, Howard M. *The Course of Modern Jewish History.* New York: Vintage Books, 1977.

Schauss, Chaim. *Dos Yontef Bukh.* Published by the author, New York, 1933.

Schauss, Hayyim (tr. by Samuel Jaffe). *The Jewish Festivals: History and Observance.* New York: Schocken, 1962.

Schechter, Solomon. *Aspects of Rabbinic Theology.* New York: Schocken Books, 1909/1961.

Siegel, Richard, Michael Strassfeld, and Sharon Strassfeld. *The First Jewish Catalogue.* Philadelphia: The Jewish Publication Society of America, 1973.

Strassfeld, Michael. *The Jewish Holidays: A Guide and Commentary.* New York: Harper & Row, 1985.

Strassfeld, Sharon, and Michael Strassfeld. *The Second Jewish Catalogue.* Philadelphia: Jewish Publication Society of America, 1976.

Wiener, Shohama, ed. *The Fifty-Eighth Century: A Jewish Renewal Sourcebook.* Northvale, N.J.: Jason Aronson, 1996.

Wine, Sherwin T. *Judaism Beyond God: A Radical New Way to Be Jewish.* Farmington Hills, Mich.: Society for Humanistic Judaism, 1985.

Index